12⁹⁵

Urban and Regional Economics

Structure and Change

M. Jarvin Emerson
Kansas State University

F. Charles Lamphear
University of Nebraska

Allyn and Bacon, Inc.   Boston

To Anne and Kay

©Copyright 1975 by Allyn and Bacon, Inc.
470 Atlantic Avenue, Boston, Massachusetts 02210

Printed in the United States of America.

Library of Congress Cataloging in Publication Data

Emerson, M.   Jarvin.
  Urban and regional economics.

  Includes bibliographical references and index.
  1. Urban economics. 2. Regional economics.
I. Lamphear, F. Charles, joint author. II. Title.
HT321.E45.   330.9   74-30454

ISBN 0-205-04694-0

Contents

Contents

Preface

During the last few years courses in urban and regional problems have sprouted in various forms in the majority of colleges and universities. The relevance of the problems nurtured strong interest in the courses, but the lack of material providing analytical frameworks to deal with the problems proved frustrating for both student and professor.

This book was written in response to the need for an integration and assembly of materials in diverse areas which would provide analytical insights into the functions and malfunctions of urban and regional economics. Since the fields of urban economics and regional economics are barely beyond an embryonic stage of development, an analytical framework is more provisional than in older areas of inquiry. The rapid evolution of theories and analytical techniques partially explains and is explained by the mushrooming interest in the area.

A unique feature of this book is a blend of urban and regional economics. A merger between the two closely related areas of investigation would seem unnecessary except that they have tended to develop on somewhat different tracks even though they share a similar, if not identical, goal. The domain of urban economics has primarily been the internal workings of the city with minimal attention to the influence of external forces on the city. Regional economics, deriving much of thrust from location theory, has been more interested in external linkages. Both areas, however, are concerned with problems and processes of subnational economic performance. Our intent is to view cities, towns, and rural areas in their regional and interregional setting as well as to examine their internal structure and problems.

The book is intended for students who have completed only

an introductory economics course. Most of the economic theory is developed on the empirically validated assumption that the student remembers little from that introduction to economics. Because of its relatively self-contained nature, the book could also be used in planning, geography, social science, and engineering courses on urban and regional problems and analysis.

Theory, problems, and policy are the three main themes of the book, with a light sprinkling of analytical techniques. Input-output analysis, an extensively used technique at the subnational level, provides an initial descriptive and analytical framework. The location of economic activity is explored for firms, industries, and cities to develop an understanding of the overall spatial structure of the economy. This leads to a consideration of change in the spatial structure: the economics of growth and decline. After considering the spatial structure of urban areas, the book moves into the economic bases of major urban problems. The final section reviews policy responses to these problems drawing on the economic relationships considered in earlier chapters.

As is the case with a venture of this kind, we must acknowledge several important contributions. John R. Moore, Richard L. Pfister, and James R. Prescott read the entire manuscript and made numerous useful comments. Our colleagues reviewed parts of the manuscript, and several hundred students served as highly responsive experimental subjects. Velda Deutsch provided highly competent secretarial assistance. Our use of facilities of the Harvard Economic Research Project, to which one of the authors was attached during part of the writing process, is gratefully acknowledged. The burdens of authorship were lightened by the patience, help, and understanding of our families.

M. J. E.

F. C. L.

1

Introduction

In 1790 when the embryonic American nation first instituted a system of comprehensive censuses, the population was 3.9 million persons occupying a land area extending largely from southern Maine to northern Georgia. All but ten percent of the people lived in small villages and remote clearings connected by foot paths and horse trails. The economy was basically agricultural, and it took the efforts of five farmers to feed themselves and one other. Only six cities had populations exceeding 8,000.

Less than two centuries later the same nation supports a population of over 210 million with an economic capacity to produce a gross national product in excess of $1 trillion. Today, much of the nation's economic capacity is located in its urban areas, where over 70 percent of the people live and work on less than three percent of the nation's total land area (excluding Alaska and Hawaii). Agriculture accounts for less than ten percent of the total work force—a situation made possible by the remarkable gains in agricultural productivity. Today's farmer feeds himself and 12 others.

A NATION OF SUB-ECONOMIES

The nation is an interlocked mosaic of unique subnational economies. New York, Philadelphia, Appalachia, Cheyenne, the Ozarks, Orlando, New England, Los Angeles, the Mesabi Range, Burr Oak, Nashville, Chicago, Waco, Bangor, the Northeast Corridor,

1

and Gatlinburg—all are subnational economies, each with a distinctive structure, performance, and problems. Let us consider a few examples in broad fashion.

An economic giant with national and international influence, the New York region possesses both great vitality and great problems. In the last few decades New York has experienced a transformation that has left its economic structure bearing little resemblance to the one that brought it worldwide influence, yet that influence remains. However, some view New York as an unsavory mix of traffic congestion, pollution, slums, and poverty.

The birthplace of the American industrial revolution, New England experienced serious reversals in its comparative advantage in the production of a wide variety of industrial products. Economic stagnation and decline occurred, followed later by a rejuvenation around the scientific and technical expertise spun off from its universities and research centers and aided by cultural amenities.

A significant portion of the new industry in the rapidly growing southern region of the United States moved from the New England region. The transformation of the South, epitomized by Atlanta, has brought rising prosperity to a previously lagging region.

In 1971 a $300 million tourist enterprise opened near Orlando, Florida, setting off economic tremors to be felt for years in the region. Other areas in Florida have boomed from recreation and retirement developments.

Of the chronically economically depressed regions, Appalachia usually heads the list. A declining resource base and technological change have resulted in severe unemployment and poverty problems. The problem is compounded by a historic, persistent deficiency in investment in the education and training of the labor force and in such public facilities as transportation, electrical power, and waste treatment.

The tidal wave of migrants into California has diminished only recently. In the process, the Los Angeles–Long Beach region became the symbol of economic opportunity, urban sprawl, and air pollution.

These vignettes could continue, only with diminishing returns. However, they do provide an intuitive feel for the scope of this book. We are interested in examining the structure, performance, problems, and policies of urban-regional economies of the United States. We now turn to a brief explanation of the approach of this investigation.

URBAN-REGIONAL ECONOMICS

Common to all subnational economies is the subject of location, which is the spatial (or geographic) dimension of economic activity. Because location is an important consideration of businesses and households, we wish to pose several key questions which are basic to a study of economic structure and change at the subnational level. Why do people and businesses choose to locate in certain areas? Or what are the factors which influence the location of individual activities? How can we account for the fact that the national economy is presently characterized by a few very large urban fields of high population density and vast agricultural areas of low population density? Will the future bring a more uniform geographic distribution of activity? Viewed from a macroeconomic level, what economic factors account for the above-average (or below-average) growth rates of some areas? More generally, how is it possible that within the same national economy some areas seem to grow at the expense of other areas? The pressing need for answers to these and similar questions as they relate to subnational economies have formed the basis of study which we shall call urban–regional economics. Basically, *urban-regional economics is the study of the structural formation and change of economic areas (or regions) with emphasis on the spatial configuration of economic activity and on the interrelationships of economic activity among areas of the same national economy.*

Urban economics and regional economics have been treated both as a combined subject of urban-regional economics and as separate subjects. One reason for the separation of the two subjects is that some urban scholars have been more concerned with those socioeconomic problems—such as crime, traffic congestion, poverty, inadequate housing, pollution, etc.—which are more dominant within urban areas than with the larger issue of urbanization or the formation of a national system of cities. A second and more historic reason for this separation can be traced to the early development of location theory, which dates back to the early 1800s. The main concern of classical location theory was the location of a single plant. A later extension of location theory considered the formation of market areas, industrial interdependence, and the formation of a system of cities. Also considered was the locational significance of agglomeration economies (i.e., the direct and indirect economic benefits of the geographic concentration of economic activity). In recent years, this work has found its way into college classrooms as courses in location economics and regional economics. But, also in recent years, some urban and regional economists have combined the work of the location theorists with urban economics in order to understand better the whole process of urbanization and how this process may lead to certain economic problems unique to urban regions.

This text represents an attempt to bring together some of the basic work of the location theorists with regional growth theory in order to gain some insight into the formation of spatial economic structure. This approach should enable us to understand better why the dynamic workings of the private-market system have literally dichotomized our nation into two basic regions—urban regions and rural regions. Furthermore, this understanding should enable us to form some intelligent opinion as to the social value of this outcome.

Is urban-regional economics a new economics? There are some of us who would like to answer yes to this query, but the correct answer is no. Urban-regional economics is simply an extension of traditional economics, where the extension is the introduction of the distance variable. Many of the principles and tools of analysis learned in traditional economics are found in urban-regional economics. As examples, the laws of supply and demand and the use of marginal analysis (e.g., marginal cost and marginal revenue) from traditional economics are found to be quite useful in urban-regional economics. What has been added in urban-regional economics, as already indicated, is the dimension of space, which raises the general "where" question of production and consumption.

Since urban-regional economics is part of economics, the same basic facts stated and general questions raised in traditional economics must be included here. The basic facts are: (1) we live in a world where society's wants for goods and services are virtually unlimited, and (2) economic resources—used in the production and consumption of goods and services—are limited and oftentimes immobile. With limited resources and unlimited wants, any economic system must solve the general what, how, how much, for whom, and where questions of production and consumption. Our discussion of these questions shall be limited to a comprehensive study of the combined workings of the private market and government of the United States. However, appropriate examples of urban-regional growth and policy in other nations will be examined to illustrate alternative experiences. England's new towns and France's regional planning are two such examples.

ECONOMIC REGIONS

A term used most frequently in economic analysis at the sub-national level and a term used extensively throughout this book is *region*. In fact, we have used the term in our title. What does the term mean? Does it have economic significance?

A region is a spatial economic entity whose configuration permits meaningful descriptive and analytical statements to be made about it. There are two basic types of economic regions: homogeneous regions and nodal economic regions. Common to both types is the notion of a contiguous geographic plain, meaning all areas of the region are connected.

A Homogeneous Region

One basic economic region is a land area that is quite homogeneous in its economic features. One obvious example of a homogeneous economic region is the farm belt of much of Iowa, Kansas, and Nebraska, and portions of Minnesota, Wisconsin, Illinois, Ohio, and Missouri. A drive through this area of the country reveals mile after mile of cropland where the same major crops are grown. The geographic landscape of this part of the country is dotted with many small urban communities primarily serving the needs of agriculture. Because of the near homogeneous feature of the area, any change in federal farm policies or in markets for farm products will affect all parts of the region in about the same way.

A Nodal Economic Region

The second basic type of region is based upon the concept of economic nodes. Economic nodes are centers of economic strength that transmit their energies for economic growth to neighboring areas. Conversely, economic energy is transmitted from the neighboring areas to the economic nodes. Regions defined on the basis of economic nodes are characterized more by the interdependence of the units that comprise the region than by homogeneity. In fact, many of the units that comprise the region can appear quite dissimilar. The neighboring units are dependent upon the economic node as both a market and a source for goods and services for production and consumption. Similarly, an economic node is dependent upon its neighboring areas for resources and markets.

The best example of a nodal economic region is a city and its surrounding community. The surrounding community is a major source of labor and other resource inputs needed in the city's production of goods and services. In addition, it serves as a major market area for many of the city's goods and services.

The geographic size of a nodal region will depend upon the magnitude of its node. As we think of economic nodes as cities, it is obvious that some cities are larger than others. Consequently, a city of four million will have a larger trade community than some smaller city.

From the foregoing discussion of economic regions, you may have wondered about regional boundaries. Are the boundaries of a nodal region so well-defined that the boundary of one region coincides with the boundary of an adjacent region? The answer is an obvious no. Apparent to all of us is the fact that many cities trade across other cities, thereby serving common trade areas. But, conceptually, we should expect to find a dominant "pairing-up" of trade areas with cities (or economic nodes). More will be said about this in Chapter 6.

The Matter of Significance

The significance of a regional approach to economics is two-fold. First, the notion of economic space is manifested in the concept of a region (recall the definition of a nodal region). A study of an economic system is not complete until consideration is given to the spatial dimension of economic activity. The combined workings of the private market and government can lead to subnational economies which are uniquely different. Second, the notion of an economic region has significance because it has policy implications. Policies that deal with economic matters can best fulfill their stated objectives if the jurisdictional area conforms to an economic region rather than to an existing governmental unit encompassing a larger or smaller area. An excellent example of much-needed economic policy at the regional level is found in our metropolitan areas. Because of present fragmented urban government, it is next to impossible to deal with the urban transportation problem on an urbanwide basis. (This and other related urban topics will be discussed in Chapters 13, 14, and 15.)

THE PLAN OF STUDY

In order to understand the function of a regional economy within the national economy, we begin in Chapter 2 with a discussion of an economic accounting system (i.e., a system of input-output accounts) which can be used to record the various interdependencies among the activities of a region. In addition, it will be shown how the system of accounts links a region's economy with the national economy through the region's imports and exports. The discussion of input-output accounts and their potential use is continued in Chapter 3.

The internal economic structure described by an input-output framework is the product of numerous location decisions by business firms, for each region has a different industrial mix determined by producers responding to supply and demand forces in the market place. Why, for instance, did the textile industry move from New England to the South after World War II? Why did so many new firms locate in Houston during the 1960s? Each of these questions has the same theme: What determines the location of economic activity? This central question is considered in Chapters 4 and 5 as we turn to a discussion of the economics of location and industrial interdependence in space. It will be shown in subsequent chapters that the economics of location is an integral part of regional capital formation, or alternatively, the region's economic structure.

Much in Chapters 4 and 5 is extended in Chapter 6 with a discussion of a national system of cities and the economics of concentration. Even the most cursory observation of the economic landscape would indicate that there is some kind of geographic distribution of cities based on city size. Can economics provide us with at least a partial answer as to why a city-size distribution exists? The first part of Chapter 6 undertakes to answer this query. The chapter concludes with a discussion of the factors which have contributed to concentration. Problems which are associated with high concentrations of economic activity are discussed in later chapters. A basic understanding of Chapters 4, 5, and 6 is critical to a later discussion of intraurban structure and urban problems.

Our analysis then moves to the dynamics of location of production in Chapter 7. The basic objective of Chapter 7 is to begin a study of the reasons why a region's economic structure tends to change over time. (This discussion is continued in Chapters 8 and 9, where we consider external linkages.) With the locational principles developed in Chapters 4 and 5, we examine the historical patterns of change and the factors precipitating these changes. We then focus on some theories of regional economic growth. Finally, we consider the hierarchical nature of the structure of development— the families of industries whose development tends to be linked together. With these ideas as a platform, we explore several systematic models of location dynamics. An input-output framework, which is first discussed in Chapter 2, is central to this discussion.

In Chapters 8 and 9 we turn to a discussion of a region's economic ties with the nation and the world. Since a regional economy is but part of a larger national and international economy, its economic well-being is highly dependent on its external linkages. These external ties are trade (exports and imports), capital flows, and migration. Each of the region's external ties is considered in detail, starting with regional exports and imports in Chapter 8 and ending with a discussion of migration in Chapter 9.

Chapters 10 and 11 discuss the economic structure of an urban-regional economy. Following a brief discussion of present and expected growth of urban areas, the rest of Chapter 10 is devoted to a descriptive analysis of intraurban structure. A theoretical analysis of intraurban structure is presented in Chapter 11.

Chapter 12 focuses on the role of the public sector, particularly in urban regions. The public sector makes investment decisions not too unlike those made in the private sectors. These investment decisions (or the lack of them) effect the economic structure of a region; therefore an examination of decision-making practices in the public sector is necessary in a comprehensive study of urban-regional economics. In addition to a discussion of taxation and public services, considerable attention is given to the notion of a public good and the meaning of economic efficiency. The discussion of economic efficiency is an important step in our understanding of a discussion of the major urban economic problems.

Using the frameworks developed in the first 12 chapters, the remaining six chapters examine the major problems of metropolitan and nonmetropolitan regions and the rationale for policies to alleviate these problems. Urban poverty and housing is analyzed in Chapter 13. Problems of urban transportation and pollution are considered in Chapter 14 along with some potential solutions to these problems. Chapter 15 examines problems of urban government and land use. The unique problems of nonmetropolitan regions are discussed in Chapter 16.

In Chapter 17 the development of new towns and new communities is evaluated as an alternative mode for alleviating some of the urban problems. This "start fresh" approach has been attempted both in the United States and Europe with some success.

Finally we consider alternative futures for the spatial distribution of economic activity. Trends, constraints, and controls are examined for their role in shaping the economic landscape. The role of planning as an instrument to shape the future is discussed.

2

Regional Interindustry Structure

A regional economy consists of an assortment of economic activities. Chemical plants, barber shops, printers, steel mills, banks, automobile assembly plants, data-processing firms, ice cream stores, grocery stores, breweries, and dozens of others comprise its industrial mix. In order to examine the functioning of a regional economy, we must develop a method of describing and analyzing such economic activities as these, activities which make up a region's economic structure. We want to know not only how a regional economy functions but also how it grows or declines.

THE CARVING OF ECONOMIC RELATIONSHIPS

In economics, as in most scientific studies, we are immediately confronted with myriad forms of information that tell us something about the economy, and the difficult task is to select the proper parts of the economy to investigate. Thus, when we study economic fluctuations, we divide the economy into major income and expenditure components and study the relationships among them. Occasionally we discover that changing the dissection scheme will yield keener insight into the causes of performance variations in the economy.

The task in this chapter is to set forth a procedure for slicing

10

a regional economy into components that will permit an examination of the industry mix and the linkages among the numerous industries which comprise that regional economy. This approach will also allow us to add other components (particularly linkages with other regions) which can be integrated into the initial framework.

In a national economy we would be concerned with a national income-accounting system which would monitor changes in production, income, and expenditure. However, for an urban-regional economy the concern is less with cyclical stability and more with structural change and growth. At the regional level the policy variables are both different and fewer than at the national level. Consequently the economic relationships of interest for a regional economy take on a different form, and the information requirements are similarly modified. Income and product accounts are not ignored; rather, they receive a different emphasis.

A popular approach in the study of urban-regional economics is the regional input-output model. More than 100 such models have been developed for subnational economies in the United States in recent years. These range from those that contain only a handful of sectors to a model of the Philadelphia region with 496 sectors.

AN INPUT-OUTPUT SYSTEM OF ACCOUNTS

The main theme of an input-output or interindustry table is *economic interdependence*. In a highly specialized economy such as that which characterizes the United States and its geographic components, several stages of production are involved in delivering a product or service to the ultimate consumer. Since numerous industries sell the majority of their output to other industries rather than to final markets, this intermediate production demand represents a sizeable portion of the total activity of an economy. Nationally, for instance, interindustry transactions represent more than 50 percent of total dollar-value transactions. Thus the activity of one industry may depend upon the activities of several other industries. These are the interrelationships that are captured in an input-output investigation.

An input-output model divides the economy into industries or sectors and then establishes the magnitude of the flows of products and services between them, flows representing an industry's purchases from and sales to other industries, individuals, or government. Although a regional input-output table also links the regional economy with other regions and the national government, the primary emphasis of this chapter is the region's internal structure as represented by an input-output matrix. Later we will focus on the region's external ties.

The input-output accounting system also can encompass within its rows and columns a variety of measures of regional economic performance such as gross regional product, regional personal income, and savings and capital formation.

We will begin with the individual firm's relationship to the overall framework and proceed to develop and interpret the three tables which are basic to an input-output system. In order to grasp the meaning of economic interdependence and interindustry linkages, we begin with a simple hypothetical illustration of a firm's "backward" and "forward" linkages with other economic sectors. This will expedite our discussion of the input-output transactions table which follows.

A FIRM'S INPUT AND OUTPUT LINKAGES

Suppose we start with an individual firm, unimaginatively called firm X. Firm X buys a variety of inputs to produce its output and sells its output to a variety of markets. In Figure 2-1 the firm's transactions are categorized in a manner useful for our purpose. Firm X appears in the center of the diagram with the supporting sectors (inputs) listed to the left and the various markets (outputs) listed to the right.

To produce its output a firm purchases raw materials, semi-finished goods, trade, financial services, and business services within the region. In addition, it pays wages to its employees, depreciates some of its capital, makes a profit (or loss), and pays taxes. The firm may also purchase inputs from firms outside of the region (imports). The output produced from these inputs may be sold to a variety of market types such as other regional firms, consumers in the region (households), capital formation, government, and out-of-region markets (exports).

Individual firm information of this type constitutes an input-output transactions matrix.

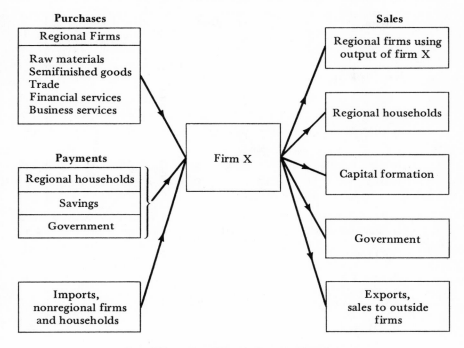

Figure 2-1 Firm flows in input-output form

TRANSACTIONS TABLE

In order to illustrate a transactions table, imagine that we have an urban-regional economy whose structure we want to simulate. Since even hypothetical economies should not suffer from an identity crisis, we will label our simulated economy Simcity. Suppose we group all the firms in our hypothetical economy into three industries: manufacturing, trade, and services. Using information of the type described for firm X, we can construct an *input-output transactions matrix* for our hypothetical regional economy, as shown in Table 2-1.

Each *column* of Table 2-1 shows the *purchases* or *payments* made by that column sector. For instance, the manufacturing sector, column 1, purchases $18 million from other manufacturing, $9 million from trade, and $11 million from services, and makes payments of $41 million to households, $15 million to gross savings, $6 million to government, and buys $20 million of goods and services from outside the region (imports). These total $120 million of inputs by the manufacturing sector to produce its output.

TABLE 2-1. *Simcity Transactions Matrix (millions of dollars)*

Sales \ Purchases	Processing Sectors			Final-Demand Sectors				
	1. Manufacturing	2. Trade	3. Services	4. Consumer Expenditures	5. Capital Formation	6. Government	7. Exports	8. Total Output
Processing Sectors								
1. Manufacturing	18	10	8	28	12	14	30	120
2. Trade	9	8	11	13	4	4	6	55
3. Services	11	6	12	24	2	3	12	70
Payments Sectors								
4. Households	41	21	23	5	5	15	10	120
5. Gross Savings	15	3	5	6	0	−6	17	40
6. Government	6	3	4	20	0	22	0	55
7. Imports	20	4	7	24	17	3	5	80
8. Total Inputs	120	55	70	120	40	55	80	540

Each *row* indicates the *sales* of that row sector to the column sector. Again focusing on manufacturing, manufacturing sells $18 million to other manufacturing, $10 million to trade, $8 million to services, $28 million to consumer expenditures, $12 million to capital formation, $14 million to government, and $30 million to customers outside the region (exports). Its total output of $120 million is exactly equal to its total inputs of $120 million. By definition this is true of each row and column total for each sector.

A portion of the purchases made by the manufacturing sector is from nonproducing-type sectors such as gross savings and government. The same is true of a portion of the sales by the manufacturing sector. These differences are compartmentalized in the transactions table so that the transactions table has three major parts. First, the upper left-hand corner of the table, which is set-off by double-ruled lines, contains the *processing sectors* which are the sectors within the region that produce goods and services. Second, rows 4–7 are the *payments sectors*, which include payments made by industries to households (wages, rent, interest, and profit), gross savings (depreciation and retained earnings), government (taxes and fees), and imports (out-of-region purchases). Third, columns 4–7 are the *final-demand sectors*, which represent the various final markets for the output of the region's industries. In the example in Table 2-1, the final-demand sectors are consumer expenditures by the region's residents, capital formation (including changes in finished-goods inventory), sales to government (federal, state, and local), and sales to nongovernment markets outside the region.

Compartmentalizing the transactions table may also be viewed as a division into exogenous and endogenous sectors. An exogenous sector is an income-determining sector, in contrast to an income-determined or endogenous sector. An exogenous sector is one whose activity level is determined outside the urban or regional economy being examined. For instance, federal-government spending in the region is exogenous to the regional economy; it is determined outside the region. Similarly, export demand is determined outside the system. In the case of the input-output model, the final-demand sectors are considered exogenous and the processing sectors endogenous. Classification of sectors as exogenous and endogenous depends on the definition of the "system" being considered. Household income and spending is considered as either exogenous or endogenous.

The transactions matrix is an accounting system and as such is based on certain accounting conventions. The most important of these are as follows:

1. All transactions are valued in producer's prices, rather than in purchaser's prices. The differences between the former and the latter are marketing and related costs. Individual marketing costs, such as transportation and retail and wholesale trade, are charged to the purchaser as a direct purchase from these sectors, rather than as part of the purchase price of the commodity.
2. The output and associated transactions of the retail and wholesale sectors are treated on a gross-margin basis, which is roughly gross sales minus costs of goods sold. For instance, if a machinery manufacturer purchases fabricated-metal parts from a wholesaler, the transaction is treated as if he were purchasing a marketing service from the wholesaler (the wholesaler's margin) and the parts from the fabricated-metal industry. If the transactions

15

were not handled in this manner, many interindustry links would be blurred by showing them flowing first to a trade sector and then to the processing or final-demand sector.

3. The input-output table contains only purchases used in current production; it excludes capital expenditures. The capital that is "used up" in current production appears as depreciation and is included in the gross-savings sector. For industries selling capital goods, the goods are shown as sales to gross private investment rather than to the industry making the purchase.

DIRECT-REQUIREMENTS TABLE

The transactions matrix is not only a useful way to organize a multitude of economic relationships in a systematic manner, but also it can be transformed into analytical matrices if we introduce a few assumptions about production.[1]

First, assume that we have constant returns to scale. In other words, with a given combination of inputs, the relationship between inputs and output is proportional; that is, if the quantity of each input is doubled, the output is also doubled. Second, assume that we have fixed production coefficients, which means that the amount of inputs purchased by each sector depends only on the output level of that sector. Third, assume that there is no substitution of production factors.

These assumptions allow us to transform the transactions data in Table 2-1 into direct requirements or "production recipes" for each of the processing sectors, as shown in Table 2-2. Each column in Table 2-2 indicates the required purchases of the column industry from the row industries in order for the column industry to produce $1.00 of output. According to our assumptions, each and every dollar of output is produced with the same mix of inputs or production recipes. For example, the manufacturing sector in Table 2-2 requires $.150 of inputs from other manufacturers, $.075 of inputs from trade firms, and $.092 of inputs from services, and makes payments to households (primarily wages and salaries) of $.342, has gross savings of $.125, pays taxes of $.050, and imports (from outside the region) $.167 of its needed inputs in order to produce an average

---

1. For a more complete discussion of the assumptions underlying the input-output model, see Hollis B. Chenery and Paul G. Clark, *Interindustry Economics* (New York: Wiley, 1959).

TABLE 2-2. *Simcity Input-Coefficients Matrix*

	1. Manufacturing	2. Trade	3. Services
1. Manufacturing	.150	.182	.114
2. Trade	.075	.145	.157
3. Services	.092	.109	.171
4. Households	.342	.382	.329
5. Gross Savings	.125	.055	.071
6. Government	.050	.055	.057
7. Imports	.167	.073	.100
	1.000	1.000	1.000

$1.00 of output. These ratios are called input coefficients. They reflect purchases made from other regional suppliers, since inputs purchased outside of the region are all included in the import category. In this way a regional input-output system differs from most national input-output tables which generate technical production coefficients. For national output tables, technical coefficients are a reflection of the current state of technology. For regional tables, the input coefficients are a product of both technology and regional trade.

Total-Requirements Table

The primary reason for the previous discussion concerning direct requirements was to provide an intermediate step necessary in arriving at a procedure for measuring both the *direct* and *indirect* requirements of changes in demand for the output of a region's industries. Such measurement is crucial to an understanding of urban-regional change.

The Simcity input-coefficient table told us the direct requirements necessary for each of the producing sectors to produce an additional $1.00 of output. For instance, from column 1 of Table 2-2 we can compute the additional purchases required of the manufacturing sector in order to produce an additional $10,000 of output. This increase would require purchases from manufacturing, trade, services, and so forth. But in order to supply these additional requirements, each of the supplying sectors must increase its production. These suppliers in turn will need to purchase inputs to meet the demands upon them. The chain of transactions would continue, with each successive round of transactions becoming smaller than the preceding because of the leakages of purchasing power from the regional economy.

Since the related concepts of industry interaction and economic impact are vital to an understanding of regional economic change and growth, we need to examine these concepts in some detail. Specifically, we will use a method of successive approximations to trace out the various rounds of transactions if the manufacturing sector increases its output by $10,000.

We know from column 1 of Table 2-2 that certain direct inputs are required in order for the manufacturing sector to produce $1.00 of output. Because of our constant-input assumption, this relationship remains proportional as we expand output. Thus, the direct requirements (or inputs) associated with $10,000 of output can be determined by multiplying the input coefficients for the manufacturing sector times the $10,000. The computed direct requirements (by sector) are recorded in column 1 of Table 2-3.

TABLE 2-3. *Increased Production Requirements Resulting from a $10,000 Increase in Manufacturing Output,*

Rounds 1 and 2

| Purchases From | Direct Requirements— Round 1 (1) | Indirect Requirements—Round 2 | | | |
		Manu- facturing (2)	Trade (3)	Services (4)	Total (5)
Manufacturing	$1,500	$225	$136	$105	$467
Trade	750	112	109	144	365
Services	920	138	82	157	377

For example, notice that from column 1 of Table 2-3, $1,500 worth of product from the manufacturing sector is required by the manufacturing sector for the production of an additional $10,000 of output (0.150 × $10,000 = $1,500). In addition, the manufacturing sector will purchase an additional $750 from the trade sector and $920 from the service sector.

If the calculation of direct requirements (the first round of transactions) were all that were necessary in tracing the economic impact associated with the manufacturing sector's initial increase of $10,000 of output, the task would be simple indeed. However, the increase in output for the manufacturing sector requires those sectors supplying inputs to the manufacturing sector to increase *their* level of input requirements because of an increase in demand for their products. New input-requirement levels for these sectors, however, imply new output levels for their suppliers. The whole process has numerous rounds which require a large number of calculations in order to estimate the total impact. As we illustrate the process by which we obtain the indirect requirements from the direct requirements of Table 2-2, each successive round will refer to the various stages of calculations and the various sets of requirements obtained. For example, round 1 will be used to refer to the direct requirements shown in column 1 of Table 2-3. Round 2 will be used to refer to the first round of indirect requirements, round 3 for the second round of indirect requirements, and so on.

The calculation of total requirements resulting from the initial increase of $10,000 of output by the manufacturing sector will be carried through three rounds in Tables 2-3 and 2-4. The derivation of the first round of transactions (show in column 1 of Table 2-3) has already been discussed. Using the information in column 1, round 2 can be calculated. For example, the direct input requirement from the manufacturing sector of $1,500 requires an additional increase in output for the manufacturing sector. What are the inputs required for this additional production? Reading from column 2 of Table 2-3 for the manufacturing sector, they are $225 from manufacturing, $112 from trade, and $138 from services. These input requirements are calculated by multiplying the $1,500 by the appropriate input coefficient for the manufacturing sector as shown in Table 2-2. Reading from Table 2-2, the manufacturing sector will

TABLE 2-4. *Increased Production Requirements Resulting from a $10,000 Increase in Manufacturing Output,*

Rounds 2 and 3

Purchases From	Indirect Requirements— Round 2 (1)	Indirect Requirements—Round 3			
		Manu- facturing (2)	Trade (3)	Services (4)	Total (5)
Manufacturing	$467	$70	$67	$43	$180
Trade	365	35	53	59	147
Services	377	43	40	64	147

purchase $0.150 from the manufacturing sector, $0.075 from the trade sector, and $0.092 from the service sector in order to produce $1.00 of output. To determine the input requirements associated with an increase of $1,500 of manufacturing output, the figure of $1,500 is multiplied by each of these input coefficients.

The other entries for round 2 are determined in a similar manner. For the trade sector, take the direct requirement of $750 and multiply this value times the input coefficients for the trade sector shown in Table 2-2. These second-round transactions are recorded in column 3 of Table 2-3. Finally, the second-round transactions associated with the service sector are shown in column 4 of Table 2-3. These dollar figures are calculated by multiplying $920 times the appropriate input coefficient for the service sector as shown in Table 2-2.

The sector totals for the second round of transactions are found by summing across columns 2 through 4. These totals (by sector) are entered in column 5 of Table 2-3. The sector totals in column 5 represent additional outputs induced by the manufacturing sector's initial increase in output of $10,000.

Let us carry our illustration through one more round. To compute the third round of transactions, the sector row totals for the second round of transactions (column 5 of Table 2-3) are viewed as additional increases in output; therefore, additional inputs are required. For example, because of the transactions considered in round 2, the manufacturing sector must increase its output by an additional $467. Therefore, the manufacturing sector will have to increase its purchase of inputs in order to produce this additional amount of output. The third round of transactions for the manufacturing sector is calculated by multiplying the input coefficients for the manufacturing sector (Table 2-2) by the $467. These figures are entered in column 2 of Table 2-4. The entries for columns 3 and 4 are determined by repeating the process used to complete column 2 of Table 2-4. The last step in determining the third round of transactions is to total the figures in columns 2 through 4 of Table 2-4 for each sector. These totals (by sector) are entered in column 5 of Table 2-4.

Although we have considered only the first three rounds of transactions, it is important to keep in mind that the impact associated with the initial $10,000 of increased output by the manufacturing sector does not stop at the end of the third round. Additional rounds of spending and respending will occur. The size of each successive round of transactions, however, becomes smaller and smaller since each round is "dampened down" by the leakage of transactions from the regional economy. The major type of leakage is the purchase of inputs from suppliers outside the region. Therefore, a point is reached where the round-by-round transactions associated with some initial change in the regional economy (e.g., an increase of $10,000 in the manufacturing sector's output) become negligible.

The foregoing discussion of the calculations may have seemed similar to a shaggy-dog story. Fortunately, the relationships we have been discussing can be expressed as a system of simultaneous equations and solved on a computer in a matter of seconds. Even for a very large table, the total-requirements table can be calculated in only a few minutes with a computer.

An interaction matrix, which shows the total transactions (direct and indirect requirements) for each of the producing sectors to deliver an additional $1.00 of output to final demand, is presented in Table 2-5. The columns show the total requirements in order for the column sector to produce and sell an additional $1.00 of output to final demand.

TABLE 2-5. *Interaction Matrix (Direct- and Indirect-Output Effects)*

	Manufacturing	Trade	Services
Manufacturing	1.226	0.289	0.224
Trade	0.136	1.231	0.252
Services	0.154	0.194	1.265

Before introducing an expanded interaction matrix which includes the effects of consumer income and spending, let us consider two examples using the information in Table 2-5.

In the Simcity transactions matrix, recall that the *final demand* for the output of the processing sectors was divided into four categories: consumer expenditures, capital formation, government, and exports. If we sum these four sectors for each processing sector, we arrive at total final demand of $84 million for the manufacturing sector, $27 million for the trade sector, and $41 million for the services sector. Our purpose in calculating total final demand for each industry is to illustrate an extremely useful relationship among final demand, the interaction matrix, and total output. Since each column in the interaction matrix indicates the total-output requirements for the column industry to deliver $1.00 of output to final demand, if we multiply each column in the interaction matrix by the corresponding final-demand value and then sum across the rows, the result will yield total output for each industry. For instance, if we multiply column 1 of Table 2-5 by $84 million, column 2 by $27 million, and column 3 by $41 million, then add up the values in each row, we find that the total output is $120 million for the manufacturing industry, $55 million for the trade sector, and $70 million for the services sector. These are the same total-output values which we started with in Table 2-1.

This relationship allows us to trace the *impact* of any change in the final demand for the output of a regional economy. Suppose that the Simcity manufacturing sector experiences an increase of $10 million in export demand. Exports increase from $30 million to $40 million and final demand for manufacturing increases from $84 million to $94 million. Using the procedure outlined above, we find that the output of the manufacturing industry increases from $120 million to $132 million, trade from $55 million to $56 million, and services from $70 million to $72 million.[2] The ability to measure the impact of a change in demand in this manner allows us to see how interdependence or linkages within the regional economy tend to amplify any change in demand for the output of the region's industries.

The interaction in the regional economy occurs not only from interindustry effects in the industries producing goods and services but also through income and expenditures of households. If an industry experiences an increase in demand, it must hire more labor services as well as purchase more inputs from other industries. This additional income received by households increases consumer expenditures for goods and services; additional demand is *induced* by the initial increase in demand. These additional induced effects can be measured in an interaction matrix similar to Table 2-5. By including the household row and column in an interaction matrix, we have the results indicated in Table 2-6. The interpretation and use of this matrix is the same as for Table 2-5, except that with households included in the interaction matrix we exclude households from our final-demand summation. As would be expected, the values in Table 2-6 are larger than in Table 2-5, indicating greater total effects than was the case when only interindustry requirements were included.

2. Results are rounded to the nearest $1 million.

TABLE 2-6. *Interaction Matrix Including Households*

	Manufacturing	Trade	Services	Households
Manufacturing	1.516	0.642	0.552	0.557
Trade	0.309	1.441	0.447	0.331
Services	0.402	0.496	1.545	0.476
Households	0.801	0.973	0.905	1.537

Other sectors, made endogenous (determined by) rather than exogenous (determining), might also be included in the interaction matrix. For instance, local government activity may be viewed as determined by the overall level of final demand for the goods and services produced in the region, rather than as an exogenous factor.

SUMMARY

The input-output relationships which we have described in this chapter are a convenient representation of the linkages among industries in a regional economy. But why are these industries where they are? And how important are linkages in determining industry location? Answers to questions of this sort are considered in detail in Chapters 4 and 5, but we need to make some preliminary observations.

Certain kinds of industries tend to develop in "families" in a given location. A firm may favor a given location because of other firms to which it can sell or from which it can buy. In other words, the firm is attracted by potential input-output linkages. The existence of suppliers or markets in a regional economy has an impact on the regional production function as viewed by other firms. Industrial complexes emerge largely because of these types of linkages.

The input-output system has the additional capability of reflecting regional input costs and differences in technology via the input-coefficients matrix or direct-requirements matrix.

REFERENCES AND SUPPLEMENTAL READING

P. J. Bourque and M. Cox, *An Inventory of Regional Input-Output Studies in the United States* (Seattle: University of Washington Graduate School of Business, Occasional Paper No. 22, 1970).

P. J. Bourque, *et al.*, *The Washington Economy: An Input-Output Study*, Business Studies No. 3 (Seattle: Graduate School of Business Administration, University of Washington, 1967).

H. B. Chenery and P. G. Clark, *Interindustry Economics* (New York: John Wiley, 1962).

M. J. Emerson, *The Interindustry Structure of the Kansas Economy* (Topeka: State of Kansas, 1969).

W. Isard and T. W. Langford, *Regional Input-Output Study* (Cambridge: The M.I.T. Press, 1971).

W. Leontief, *Input-Output Economics* (New York: Oxford University Press, 1966).

William H. Miernyk, *The Elements of Input-Output Analysis* (New York: Random House, 1965).

C. M. Tiebout, *The Community Economic Base Study*, Supplementary Paper No. 16, (New York: Committee for Economic Development, 1962).

3

Monitoring Urban-Regional Performance

The input-output model described in the previous chapter can serve as a framework for a variety of analyses of urban-regional economies. As indicated in the previous chapter, input-output models have been developed for more than 100 regions, ranging from large metropolitan areas to small towns. A number of factors explain the widespread development of such models, including the potential for numerous analytical extensions. A few of the basic types of analyses will be presented in this chapter as background for subsequent applications in later chapters. In describing some of the major uses of a subnational input-output model, we will draw heavily on actual cases.

REGIONAL INCOME ACCOUNTING

Since the transactions table is in essence an economic-information system, it provides us with several measures of the economic performance of an urban-regional economy in one data package. Two of the more common measures of economic perform-ance, gross product and personal income, can be obtained from the transactions table. In addition, the transactions table records the region's external trade (i.e., imports and exports), sheds some light on capital sources and capital formation, and shows the expenditure pattern of the region's residents. In simple terms, the transactions table is a numerical description of the internal and external transactions of an economy for some point in time. We will take a brief look at the major components of regional income accounts.

Gross Product

The regional counterpart of gross national product is *gross regional product*. Thus, the definition of gross national product can be used to measure gross regional product. Broadly defined, gross regional product is the market value of all current goods and services produced within the region. As with gross national product, gross regional product can be measured by using either an income or an expenditure approach. Summing the incomes from all the sources that are derived from current production within the region is one way of measuring gross regional product. Incomes, of course, refer to the wages, rents, interest payments, and profits created in the current production of all goods and services within the region. Similarly, expenditure data such as consumer spending (the household column), gross investment, government purchases, and exports can yield gross regional product.[1]

Personal Income

By definition, personal income is the current income received by persons from all sources. In addition to earnings from gross regional product, it includes transfer payments from government and business. Regional personal income can be readily obtained from the transactions table. Regional personal income is simply the sum of the household row of our input-output transactions table. In the example, Simcity personal income is $120 million. Row 4, the household row, also indicates the sector of origin of the region's personal income.

1. The Simcity matrix is too highly aggregated to yield meaningful straightforward calculations of gross regional product. In the process of reducing a transactions matrix to small but illustrative size, certain trade-offs were necessary.

Interregional Trade

The transactions table also provides substantial insight into the nature of the region's external trade. For instance, the region's three processing sectors export $17 million more than they import. That difference can be obtained by adding the exports of the three producing sectors and subtracting the imports of the same three sectors. But for all sectors in the region, imports exceed exports by the amount which appears in the cell corresponding to the export column and gross-savings row, which is, coincidentally, $17 million. A thorough explanation of this relationship is delayed to Chapters 7 and 8. At this point we are simply suggesting some of the ways in which the transactions table yields numerical values of important measures of economic performance. We will return to interregional trade and capital flows later in the book.

IMPACT ANALYSIS

What will be the impact on a region's industries of an increase in military spending? What will be the impact on employment of a decline in the demand for textile products produced in the region? What will be the impact of a new chemical plant in the region?

These are a sample of frequently asked questions which can be answered by the analytical potential of an input-output system. This section offers an explanation of the procedures for using inter-industry analysis to measure the impacts of actual or anticipated developments affecting a region's economy.

Output Multipliers

If one industry experiences a change in demand for its output, not only will its output change but so will the outputs of other industries in the region. For instance, if the export demand for manufactured products in Simcity increases by $10 million, the direct- and indirect-output requirements of the manufacturing sector will increase $12.26 million, the trade sector will increase $1.36 million, and the services sector will increase $1.54 million. These values were obtained by multiplying the values in column 1 of Table 2-5 by the $10 million increase in export demand.

The total output increases of all industries as a result of the increased final demand of $10 million is $15.16 million. This latter figure could have been determined by multiplying the $10 million by a corresponding *output multiplier*, which is obtained for each industry in Table 2-5 by summing each column. The output multiplier for the manufacturing sector is 1.516, which indicates that total output of all industries in the Simcity economy will increase 1.516 times as much as an increase in final demand in the manufacturing sector. Similarly, the output multiplier for trade is 1.758 and for services is 1.741.

It should be recalled from Chapter 2 that the selection of sectors to be included in an interaction matrix depends on several factors, including theories of income determination, geographic area, and analytical purpose.

Income Multipliers

Several types of income multipliers have been developed to measure the impact of a change in final demand on income. Two of these will be illustrated here.

The *simple-income multiplier* compares the additional income generated as a result of additional output increases with the direct increases in income in the sector experiencing the change in final demand. Calculation of a simple-income multiplier involves two steps.

1. For the industry in question, the coefficients in that industry's column in the table of direct and indirect requirements (Table 2-5) are each multiplied by the corresponding household-row coefficient (Table 2-2). For the manufacturing sector the calculation is

   $(1.226) (0.342) + (0.136) (0.382) + (0.154) (0.329) = 0.522$

2. The result of the first step is then divided by the corresponding direct-income requirement (Table 2-2). For the manufacturing sector this is 0.342, so that the simple-income multiplier is 0.522/0.342, or 1.526.

The *full-income multiplier* measures the overall increase in income generated by a dollar increase in final demand compared with the direct increase in income in that sector. Again using the manufacturing sector as an example, the numerator of the ratio is obtained from row 4, column 1 of Table 2-6 (0.801), and the denominator is obtained from row 4, column 1 of Table 2-2 (0.342). The full-income multiplier for the manufacturing sector is 0.801/0.342, or 2.342.

Employment Impacts

By making a simple conversion of the matrix of direct- and indirect-output requirements, employment impacts may also be obtained. If the employment in each industry is known, employment/output ratios can be computed for each industry. If the matrix of direct- and indirect-output requirements is multiplied by these values (each element in a row multiplied by the sector's employment/output ratio), the result is a matrix showing the direct- and indirect-employment requirements per dollar of output. Using the same procedure discussed above for output impacts, it is possible to calculate employment impacts.

EXAMPLES OF IMPACT MEASUREMENT

Hundreds of impact analyses have been conducted using a regional input-output model. Two examples are sketched to indicate typical procedures. The first is based on a Philadelphia regional input-output model and the second on a Kansas input-output model.

The Impact of Military Spending on Philadelphia

By far the largest regional input-output table constructed to date is for the Philadelphia region, with over 500 sectors (496 endogenous sectors).[2] Among its many uses has been to determine the impact of Vietnam War expenditures on the Philadelphia economy. The procedures used were similar to those outlined above.

Although it is impractical to recreate the impact on each of

2. Walter Isard and Thomas W. Langford, *Regional Input-Output Study* (Cambridge: M.I.T. Press, 1971).

the 496 sectors of the economy, it is possible to summarize the results of a "no Vietnam War" situation. In Table 3-1 each government sector is identified by a Standard Industrial Classification number. The names of the sectors are not necessary to the point being made. Corresponding to each government sector are the changes in employment, local purchases, and direct and indirect (total) impacts had there been no Vietnam War spending.

The results in Table 3-1 were obtained by projecting the expenditures in each government agency in 1968 assuming there had been no Vietnam War. These projections of employment, payroll, and total and local expenditures were made from past trends and agency interviews and were subtracted from the actual 1968 figures and converted to percentages, which appear in the first two columns of Table 3-1. The column totals indicate that federal employment would have been 10.2 percent lower and federal expenditures locally would have been 19.7 percent lower. The last column shows the value of inputs directly and indirectly required of the Philadelphia region by each government sector. This measure of total impact shows total output declines by $1.278 billion in the region.

Impact of a New Plant

The construction of a new plant in a region has an initial impact on industries in the region supplying construction inputs and a different impact once it begins operations. Its addition to the economy also causes structural change, but we will defer that discussion to Chapter 7. At this point we are concerned about impact analysis with an input-output model.

In 1973 a utility company announced that it planned to construct a fossil-fuel electric-generating plant in a rural area in northeast Kansas. The plant was to be constructed in four units at a total cost of $750 million. What would be the impact of such a generating facility on the immediate region and on the state?

First-Unit Impact.[3] The direct construction of the first generating unit is expected to cost $165 million, of which nearly $114 million will be spent on equipment purchased outside the state and $51 million on equipment and field construction within the state. The

---

3. This material is based on a report entitled *A New Electric Energy Center for the Kansas Power and Light Company*, Topeka, Kansas, 1973.

TABLE 3-1.   *Impact on the Philadelphia Region of Vietnam War Expenditures, 1968*

Sector	Employment (percent)	Local Purchases (percent)	Total Impact (dollars)
9101	+ 64.76	+ 64.88	+ 24,690,663
9102	+ 5.00	+ 4.76	+ 32,375,754
9103	0.00	0.00	0
9104	+ 4.98	+ 4.98	+ 6,424,369
9105	+ 14.98	+ 15.00	+ 11,999,002
9106	− 7.34	− 7.34	− 3,849,844
9107	0.00	0.00	0
9108	0.00	0.00	0
9109	0.00	0.00	0
9110	0.00	0.00	0
9111	+ 20.69	+ 92.24	+ 250,264,277
9112	+ 13.35	+ 13.35	+ 2,262,756
9113	+ 28.25	+ 28.27	+ 17,800,343
9116	− 33.36	− 33.30	− 61,699,644
9117	—	− 65.75	− 307,069,950
9118	− 4.14	− 4.14	− 3,932,432
9119	—	− 55.92	− 60,525,423
9120	−100.00	−100.00	− 217,311,119
9121	—	− 46.85	− 375,304,650
9122	− 40.64	− 37.56	− 31,369,832
9123	—	− 83.66	− 56,430,039
9124	− 13.79	− 15.75	− 13,151,614
9125	—	− 21.75	− 64,492,068
9126	− 10.10	− 10.10	− 6,001,120
9128	0.00	0.00	0
9129	− 36.67	− 61.58	− 40,658,028
9130	− 5.32	− 23.39	− 85,656,542
9131	0.00	0.00	0
9132	0.00	− 16.50	− 46,788,023
9133	0.00	0.00	0
9134	0.00	0.00	0
9135	− 34.70	− 34.70	− 51,352,610
9136	− 54.02	− 47.22	− 15,988,914
9138	− 13.89	− 19.54	− 182,074,370
TOTAL	− 10.22	− 19.71	−1,277,839,058

SOURCE: Walter Isard and Thomas W. Langford, Jr., "Impact of Vietnam War Expenditures on the Philadelphia Economy," *Regional Science Association Papers*, Vol. 23, 1969, p. 230.

$51 million expenditures are estimated to be divided as indicated in Table 3-2.

TABLE 3-2. *Expenditures Affecting the Kansas Economy,*
First Generating Unit

Expenditure	Amount ($ million)
Wages	40.0
Contractor's overhead	8.5
Pumps and fans	0.9
Concrete	1.5
Paint	0.2
TOTAL	51.1

SOURCE: *A New Electric Energy Center for the Kansas Power and Light Company,* Topeka, Kansas, 1973. Appendix C.

The $40 million in wages to be paid to construction workers on the site are assumed to be paid to workers residing in Kansas at the time. This is not to suggest that all construction labor will be drawn from Kansas. Workers will undoubtedly be drawn from a multistate area, if not from the nation. However, the expenditure categories presented above refer only to the Kansas component of each expenditure. Excluded is nearly $114 million of purchases made outside the state for the construction of the first unit.

The impact analysis is concerned with only the Kansas expenditures because the non-Kansas purchases are "leakages" from the income-expenditure stream for Kansas and consequently have little, if any, impact.

In addition to the $40 million in wages, $5 million of the contractor's overhead was allocated to personal income in the form of interest, profits, and other wages and salaries and $3.5 million was assigned to business services.

The additional personal income exerts a multiplier effect on the Kansas economy and on the seven-county region of primary impact. As discussed in the previous chapter, these direct and indirect effects can be measured by input-output analysis. Table 3-3 summarizes the results.

TABLE 3-3. *Selected Economic Impacts Upon Kansas and the Seven-County Region,*

First Generating Unit

Impacts	Kansas	Seven-County Region
From construction		
Additional industry output, ($ million)		
Agriculture	4.5	0.9
Mining	6.4	4.3
Other construction	4.6	4.1
Manufacturing	27.5	10.4
Transportation	5.8	4.8
Utilities	4.4	3.9
Trade	17.9	14.0
Finance, insurance, real estate	14.1	9.4
Services	18.4	13.5
Total industry output	103.6	65.3
Additional personal income, ($ million)	67.2	57.8
Additional employment, (number)	840	560
From annual operation		
Additional industry output, ($ million)	4.1	3.5
Additional personal income, ($ million)	3.2	2.7
Additional employment, (number)	210	140

SOURCE: *A New Electric Energy Center for the Kansas Power and Light Company,* Topeka, Kansas, 1973. Appendix C.

State personal income will increase $67.2 million as a result of construction of the first unit. Personal-income gains in the seven-county region will be less than those for the state as a whole because the region will supply a smaller share of the goods and services purchased directly and indirectly by construction employees. The gain in regional personal income is estimated at $57.8 million.

The major portion of total spending for the project is for purchases supplied outside Kansas. But about $6 million of purchases are made in the state. The combined effects of these purchases and wages will result in an estimated increase in state output of $103.6 million. Because of greater "leakages," the output effects in the region will be only $65.3 million during the construction of the first unit.

The major expense of operating the first unit is $2 million in annual wages. The total additional industry output resulting from this additional payroll is estimated at $4.1 million for the state and $3.5 million for the region. The annual personal-income gain is expected to be $3.2 million for the state and $2.7 million for the region.

The additional employment indicated in Table 3-3 is the approximate magnitude of the number of employment opportunities that might be expected in the state and region as a result of construction and operation. Plant-related jobs are included in the totals shown.

Four-Unit Impact. Total direct construction cost of the four-unit facility is estimated to be $615 million. Nearly $425 million of the total will be as purchases of goods and services from outside the state and will have little impact. The remaining amount, approximately $190 million, will be spent in Kansas. The anticipated breakdown is indicated in Table 3-4.

TABLE 3-4. *Expenditures Affecting the Kansas Economy,*
Four Generating Units

Expenditure	Amount ($ million)
Wages	149.0
Contractor's overhead	31.5
Pumps and fans	3.3
Concrete	5.6
Paint	.7
TOTAL	190.1

SOURCE: *A New Electric Energy Center for the Kansas Power and Light Company*, Topeka, Kansas, 1973. Appendix C.

The impacts were calculated in the same manner as for the first unit and are presented in Table 3-5. Output increases of all state industries will total $386.2 million, $243.5 million of which will accrue to the seven-county region's industries. The four-unit facility will add $254.3 million of personal income to the state during its

TABLE 3-5. *Selected Economic Impacts Upon Kansas and the*
           Seven-County Region,

Four Generating Units

Impacts	Kansas	Seven-County Region
From construction		
Additional industry output, ($ million)		
Agriculture	16.8	3.4
Mining	23.9	16.1
Other construction	17.1	15.2
Manufacturing	102.5	38.8
Transportation	21.6	17.9
Utilities	16.4	14.5
Trade	66.7	52.2
Finance, insurance, real estate	52.6	35.1
Services	68.6	50.3
Total industry output	386.2	243.5
Additional personal income, ($ million)	254.3	219.2
Additional employment (number)	1260	840
From annual operation		
Additional industry output, ($ million)	6.2	5.2
Additional personal income, ($ million)	4.8	4.0
Additional employment (number)	315	210

SOURCE: *A New Electric Energy Center for the Kansas Power and Light Company,* Topeka, Kansas, 1973. Appendix C.

construction, with personal income in the primary impact region increasing $219.2 million.

The operations of the four-unit plant will add $6.2 million annually in output to all state industries, including $5.2 million to the region. Annual state personal income will be $4.8 million greater. The region's personal income will be $4.0 million greater.

CONSISTENT PROJECTIONS

Long-run decisions, planning, and policy questions frequently involve resource commitments extending over several years. Invest-

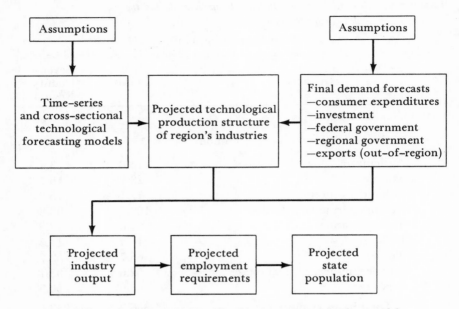

Figure 3-1   Schematic diagram of input-output projections model

ment decisions in development and related capital requirements require some judgment about the future. Projections from an input-output model can be made for such purposes.[4] Such projections are mutually compatible because the model generates "consistent forecasts," forecasts of variables which are consistent with each other. While consistent forecasts do not guarantee correct ones, they do require the sum of the separate forecasts to be identical to the total forecast.

A schematic diagram of an input-output projections model is presented in Figure 3-1.

The projections model requires two types of intermediate projections: technological change and final demand. Regardless of the technique, technological forecasting is a demanding exercise. It can be accomplished by using both time-series and cross-sectional data. The latter is usually the "best-practice technique," which arrays the firms in the industry from most efficient to least efficient

4. Two examples of projections from regional input-output models are Charles M. Tiebout, "An Empirical Regional Input-Output Projection Model: The State of Washington 1980," *Review of Economics and Statistics*, 51 (1969), pp. 334–40, and M. Jarvin Emerson, *Interindustry Projections of the Kansas Economy* (Topeka: State of Kansas, 1971).

and expects the average technology in the industry to move in the direction of the most efficient firms.

Final-demand projections are made for capital formation, government sectors, and exports. The latter necessitates a tie-in with national markets. Once new technologies have been projected and adjusted for probable changes in out-of-region purchases, the resulting direct- and indirect-requirements matrix is multiplied by the new final-demand projections to obtain projected output levels for each industry. By projecting productivity changes in each industry, new employment/output ratios can be determined which will yield the corresponding employment for each industry. The employment projections are consistent with the output projections. From the employment projections, labor-force participation rates will yield a regional population projection.

SIMULATING DEVELOPMENT

What would happen if a new electronics firm moved into the area? What would happen if a petrochemical complex formed in the region? What would happen if the textile industry moved out of the region?

In addition to estimating short-run impacts from changes in the demand for the region's output, the input-output model is capable of simulating the effects of long-term development. Simulations were made for six industries that might have developed in the West Virginia economy.[5] These were book printing, electronics assembly, plastic wood, flyash brick, sulfuric acid, and petroleum production from coal.

Starting with the input-output data for the base year, projections of the input coefficients were made for a decade later. This provided two static pictures of the West Virginia economy, present and future. For the six sectors to be simulated, data were obtained from other regional input-output tables which had such industries or from expected characteristics of the industry. These six sectors were then added to the "future matrix," thereby allowing calculations of the output effects of these industries on each industry in the state.

The impact of the addition of the six simulated sectors on the West Virginia economy was calculated assuming final demand of

5. William Miernyk, *et al. Simulating Regional Economic Development* (Lexington, Mass.: Heath Lexington, 1970).

37

$100 million for each sector. The results indicated that the $600 million of additional sales to final demand by these simulated industries would increase total gross output of the West Virginia economy by $1.5 billion. The total effect of each sector is indicated in Table 3-6.

TABLE 3-6. *Summary of Direct and Indirect Impacts on the West Virginia Economy of Simulated Sectors*[1]

Sector	Change in Total Gross Output[2]	
	Millions of Dollars	Percent Change
Sulfuric acid	$ 381.8	1.25%
Petroleum from coal	296.9	0.97
Electronics complex	220.3	0.72
Flyash brick	218.9	0.72
Plastic wood	218.9	0.72
Book printing	210.8	0.69
Total change	1,547.7	5.08

SOURCE: Reprinted by permission of the publisher, from *Simulating Regional Economic Development* by William H. Miernyk, *et al.* (Lexington, Mass.: Lexington Books, D. C. Heath and Company, 1970).
[1]Changes in total gross output due to introduction of simulated sectors with assumed sales to final demand of $100 million by each sector.
[2]Detail might not add to total because of rounding.

Such a simulation technique identifies not only the magnitude of impact of a potential new industry but also the impact on other industries in the region. For development planning, such simulations can be useful, as will be discussed later. Our interest at this point is in demonstrating the multiplier effects of a new industry on a regional economy.

SUMMARY

Regional input-output models can yield a wealth of data on the structure and performance of a regional economy. Regional income-and-product accounts can be obtained, as well as detailed data on the region's imports and exports.

Impact analyses can be accomplished with the interaction matrices described in Chapter 2 and the multipliers derived from them. The impact of a change in the external demand for a region's products or of a new plant location in the region are examples which can be measured with an input-output system.

Input-output can also be the core of a projections model for the region. Consistent projections can be made with the interdependency framework.

REFERENCES AND SUPPLEMENTAL READING

Roland Artle, *Studies in the Structure of the Stockholm Economy: Toward a Framework for Projecting Metropolitan Community Development* (Ithaca, N.Y.: Cornell University Press, 1965).

J. R. Barnard, *Design and Use of Social Accounting Systems in State Development Planning* (Iowa City: Bureau of Business and Economic Research, University of Iowa, 1967).

M. Jarvin Emerson, *Interindustry Projections of the Kansas Economy* (Topeka: State of Kansas, 1971).

Werner Hochwald, Herbert E. Striner, and Sidney Sonenblum, *Local Impact of Foreign Trade* (Washington, D.C.: National Planning Association, 1960).

Walter Isard and Thomas W. Langford, *Regional Input-Output Study* (Baltimore: Johns Hopkins, 1972).

William H. Miernyk, "Long-Range Forecasting with a Regional Input-Output Model," *Western Economic Journal*, Vol. 6, No. 3, June 1968, pp. 165–176.

William H. Miernyk, *et al. Simulating Regional Economic Development* (Lexington, Mass.: Lexington Books, 1970).

Harry W. Richardson, *Input-Output and Regional Economics* (New York: Halsted Press, 1972).

Charles M. Tiebout, *The Community Economic Base Study*, Supplementary Paper No. 16 (New York: Committee for Economic Development, 1962).

4

Location Analysis

The urban-regional economic structure as described by the input-output framework is the product of numerous location decisions by firms. A firm must acquire inputs and dispose of its output, but to accomplish this some locations are better than others. How are these better locations determined?

The primary purpose of this chapter is to develop a theoretical framework which will make possible a general understanding of the economic forces that shape the economic structure of a region. Several questions regarding plant location (and location decisions) were raised in Chapter 1. Why did the textile industry move from New England to the South after World War II? Why did the Chicago stockyards decide to cease operations in 1970? Any attempt to answer these and similar questions of location requires some knowledge of how locational decisions are made.

In order to set the stage for our fairly abstract discussion of location, we need to begin with a historical sketch of areal location patterns. This will be followed with a brief discussion of the spatial nature of transportation costs. This general overview of spatial economic activity will pave the way for the development of a theoretical analysis of plant location.

AREAL LOCATION PATTERNS

Needless to say, there are notable differences in the basic economic activities of regions. Generally speaking, today's areal pattern of economic activity stems partly from the geographic inequality of the nation's natural resources. In early settlement periods of this country, the availability of natural resources (raw materials) was important for the development of local industry; however, recent technological advances have lessened this influence.

The regional development of the United States can be divided roughly into three periods of differing resource orientation in the location of economic activity. The dating of these periods is only approximate. The first period, from colonial time to 1850, was the early agricultural period; the second, from 1850 to 1950, was the minerals period, with its associated growth in manufacturing activity; and the third period, since 1950, is the amenity-resource period.

The agricultural period was characterized by the opening up of new land for farming and the development of transportation networks primarily designed to move agricultural commodities to market centers. The economic landscape formed by the location of market centers and transportation systems during this period conditioned much of the location of economic activity in later periods.

The agricultural period created new input requirements in the economy, and these shaped a new set of location forces in the minerals-manufacturing period. New industry locations were oriented toward mineral resources, shifting as the resources were depleted.

By about 1950, several changes occurred to decrease the importance of natural resources. As a result of technological change, raw materials as a percentage of output value declined in importance, thus weakening the locational ties to raw materials. Markets became the dominant location factor and amenity resources emerged as an important location force. Climate and cultural attractions, two examples of amenities, affect the quality of life and have served as locational magnets in recent times.

TRANSPORTATION COSTS

We can easily recognize that the production and marketing of goods involve some transportation costs. Although the importance of transportation costs may have diminished over time as a result of better transportation technology and greater economic density, these costs continue to have a significant impact in shaping the economic landscape.

Transportation costs, as related to the production of goods and services, have two distinct components: procurement costs and distribution costs, or alternatively, transportation costs associated with inputs and transportation costs associated with outputs. The general behavior of these transportation costs can be seen in Figure 4-1,

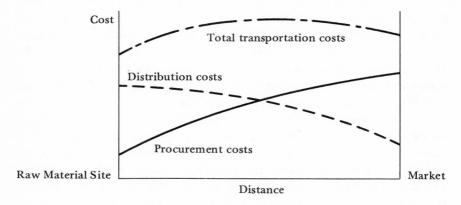

Figure 4-1   Structure of transportation cost

which represents a simple case of one raw-material source and one market. Procurement costs rise as distance from the raw material source increases, while distribution costs fall as distance to the market declines. Total transportation costs are lower at either the raw-material source or the market, but almost never are they lower at an intermediate location. Only a break in the mode of transportation or an artificially created freight-rate situation would allow an intermediate-site location. The former would occur, for instance, if the mode of carrier changes from railroad to water transportation. The latter is seen in a milling-in-transit privilege, which allows grain to be moved to a specified location, be milled, and continue to its destination with a through rate applied as if no stop were made. Otherwise, intermediate locations represent additional handling costs.

THE ECONOMICS OF LOCATION

To begin a discussion of the economics of location, we will assume that the goal of business is to maximize profits. Thus, profit is the basic factor underlying, for instance, the decision either to relocate or to expand a plant at its present location. Certain non-economic factors, such as pleasant surroundings and high-quality schools, may also play a role in the final selection of a location site. But if noneconomic considerations are incompatible with a profitable location, noneconomic considerations will be disregarded in the final selection of the maximum-profit site of location. In many instances, however, the maximum-profit site of location is actually an area (e.g., an urban area) where the quality of noneconomic factors varies substantially within the area. In such a case, noneconomic factors can become the final "swing" factors as to the choice of a site within the area. In a final section of this chapter, we will consider some alternatives to profit-maximizing behavior. Incidentally, it is quite probable that at any given time there will be more than one maximum-profit site of location. Additionally, uncertainty about the future and imperfect information make it extremely difficult to know which location site is the one that will yield maximum profits. But, to begin our discussion of the economics of location, we will confine the discussion to the notion that there is a single maximum-profit site of location and that businessmen are making location decisions on the basis of perfect information. The matter of uncertainty will be treated at the end of this chapter.

Cost Considerations (Supply)

Let us begin the analysis of plant location with an examination of the nature of production and production costs among alternative sites. More specifically, the task before us is to determine the minimum-cost site of production.

We begin this discussion with a case that is very simple to imagine. Suppose we have an operation that requires three resource inputs for production—labor, services, and materials. Let us assume that three alternative sites,—A, B, and C—are being considered. Let us add that there are regional differences in the quality of each resource, so that the input-output relationships differ at each site. Our hypothetical problem can be made quite explicit by the simple numerical example that is shown in the input requirements of Table 4-1. (Table 4-1 is similar to the input-coefficient table of Table 2-2). The column figures for site A show that 1 unit of output requires 20 units of labor, 4 units of services, and 12 units of materials. Shifting to site B, 18 units of labor, 6 units of services, and 14 units of materials

TABLE 4-1. *Input Requirements for One Unit of Output*

Inputs	Site A	Site B	Site C
Labor	20	18	21
Services	4	6	4
Materials	12	14	14

are required to produce 1 unit of output. The figures in column 3 (site C) show yet a different set of input requirements.

In light of Table 4-1, it is important to note that the input requirements represent one combination of inputs needed to produce one unit of output. Certainly it is possible to conceive different combinations of input requirements for *each* level of output. For example, to produce one unit of output at site A, it may be possible to substitute materials for labor. The particular combination of inputs used in production will depend on the technical nature of production and the relative prices of the inputs. We will need to say more about input-substitution possibilities later.

Before we can determine the site of minimum cost of one unit of output, we will need to know the unit prices of the inputs at each site. The per-unit prices of the inputs are shown in Table 4-2,

TABLE 4-2. *Per-Unit Cost of Inputs*

Inputs	Site A	Site B	Site C
Labor	$1.20	$1.40	$1.05
Services	3.50	3.00	3.30
Materials	5.00	4.00	4.50

where we are assuming that the producer is too small to effect changes in the prices of resources that he must purchase. Thus, for the producer the unit prices of the inputs are fixed. To determine the production costs for one unit of output at each site, the per-unit cost figures are multiplied by the number of input units used to produce one unit of output. The production-cost figures are shown in Table 4-3. To illustrate, at site A 20 units of labor are required to produce 1 unit of output, and the per-unit cost of labor at site A is $1.20. Hence the total labor cost to produce one unit of output at site A is $24.00 ($1.20 × 20 = $24.00). The remaining figures in Table 4-3 are computed in the same way. From Table 4-3 we note that the

TABLE 4-3. *Production Costs for One Unit of Output*

Inputs	Site A	Site B	Site C
Labor	$24.00	$25.20	$22.05
Services	14.00	18.00	13.20
Materials	60.00	56.00	63.00
TOTAL	$98.00	$99.20	$98.25

total cost of producing one unit of output is lowest at site A. Hence production costs—at one unit of output—can be minimized by locating at site A.

Such elementary analysis as this could be used to figure regional production costs for any level of output if constant returns to scale characterize a plant's production-cost schedule. But a plant's production-cost schedule is usually not characterized by constant returns to scale, and therefore the analysis needs to be corrected further (as in the next section).

We need to pause and see where our much-simplified analysis of the minimum-cost site of production has led us. From our discussion, we noted that the cost of production depends on the method of production (existing technology) and the relative prices of the resource inputs. Furthermore, we noted that the method of production and the relative prices of resource inputs can vary among regions. All of this suggests that spatial variations in the total cost of production can occur, and a minimum-cost site (or sites) of production exists. The task now before us is to develop these statements more fully. While a tabular portrayal was useful for introducing the topic of minimum-cost site of production, we now will need to turn to a more refined treatment of production and minimum-cost sites of production.

Production Function. An important item noted in our discussion of minimum-cost sites of production was the relationship between resource inputs and the rate of production, an example of which was the requirements table, Table 4-1. Economists refer to the relationship between resource inputs and the rate of production as a production schedule or *production function*, and define it as the relationship between quantities of various resource inputs used per period of time and the maximum quantity of the good (or service) that can be produced per period of time. Thus the production function summarizes the characteristics of existing technology at a given point in time, and it shows the technological constraints that a firm must reckon with.

When two or more variable resource inputs are used in production, the production function can be visualized as a production surface, showing various input-substitution possibilities. However, the particular combination of inputs used to produce some level of output depends on the relative prices of the inputs.

Figure 4-2 shows graphically a hypothetical production surface for a two-variable resource-input case. The three-dimensional diagram shows output on the vertical axis, and the two resource inputs are shown on the horizontal axis. An upward movement along the production surface represents an increase in the level of production. This is made possible by increasing the inputs of labor and capital. Contour curve *AB* represents a constant output of 20 units. Movements along the contour represent a substitution of labor for capital or a substitution of capital for labor. The rate at which one input can be substituted for another and still maintain the same level of output is called the marginal rate of input substitution. The production surface shown in Figure 4-2 constitutes a "family" of contours. The contours representing greater outputs are higher on the production surface, just as a contour map pictures a mountain or hill rising from a plain.

Conceptually, it is easy to transcribe a family of contours onto

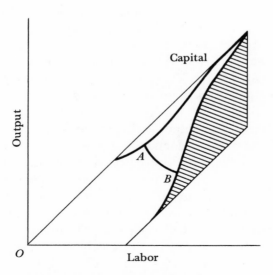

Figure 4-2 Two-resource production surface

a second diagram which more explicitly shows the input substitution possibilities at each level of output. Figure 4-3 shows three different contour curves, Q_1, Q_2, and Q_3, representing successively higher levels of output—20, 40, and 60 units, respectively. Since each point on a contour curve, say Q_1, represents a constant level of output but different combinations of inputs, they are termed *isoproduct* (equal product) curves. The isoproduct curves are shown convex to the origin to reflect diminishing marginal rates of input substitution.

While the isoproduct curves in Figure 4-3 imply an almost infinite number of combinations of resource inputs at each level of output, an isoproduct curve should be interpreted as an expression of the input substitution possibilities at different levels of output. To illustrate, a combination of 10 units of capital and 2 units of labor will produce 20 units of output. Or a combination of 4 units of capital and 6 units of labor can be combined to produce 20 units of output. Thus, Q_1 represents the various combinations of capital and labor that can be combined to produce 20 units of output. Similarly, Q_2 and Q_3 represent the various combinations of capital and labor that can be combined to produce 40 and 60 units of output, respectively.

Until now, we have stressed the relationship between input and output without consideration of input prices. The next logical

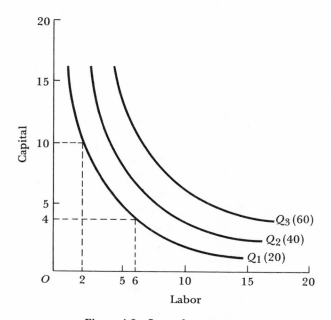

Figure 4-3   Isoproduct curves

step in the discussion of the minimum-cost site of production is to examine the relationship between input prices and the minimum-cost combination of inputs. Knowing the per-unit prices of the inputs, we can determine the minimum-cost combination of inputs at each level of production. Suppose the per-unit price of labor is $4.00 and the per-unit price of capital is $2.00. For some given level of cost outlay, we can determine the total units of labor and capital that can be purchased. To illustrate, suppose $36 (the cost outlay) is available to purchase the required inputs. Management could purchase 9 units of labor and no units of capital ($4 × 9 + $2 × 0 = $36). Or, alternatively, management could purchase 18 units of capital and no units of labor ($2 × 18 + $4 × 0 = $36). More generally, management could purchase various combinations of labor and capital, given the fixed cost outlay of $36. Economists refer to the relationship between a fixed-cost outlay and different combinations of inputs as an *isocost* curve.

The problem faced by management is one of determining how to produce a given output at the least cost (or, viewed in somewhat different terms, maximizing the level of output at the same given cost level). In Figure 4-4 the greatest amount of product

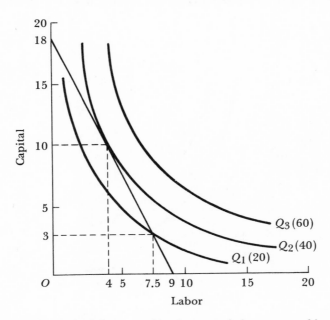

Figure 4-4   Optimal input combination to optimize output subject to a given cost

which management can get from $36 of cost outlay is 40 units of output. Any other combination of labor and capital obtainable for a cost outlay of $36 will move us to a lower isoproduct curve, and hence to a lower level of output. For example, a combination of 7.5 units of labor and 3 units of capital can be purchased for $36 and will produce only 20 units of output.

We now may go further with our analysis and consider different levels of cost outlay. For each level of cost outlay, resource inputs can be combined to maximize production, and therefore minimize production costs at that level of output, as seen in Figure 4-5. In Figure 4-5, curve EF represents the minimum-cost combinations for each of the rates of production Q_1 through Q_5, respectively. Curve EF is referred to as an expansion path, and is defined as the locus of points where output is produced at minimum cost.

Let us now summarize the major points made in the discussion of minimum cost of production. Firstly, the possibility of resource-input substitution was considered. This point was brought out in the use of the isoproduct curves. Clearly, the shape of the isoproduct curves reflects not only the existing technology of production but also the technical limitations of input substitution. Secondly, input prices and the means of determining input combinations per

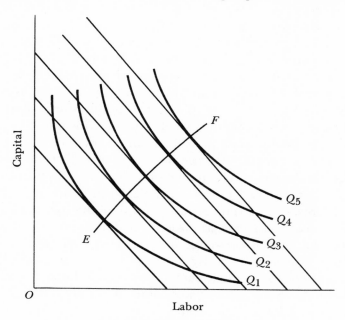

Figure 4-5   Expansion path

unit of cost outlay were shown through the use of an isocost schedule. Such a schedule was presented in Figure 4-4 where different levels of cost outlay are represented by different isocost curves. Finally, it was pointed out that by knowing the input-substitution possibilities (isoproduct curves) and the relative prices of the inputs (isocost curves), output can be maximized for a given resource outlay. Maximizing output for a given cost outlay is the same as minimizing the cost of production for a given level of output. Thus the expansion path of Figure 4-5 shows various levels of production, where each level of production represents minimum production costs. All of this paragraph can now be summarized in one general statement: It is possible to combine resource inputs in such a way that, for each level of production, the cost of production is minimized.

Now, with the general framework of production-cost minimization before us, let us apply the framework to an analysis of minimum-cost sites of production. In this study we will need to consider possible areal differences in the quantity, quality, and prices of resource inputs.

For any firm, costs vary from place to place in accordance with variations in the cost of the necessary inputs of production. The cost of labor, for example, varies from place to place according to wage rates and labor efficiency. Similarly, the costs of certain material inputs vary from place to place largely in accordance with transport costs. And transport costs themselves reflect the fact that certain resource inputs are not available locally.

Since a user of a resource input is concerned only with the final cost per unit of the input, the per-unit price of the input can be defined as the "mill" price plus the transportation charge. Thus the prices of resource inputs, which now may include transportation charges, can be shown graphically as an isocost curve.

How do areal differences in the per-unit costs of inputs affect the cost minimization of production? The best way of answering this query is with the use of a simple illustration. For the hypothetical firm which was used earlier, imagine that two sites, A and B, are now being considered as possible location sites. For production, the firm requires two resource inputs—labor and capital. Assume that labor is available locally at site A but not available locally at site B, and conversely, that capital is available locally at site B, but not at site A. Since labor is not available locally at site B, the per-unit price of labor will be higher at site B than at site A. In like manner, the per-unit price of materials will be higher at site A than at site B. It is assumed that areal differences in the price of each input reflects transport charges.

The foregoing example is illustrated in Figure 4-6. For sites A and B, the slopes of the isocost lines reflect the relative prices of the two inputs. For a specified cost outlay, the isocost line for site B has a steeper slope than the same isocost line for site A, because the input prices are different at the two sites—labor is more expensive at site B than at site A.

From Figure 4-6, we can see that for each site there is a locus of points which represents the minimum-cost combination of inputs at varying levels of output (i.e., the expansion path). However, the graphs in Figure 4-6 do not show directly which of the two sites represents the *minimum-cost site* of production. Therefore we need to view the problem in slightly different terms.

Using the expansion path, it is possible to express the relationship between production costs and output as a total-cost schedule or a total-cost curve. The total-cost curves for site A and site B are shown in Figure 4-7. A comparison of the two total-cost curves reveals that for rates of production from 0 to 200 units, the minimum-cost site of production is site B. For rates of production above 200 units, the minimum-cost site of production is site A.

Leaving price considerations aside, we have shown how location can affect the cost of production. Since areal differences in the availability, quality, and cost of certain economic resources exist, minimum-cost sites of production will occur. Thus, in the case of a

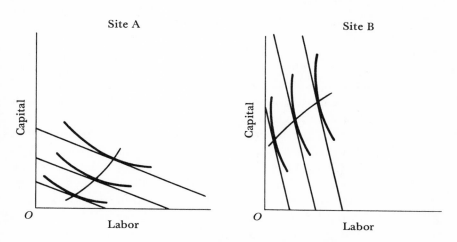

Figure 4-6   Expansion paths for different locations

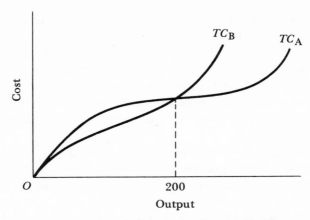

Figure 4-7 Total-cost curves for different locations

new firm, it is easy to imagine the existence of a minimum-cost site (or sites) of production—and hence the importance of location in the construction of new plants. However, what can be said about the importance of location for existing firms? Returning to our analysis for the answer, it was shown that the minimum-cost site of production can vary with the *level* of production. It then stands to reason that areal location is as important to existing firms as it is to new firms. The decision to expand the operations of an existing firm should include the decision of whether to expand operations at the present location, find an alternate or new location (relocate), or continue the present operations but expand in a newly located branch plant.

A final note to this section: Until now we have assumed that regional variations in the cost of production are due to regional differences in the availability, quality, and cost (including transportation charges) of resources. One important reason why the cost of resources can vary among regions is because of agglomeration economies. Certain agglomeration economies play an important part in determining production costs. But what are agglomeration economies? Broadly defined, the term *agglomeration economies* is applied to those internal and external remunerative benefits of the firm which stem from an areal concentration of people and activity, a concentration that may be profitable to business. In a later chapter, it will be shown that the extent of agglomeration economies depends on the particular economic structure of the region. An input-output system of accounts can be used to make explicit the structure of a region. Besides agglomeration economies, local taxes can also effect the final location decision of business. Within a state, and more particularly within a metropolitan area, significant local property-tax variations can become swing factors in business-location decisions. We shall have more to say about the effect which local taxes may have on location decisions.

Price Considerations (Demand)

Until now our discussion of location analysis has centered on the cost considerations of location. The next logical step is to examine in some detail the nature of areal demand. Here, a brief review of some basic principles of demand is helpful. We know that the fundamental characteristic of demand is that as price falls, the corresponding quantity demanded tends to rise, or alternatively, as price increases, the corresponding quantity demanded falls. The exact relationship between price and demand for some good per unit of time is determined by such factors as consumer preferences, consumer incomes, and consumer expectations. Once the relationship between price and quantity demanded is known, the effect of a change in price on total revenue (and marginal revenue) can be determined. By bringing the forces of demand and supply together, the maximum-profit level of production (and hence, the location site) can be determined. Specifically, the maximum-profit level of production is where marginal cost equals marginal revenue.

Our task is to incorporate the concept of areal markets into the traditional analysis of demand. To begin our analysis of areal demand, let us concentrate on a good that is sold entirely to household consumers. The purpose of this step is to avoid possible problems that are unique to intermediate-type market demands in the early stages of our discussion (i.e., the movement of goods from one industry to other industries). We will now make several specific assumptions to set the stage for our analysis.

1. Consumers are uniformly distributed throughout the market area. This means there is no concentration of consumers at some locality within the market area.
2. The seller of the good is located at the center of the market area.
3. Individual consumer-demand schedules are identical. This can be interpreted to mean that all consumers located in the market area have equal incomes, identical tastes and preferences, and

equal expectations. While this assumption obviously presents
an unreal situation, it does permit us to focus on a single consumer-demand schedule rather than on a series of different
demand schedules reflecting differences in such matters as consumer tastes and incomes. This assumption will be relaxed
later.

4. Transportation: (a) A single mode of transportation is available;
   (b) transportation charges per mile are uniform throughout the
   area; and (c) transportation charges are proportional to distance.
5. Consumers pay the transportation cost for moving the good to
   the site of use.

In view of these assumptions, look upon line AB in Figure 4-8
as an aggregate-demand curve for the good at *any* location within the
total market area. Specifically, the aggregate-demand curve of
Figure 4-8 is a summation of all the individual consumer-demand
schedules at some location within the market area. The linear
demand curve AB indicates the quantity of the product which consumers are willing and able to buy per unit of time within a relevant
price range. Since consumers demand more at lower prices, the line
slopes downward. To illustrate graphically the relationship between
price and quantity demanded, consider a price P_1. At price P_1,
consumers are willing to purchase Q_1 units of product per unit of
time; at price P_2 consumers are willing to purchase Q_2 units of product

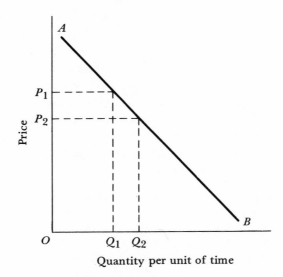

Figure 4-8 Aggregate-demand curve

per unit of time. These examples illustrate the responsiveness of consumers—quantity demanded—to a change in price. A measurement of this response is the price elasticity of demand. Simply stated, price elasticity of demand is a measure of the percentage change in quantity purchased (demanded) to the percentage change in the price of the good—all other things being constant. We shall see shortly how the price elasticity of demand can be used to measure the effect of consumer response on total revenue for an areal market.

Look upon the prices illustrated in the above example (and Figure 4-8) as seller's prices. If the seller's price is P_1, will some consumers have to pay more than P_1 for the good? The answer is yes. Let us see why.

The price to a consumer located some distance from the seller is the seller's price P_1 plus the transportation charge for shipping the good to the consumer. Since we have assumed that transportation costs are proportional to distance, let r represent the cost of moving one unit of the good one mile. Hence, the total transportation cost of moving one unit d miles is rd. Thus, it follows that the price of the good d miles from the seller is $P_1 + rd$. Or,

$$\text{Final price} = \text{seller's price} + rd$$

There should be no transportation costs for consumers located adjacent to the seller. In contrast, transportation costs will be highest in the peripheral zones of the total market area. This all suggests that while consumers have identical demands for the good, the quantity demanded will depend on the seller's price *and* the consumer's location from the seller.

Now the question to be faced is this: What effect does areal distribution of consumers have on a seller's total revenue? This is not an easy question to answer. The best way to approach the question is with the use of a *graphical demand cone*. However, before we discuss the meaning and use of a demand cone, we will need to go over once more the demand curve of Figure 4-8 with transportation costs now included.

As shown in the downward-sloping demand curve of Figure 4-8, the further a consumer is from the point of sale, the less he will purchase at any given price. This is illustrated again in Figure 4-9. Assume for the moment that the seller's price is P_o. Consumers located adjacent to the seller will purchase a total quantity of Q_o units. Thus the final price is the seller's price since there is no transportation cost. Let us now consider consumers located d miles

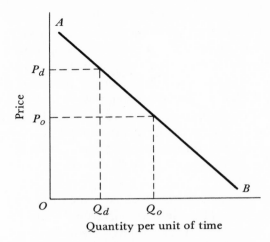

Figure 4-9   Aggregate-demand curve with transport costs

from the seller. For illustration purposes let the final price be P_d (Figure 4-9), representing a distance d miles from the seller and a transport charge, r. The consumers will demand less of the good since the final price is higher relative to the final price for purchases adjacent to the seller. The quantity demanded is shown to be Q_d units per unit of time. The difference between P_d and P_o, of course, reflects transportation costs.

It should now be obvious that because transportation costs are included in the final price of the good there is a price-demand elasticity associated with distance. In effect, Figure 4-9 shows that, with the seller's price constant, as the distance of consumers from the seller increases, the corresponding quantity demanded per unit of time falls.

Now let us return to the discussion of the demand cone. The use of a demand cone permits us to represent clearly the relationship between distance and the quantity demanded per unit of time. Given the seller's price as P_o, the total quantity demanded at varying distances from the seller is reflected in the shape of the demand cone of Figure 4-10. This figure requires some explanation. We will need to refer to Figure 4-9 in order to understand the graphic construction of Figure 4-10.

In Figure 4-9 it is shown that consumers located adjacent to the seller will purchase Q_o units at price P_o. Since point O of Figure 4-10 represents the location of the seller, the quantity Q_o is shown as

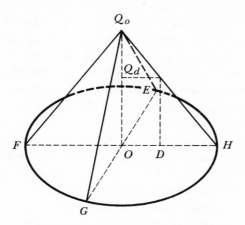

Figure 4-10 Market-demand cone

the height of the demand cone. The location of consumers some distance from the seller is measured along the base of the cone and in any direction from point O. Thus the line segment OD represents consumers located d miles to the "east" of the seller. At this location consumers will purchase Q_d units per time period. The final price of the good d miles from the seller, we recall, is P_d.

Since demand and transportation costs per mile are uniform in every direction from the seller, the quantity demanded by consumers at alternative locations from O will be the same in every direction as in the easterly direction. Remember that we have assumed that a potential consumer exists at every point in the market space. The outer base of the demand cone represents the natural boundary of the market. In effect, consumers located to the east of point H are "priced" out of the market. This is so because the final price of the good is higher than the price consumers are willing to pay. The surface height of the demand cone at any location shows the quantity demanded by the consumers at that location, given that the seller is located at O, that the seller's price is P_o, and that the transportation cost is r per unit per mile.

By knowing the area's total quantity demanded at the seller's price P_o, we can determine the total market receipts (or revenue). Total revenue equals the seller's price times the total quantity demanded. Certainly the total revenue figure is based upon a particular seller's price.

This brings us to the next question: What effect does a change in the seller's price have upon total revenue? We can answer this query with the use of the market-demand cone (Figure 4-10). For every price set by the seller, there will be a different demand cone. For instance, when the seller's price is greater than P_o, fewer units per time period will be demanded by the consumers located adjacent to the seller (point O). In fact, the quantity demanded will decrease at all points within the market area. It follows, then, that the height and base of the demand cone will be smaller, and the volume will be less. Thus, with an increase in price, the total quantity demanded will decrease; or alternatively, with a decrease in price the total quantity demanded will increase. The total market area (volume) expands or contracts depending upon the direction of the price change. Whether total revenue will be higher as a result of a price decrease depends upon whether the percentage increase in sales is greater than the percentage decrease in price. This seemingly complicated statement reduces to this:

1. When demand is price-elastic, a decrease in the seller's price will result in an increase in total revenue. This is so since the percentage change in quantity demanded (sales) is greater than the percentage decrease in price.
2. When demand is price-inelastic, a decrease in the seller's price will result in a decrease in total revenue. Why? Because the percentage increase in quantity demanded (sales) is less than the percentage decrease in price. The student should follow the same type of analysis in the case of a price increase.

As long as demand is price-elastic, total revenue will increase as a result of a decrease in the seller's price. This is indicated in Figure 4-11. When demand becomes price-inelastic, a decrease in the seller's price will result in a decrease in the total revenue. The decreasing portion of the total-revenue curve is not shown in Figure 4-11.

We may now put the concepts of location costs and areal demand together to see how the interaction of location costs and market receipts will determine the site of maximum profits. The assumed goal of businesses, we recall, is to maximize profits. To do so, they must operate at a level of activity where marginal cost equals marginal revenue. Stated somewhat differently, the maximum-profit level of activity is where total revenue exceeds total cost by the greatest amount.

Figure 4-12 brings together the cost curves and total-revenue curves for sites A and B of our earlier discussion. The total cost

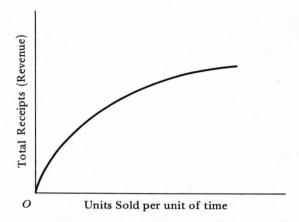

Figure 4-11 Total revenue for different-size market areas

curves for site B and site A are labeled TC_B and TC_A, respectively. You will remember that for rates of production from 0 to 200 units, the minimum-cost site of production is site B. For rates of production above 200 units, the minimum-cost site of production is site A. Though the total-revenue curves for site A and site B have not appeared in our discussion, let us imagine that the total-revenue curves TR_A and TR_B represent the total-revenue schedules for site A and site B, respectively. We must remember, of course, that a total-revenue schedule for an areal market reflects the seller's prices,

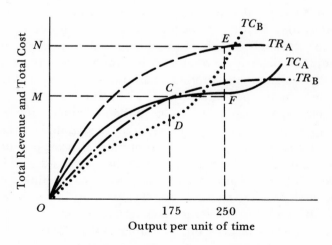

Figure 4-12 Site of maximum profits

59

transportation rates, population density, consumer demands, and consumer distance from seller.

For Figure 4-12, consider the total-revenue curve and total-cost curve for site B. Subtracting total cost TC_B from total revenue TR_B at each rate of production reveals that an output of 175 units per unit of time will yield the greatest difference CD. Shifting to the total-revenue and total-cost curves for site A, the greatest difference EF occurs with the rate of production of 250 units per unit of time. Since EF represents a greater profit than CD, the producer would locate at site A. The producer, of course, would have to set the price implied by the revenue curve to sell this rate of production. While the most profitable site and rate of production are at the minimum-cost site in this case, the most profitable site might be one at which both costs and revenues were higher and the difference was also higher than at other sites.

Although much of the foregoing discussion of location relates to the production and distribution of goods, the analysis can be extended to include the service industries. Regardless of the kind of economic activity under consideration, cost and market considerations are involved in the question of where to locate. Because of the nature of most service activities, it is expected that market considerations will have a dominant influence on their preferred place of location—that is, service activities tend to be market-oriented. This statement applies particularly to services that are administered frequently and directly to customers. A restaurant specializing in gourmet foods finds it advantageous to locate near those who have the incomes and tastes for gourmet foods. A service of this type handles an extremely perishable and high-value product that must be transmitted directly and almost instantaneously from the producer to the consumer. Another example is a medical doctor who must locate near the people who are to be served.

Since services are basically market-oriented, they tend to gravitate toward population centers. Not all population centers are of the same size, however. Many communities have populations of less than 2,000; others have populations that exceed 2 million. But certain services are found in even the smallest community. Contrarily, specialty shops, gourmet restaurants, and brain surgeons are almost always found in the larger urban communities. The location of services depends largely on two interrelated factors: threshold-market size and internal scale economies. A threshold market refers to the smallest market necessary for the enterprise to be profitable.

Closely associated with the threshold-market concept is the matter of internal economies of scale. Internal economies of scale refer to that portion of an enterprise's average-cost curve where average cost is decreasing with increasing levels of output (see Figure 5-4). While there are a number of factors that determine the nature of an enterprise's average-cost curve (these factors will be discussed in a later chapter), the important point for the present discussion is that in order for the operation to be profitable, the average revenue from the sale of the service (and hence, price) must at least equal the average cost of the operation in the long run. This means that if the spatial market for a particular service is too small to generate an average revenue at least equal to average cost, that activity will not be found in the area. In short, every service activity has some minimum-sized market that its scale economies require for the activity to be profitable. One would not typically expect to find, for example, a professional theatrical group located in a remote rural community.

Though most services are market-oriented, there are several factors that must be considered in the selection of the most-preferred population center. One consideration has already been touched upon, the matter of threshold markets. Other considerations, although related to the notion of threshold markets, include the frequency of demand for the service and accessibility. Services of infrequent use by the typical consumer must locate in large population centers so that the total demand by all residents is sufficient to make the provision of the service profitable. For example, brain surgeons are usually found only in the larger urban centers. General practitioners, on the other hand, are found in most small towns, where the demand for their services is more frequent. Turning to the matter of accessibility and modern transportation in particular, the automobile and improved highways have made it possible for most services to expand their market areas. Even the general practitioner may locate in a small town and extend his services to those who live in the smaller nearby communities. To a considerable extent, modern transportation has brought about the migration of many services from the small rural communities to the nearby larger towns. It is more convenient and far less expensive to have customers from small communities journey to service centers than to disperse these services to population centers of subminimal size.

A brief comment on cost consideration. Although the principle location consideration of the service industries is markets, cost factors are considered. Variations in land rents (or taxes) within the desired market area may cause the enterprise to select a low-rent site within the area.

Relaxing Assumptions

Uniform Distribution of Population.   Until now we have been assuming a uniform geographic distribution of population.   This assumption, along with others noted on pages 53 and 54, permitted a development of a general understanding of areal demand and areal markets.   When the assumption of a uniform population-density pattern is dropped, the size and shape of our market areas become irregular.   Realistically speaking, population distribution patterns appear as points (or nodes) within a market area, for consumers are inevitably grouped at various localities within a total market area.   While the assumption of a uniform distribution of population simplified our analysis, relaxing this assumption does not significantly change our results.   The effects of variable consumer-distribution patterns upon market areas will be noted later (Chapter 5) when we discuss industry competition and market areas.

Uniform Demands.   We assumed earlier that each consumer's demand schedule for the good under consideration is identical.   This assumption simplified our discussion of areal markets without impairing the overall validity of the conclusions.   In fact, a demand cone (and hence a total-revenue schedule) can be determined for the more realistic situation of different consumer-demand schedules for the same good.

The Centrality of Production.   On page 53 it was assumed that the producer will locate in the geographic center of his market.   For a variety of complex reasons, the site of maximum profits may not be at the geographic center of the market area.   First, the degree of competition will obviously effect the particular location of the pro-ducer.   A more rigorous discussion of the effects of competition is given in Chapter 5.   Second, the particular transportation network will partly determine the location of the producer.   Third, the topography of the area limits the number of possible locations. Finally, the particular population-density pattern of the area will be an important factor in determining the site of location.   For all these reasons, and others, the site of maximum profits may not be at the geographic center of the market area.

LOCATION IN PRACTICE

Our discussion has centered upon the development of a logical profit-maximizing framework for the location of an enterprise. But now a final question arises. Do businesses in fact follow the logical framework outlined here? Some do not. In some cases, a locational decision may be based more on personal factors than on economic factors. For example, a businessman may simply start a business in the community where he lives, where the location may or may not be the most profitable one. When competition is intense and profit margins are thin, the location of an enterprise which is based almost entirely on personal factors will likely fail in the long run unless the personal factors are compatible with economic factors. In regards to an oligopolistic (or monopolistic) situation, the location of an enterprise at a site which is not the most profitable may not end in a failure for the enterprise, even in the long run. With only moderate competition, profit margins may be so great that management need not confine their location decision only to maximum-profit location sites. Because of political and other reasons, management may decide on a profit margin which is less than the profit margin that could be earned from a maximum-profit location site. In such a case, management's decision of a location site would likely be based more on a study of comparative cost differences than on profit differences. Such a study would not be too unlike our prior analysis of cost considerations.

If the oligopolistic (or monopolistic) enterprise represents a large operation, its potential impact upon the local environment is substantial. One direct kind of impact is the attraction of other activities to the area, some which supply goods and services to the oligopolist and others which buy items as inputs for further production purposes. An indirect kind of impact would be the multiplying effect that these related businesses would have on employment and income growth in the area. The multiplying buildup of activity in the area may appear as a justification for the oligopolist's initial decision to locate in the area. This impression may not be altogether accurate. The agglomeration of activity in the area, which was prompted initially by the oligopolist's presence in the area, may still represent a spatial misallocation of resources. In other words, a reallocation of these same resources to other areas may mean a gain in net social benefits. Patterns of agglomeration and the notion of net social benefits will be topics for discussion in later chapters.

A discussion of location in practice would not be complete unless some consideration was given to the matter of uncertainty. Decisions of location do involve the long run and, therefore, uncertainty as to long-run profits. Businesses seeking to find a profitable location site must estimate the expected profits of alternative sites. In view of probable changes in economic conditions, the expected profits of a location site for today may not be the same as the expected profits of the same site in the future. Consequently, plant locators must give consideration to alternative location situations: for example, between a site which indicates a high initial return followed by an expected gradual decline in yields and a site which indicates a small financial loss for the first several years followed by an indefinite period of extraordinarily high returns. Viewing alternative locations on the basis of expected returns is not as simple as it might first appear. In addition to the knotty problem of estimating future returns, there is also the matter of existing competitive pressures, profit margins, and the financial strength of the firm. Thin profit margins, low financial reserves, and an awareness that estimated yields are only probabilities may cause management to act conservatively and select the site returning higher early profits.

REFERENCES AND SUPPLEMENTAL READING

Greenhut, Melvin L., *Plant Location in Theory and in Practice* (Chapel Hill: The University of North Carolina Press, 1956), Chapters 2, 3, 4, 5, 6, and 7.

Hoover, Edgar M., *An Introduction to Regional Economics* (New York: Alfred A. Knopf, 1971), Chapters 2, 3, 4, and 7.

Isard, Walter., *Location and Space-Economy* (Cambridge: The M.I.T. Press, 1956), Chapters 2, 3, and 4.

Karaska, Gerald J., and David F. Bramhall (ed.), *Location Analysis for Manufacturing: A Selection of Readings* (Cambridge: The M.I.T. Press, 1969), Readings 1, 2, 3, 5, 6, 10, 12, 15, 21, 22, and 28.

Nourse, Hugh O., *Regional Economics* (New York: McGraw-Hill Book Company, 1968), Chapter 2.

Richardson, Harry W., *Regional Economics* (New York: Praeger Publishers, 1969), Chapters 2, 3, and 4.

5

Spatial Competition, Pricing, and Location

To be sure, Chapter 4 was not intended to be "the practical man's guide" to plant location. Rather, our primary concern was to develop a theoretical profit-maximizing framework which would bring together the cost and price considerations of plant location. Viewed another way, Chapter 4 recognized that area variations in production costs and sales revenues do occur, and that the maximum-profit site of location is determined by comparing production costs with receipts for all alternative sites of location. Businesses maximize their profits not by locating in areas where costs are less or receipts greatest, but by locating where the margin between total costs and total receipts is the greatest.

The discussion in Chapter 4 of maximum-profit location sites was limited to a single market situation, the spatial-monopoly situation. Competition was excluded to avoid considering the complex relationship between spatial pricing and market situations (or market types) and their influence on plant location. The only spatial-pricing system mentioned in Chapter 4 was that of f.o.b. mill pricing.

This chapter will emphasize the relationship between differing market types and their influence on spatial-pricing policies. That is, the basic objective of this chapter is to see how prices and market areas are determined in the face of spatial competition. With this objective in mind we shall attempt, first, to give some simple illustrations of market areas for an assumed f.o.b. mill-pricing policy. This discussion will provide us with (1) a visual understanding of spatial competitive-market areas, and (2) a sketch of how production and distribution costs combine with competition to limit (or define) a producer's market area.

Second, the chapter presents a rigorous discussion of spatial competition and market-area determination. This section begins with a spatial-monopoly situation in which a producer sells his product under an f.o.b. mill-pricing policy. Then, the section considers the locational effects of rival producers in a monopolistic competitive situation. By moving across the spatial economic spectrum—from the spatial-monopoly situation to the spatial monopolistic competitive situation—this section prepares the way for a discussion of the economic rationale for shifting from an f.o.b. mill-pricing policy to some other type of spatial-pricing policy—uniform pricing, basing-point pricing, and zone pricing, for example.

The last discussion of this chapter emphasizes the effect on industry location of the various spatial-pricing policies.

PRODUCTION COSTS AND MARKET AREAS

If we can imagine a situation in which the product of each seller is identical to the product of every other seller for an industry group, product-demand differentiation will occur as a result of the formation of spatial markets. The logic is obvious. When the consumer price includes the seller's price plus the consumer's expense of transporting the item to the point of consumption, consumers will generally buy from the nearest seller. In general, the "friction-of-distance" factor causes consumers to pair up with sellers even when there are no real or fancied differences in the sellers' products; consequently and generally speaking, a purely competitive market situation is impossible if consumers are dispersed over a geographic market area. If in no other way, product-demand differentiation will result from the market area's spatial-pricing policies. Inevitably, the nature of competition and the significance of delivery costs for many real market situations will result in the emergence of a common spatial-pricing policy such as the "free-on-board" mill-pricing system. (You will recall from Chapter 4 that f.o.b. mill prices include a seller's price plus any delivery, i.e., transportation charges.)

Our discussion of spatial competition and market areas will

begin by considering the f.o.b. mill-pricing policy. We now turn to some market-area illustrations for a simple homogeneous goods situation, and by applying the f.o.b. mill-pricing policy, we will examine three different cost situations.

Equal Production and Transportation Costs

Market areas can be illustrated by two coordinated diagrams as in Figure 5-1. Suppose there are two sellers, S and T, and both have identical production and transport costs. The height of the vertical stems of the figure shows that each firm has production costs of $1.00; the gradients depict the transportation costs. A customer located d miles from seller S, at point D, will pay $2.00 for the item (the f.o.b. price of $1.00 plus a $1.00 transportation charge).

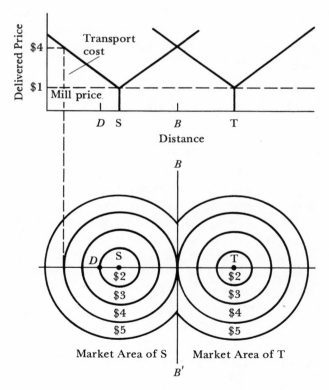

Figure 5-1   Market areas where firms have identical production and transport costs

Point *B* represents the market boundary between the two firms. To the left of *B* the delivered price of S is lower than that of T and, conversely, to the right of *B* the delivered price of T is lower than that of S. On a two-dimensional plane, the market boundary appears as illustrated in the lower part of Figure 5-1. The curves (in this case circles) represent equal delivered prices. Thus the market boundary between the two sellers is the line *BB'*.

Unequal Production Costs and Equal Transport Costs

Figure 5-1 represents only one of several possible situations. Let us consider another: S and T have identical transport rates, but the production costs at S are twice those at T. Will S be able to capture any part of the market and, if so, how much? The answer to both questions is illustrated in Figure 5-2. If the distance separating S and T is sufficiently great such that T's delivered price at S is greater than the production costs for S, S will be able to capture part of the market. The extent of S's market area is indicated in the lower portion of Figure 5-2.

Equal Production Costs and Unequal Transport Costs

In yet one other hypothetical case, let us assume that S and T have identical production costs, but that T is confronted with higher transportation costs. The resulting market areas for the two firms and their corresponding delivered prices appear in Figure 5-3. Firm T can serve only a small local market because of the rapid increase in its transportation costs for its output compared with those of S. The situation in Figure 5-3 is identical to one indicating that the product supplied at T (coal for instance) is inferior to the one at S. Since more coal is required, the overall transportation costs to the user of the coal are greater.

SPATIAL COMPETITION AND MARKET AREA DETERMINATION

The preceding discussion presented three possible cost situations for an f.o.b. mill-pricing policy: equal production and trans-

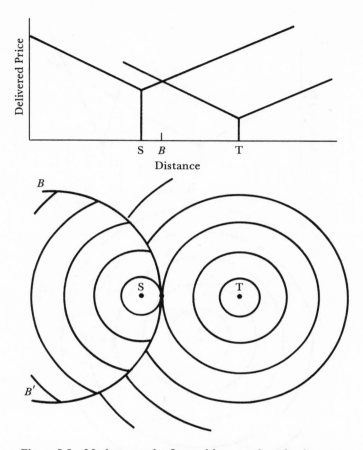

Figure 5-2   Market areas for firms with unequal production costs

portation costs; unequal production costs but equal transportation costs; and equal production costs but unequal transportation costs. Under all three conditions potential new producers will be influenced to locate their plants by the location of existing plants and their marketing areas. With this concept in mind, let us turn to a more rigorous discussion of spatial competition and market-area determination.

In discussing the first case, equal production and transportation costs, let us include the locational interdependence among competing producers under an f.o.b. mill-pricing policy. We will assume, additionally, that the total market area is a flat plain, evenly populated and geographically uniform. Obviously this is too simplified an economic situation to represent reality, but the model is

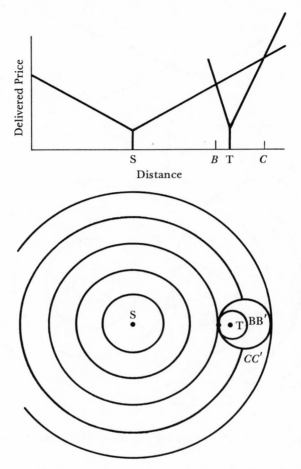

Figure 5-3   Market areas when producers have different transportation rates

convenient for discovering the locational affects of spatial competition and spatial pricing under realistic market conditions.

Spatial Competition and the Use of Marginal Analysis

In order to develop an analytic framework for a study of spatial competition, we must first digress to consider an alternative means of illustrating the maximum-profit site of location. Chapter

4 viewed a firm's maximum-profit level in terms of the greatest difference between total revenue and total cost. To best understand the nature of spatial competition and market areas, we now need to use a somewhat different approach for determining maximum profits. We need to equate marginal cost with marginal revenue for all alternative sites of location.

Figure 5-4 graphically shows the marginal-cost and marginal-revenue information for the maximum-profit site of location of a hypothetical firm. The rate of output per period of time is recorded on the horizontal axis, and the vertical axis records price, revenue, and production costs at various levels of output. We will later see that the graphic analysis of Figure 5-4 gives the same results as our total-cost and total-revenue curves of Figure 4-13.

Average and Marginal Cost. Figure 5-4 shows marginal cost (*MC*) and average cost (*AC*) curves. The latter is determined by dividing total cost by the volume of output; marginal cost, by definition, is the addition to total cost attributable to an additional unit of output when all inputs are optimally adjusted. An optimal use of resources occurs when resources are combined in such a way that the marginal physical productivity per dollar spent on one resource is equal to the marginal physical productivity per dollar spent on every other resource used in production. (The expansion path of Figure 4-6 traces out the optimal combination of resources at various levels of output.)

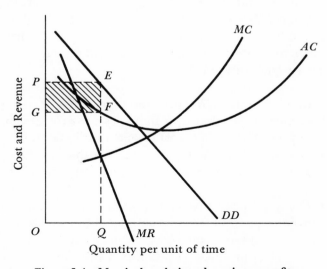

Figure 5-4   Marginal analysis and maximum profits

The preceding discussion of the optimal use of resources implies that the MC and AC curves of Figure 5-4 represent "long-run" cost curves; that is, there are no fixed resource inputs. The implication is consistent with Chapter 4, in which the discussion of plant location logically regarded all resources as variable resource inputs.

The marginal-cost and average-cost curves have the shape of conventional cost curves. As average cost decreases when output increases, marginal cost is less than average cost. When average cost increases as output increases, marginal cost is greater than average cost. Finally, if average cost is minimal, marginal cost will equal average cost.

Areal Demand. The DD (areal demand) curve of Figure 5-4 pictures the consumers' willingness to purchase a product at varying mill prices. DD can be derived from a series of demand cones similar to the one shown in Figure 4-11 if an area's population density is known, because the surface of the demand cone shows the total product demanded at all possible distances from the geographic point of sale. The cone's surface slopes downward to indicate decreasing demand with distance from the point of sale, because a delivered price will increase to reflect transportation costs. The further the buyer is from the point of sale, the higher will be the price and the lower will be the demand. In Figure 5-4, the total quantity demanded at a given mill price is simply the volume of the demand cone associated with that mill price. Accordingly, each point along the DD curve of Figure 5-4 represents a different mill price and, therefore, a different demand cone. Care must be taken by the reader to relate the concept of a demand cone with the areal demand curve DD of Figure 5-4.

Marginal Revenue. The MR curve of Figure 5-4 is the product's marginal-revenue curve; that is, it indicates the extra revenue resulting from the production (and sale) of one additional unit. After the sale of the first unit, marginal revenue is less than price, to indicate the presence of a degree of monopoly control over the seller's market.

Maximum Profits. Integrating the concepts of marginal cost and marginal revenue gives us an alternative way of determining maximum profits. Maximum profits occur when marginal revenue equals marginal cost. If a producer maximizes his profits, he will produce an output of Q units per period of time at a mill price of P per unit.

In the specific example of Figure 5-4, the maximum-profit level of production results in "excess" profits as represented by the shaded area *PEFG*. Indeed, the opportunity to earn excess profits will induce other producers to locate at other sites on the market plain—a matter that we will need to consider in a moment.

The Seller's Market Area

Our present assumptions argue that the determination of the site of maximum profits limits (or defines) the seller's market area. Though this point has already been implied in the areal-demand analysis of Chapter 4 (i.e., Figure 4-11), we need to sum up the two main reasons for market-area determination. First and foremost, the delivered price of a product (the mill price plus transportation costs) increases over distance. It is possible, consequently, that a distance is reached where consumers are simply priced out of the seller's market.

Second, diseconomies of scale in production can also delimit market areas. When diseconomies of scale in production set in at higher levels of output, the increased demands of a larger market area push production to the point at which unit production costs begin to increase. The resulting increase in mill prices will limit the size of the market area.

A Network of Market Areas

Now with the marginal analysis (i.e., the marginal-cost and marginal-revenue framework) before us, let us examine in some detail the formation of a market network which is based, in part, on an f.o.b. pricing policy. Given the set of assumptions on pages 53 and 54, the demand and cost curves for each firm within the same industry group are identical. (This conceptual uniformity allows us to develop our analysis from a single diagram without invalidating our overall conclusions.)

Firm Entry. If an original producer enjoys excess profits, additional producers will be logically encouraged to locate somewhere on the market plain, and to minimize competition (and enjoy similar monopoly advantages) each new producer will attempt to find a site

73

away from existing rivals. The influence of agglomeration economies (Chapter 6) may otherwise affect the location decision. Schematically, dispersal of firms can be pictured as a market plain covered with circular markets as shown in Figure 5-5. Figure 5-4 represents the maximum-profit situation for each producer located on the market plain. Since no effective market competition exists at this stage, each producer realizes excess profits.

Effective Spatial Competition. However, the existence of excess profits will attract additional producers. As they enter the market, they will locate in areas not served by the existing producers, the shaded areas of Figure 5-5. As these new producers locate they will begin to encroach upon the market areas of established producers by offering lower prices to consumers for whom they will now be the closest producers. The emergent consumer-producer relationships assume consumer rationality—assume, that is, that consumers know the alternatives and choose the cheapest among them, because the quantity they can consume will then be larger. So long as the final consumer price includes transportation charges, nearby sellers have a price advantage over distant sellers; thus, consumers located on the periphery of an established producer's existing market area will now purchase from the new producer located in the adjacent shaded portion of the market plain.

The entire process of changing markets can be graphically presented as in Figure 5-6. The three large circles (for producers A, B, and C) represent an areal market pattern before effective

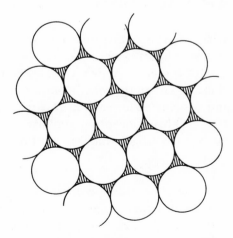

Figure 5-5 Market network before equilibrium

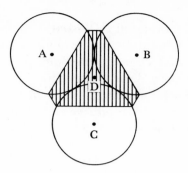

Figure 5-6   Effective competition

spatial competition.   As a fourth producer locates at site D, the consumers located in the shaded area will buy from him since it is cheaper to buy from the new producer than from the producers located at sites A, B, and C.   Consequently, the producers at sites A, B, and C lose a portion of their initial markets to the new producer located at site D.

Price and Output after Effective Spatial Competition.   As new producers continually encroach upon the market areas of existing producers, the spatial monopoly demand curve (*DD* of Figure 5-4) is replaced by a spatial monopolistic competitive demand curve (*DD'* of Figure 5-7); that is, the transition from the initial *DD* (spatial monopoly

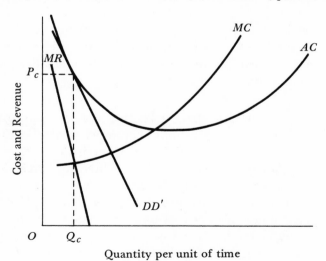

Figure 5-7   Equilibrium price and output

demand) curve to the eventual DD' (spatial monopolistic competitive demand) curve comes about by the free entry of additional producers. With maximum spatial competition, implied in the notion of free entry, the spatial monopolistic competitive demand curve becomes tangent to the average-cost curve, as shown in Figure 5-7. Such a situation is identical for each producer and represents the equilibrium position at which no excess profits are earned and no new producers will enter.

For Figure 5-7, the spatial monopolistic competitive price and output for each producer is P_c and Q_c, respectively. A comparison of Figure 5-7 to Figure 5-4 shows that with free entry, production takes place on a smaller scale and at a higher price. How can this be? This is explained by the DD demand curve of Figure 5-4. The shape and position of DD portrays a series of area markets (i.e., a particular area market for each mill price indicated along the areal-demand curve). As firm entry takes place and rival producers encroach upon the markets of existing producers, the areal-demand curve for each producer shifts toward the origin (Figure 5-7), to reflect a decreasing demand for each producer's product. Also, as each producer's areal-demand curve shifts toward the origin, consumer demand becomes more price-inelastic because, even with a transition from spatial monopoly to spatial monopolistic competition, the individual producer does not face spatial competition within his market at relatively high prices. He is protected from rival producers by both their higher transportation charges and their rising unit costs at lower levels of production. The important effects of this are that firms respond to an increase in spatial competition by increasing the mill price of their product and by selling a smaller volume of output per unit of time.

The Exact Shape of Market Areas. Though the foregoing discussion suggests that free entry and rational consumer choice leads to hexagonal market areas, free entry could result in a different shaped spatial-market pattern. Recent theoretical literature on spatial competition and market networks has sufficiently demonstrated other possible market networks, such as a triangular market pattern.[1]

Though much has been written on areal-market patterns, an extensive review of the literature is not crucial for a general understanding of the formation of a spatial-market pattern. One point,

1. Edwin S. Mills and Michael R. Lav, "A Model of Market Areas with Free Entry," *Journal of Political Economy.* (June, 1964), pp. 278–88.

however, should be singled out—the matter of excess profits. Contrary to our conclusion of average cost-pricing under conditions of equilibrium (Figure 5-7), some economists note that free entry will not usually eliminate all excess profits when the friction-of-distance factor is the source of market imperfection. Simply put, spatial competition may cease before price is exactly equal to average cost, because a portion of excess profits is inadequate to make the entry of an additional firm profitable. In a sense, the portion of excess profits that remains after free spatial competition is a form of economic rent, a return above the "normal" return for all factors of production, and this excess return may not be eliminated in the long run. For our present discussion of spatial competition and market-area determination, we will assume that excess profits are eliminated with maximum free entry. This assumption will simplify our discussion without invalidating its conclusions.

SPATIAL COMPETITION AND OTHER PRICING POLICIES

The preceding discussion of spatial competition indicated that the free entry of rival producers determines the spatial-market pattern for an industry group that follows an f.o.b. mill-pricing policy. Spatial-market differentiation was shown to continue until all excess profits are eliminated from the industry group. And the spatial monopolistic competitive industry was said to be in a state of equilibrium where each seller's price equals his average costs at a maximum-profit level of production.

Though maximum free entry was considered, it was indicated that consumers still pair up with sellers because of the friction-of-distance factor. That is, each seller has his own particular market area which affords him some monopoly power. Will this market imperfection lead to some other type of pricing policy? To answer this question, let us consider the possibility of a uniform pricing policy.

Uniform Pricing

In situations where distribution costs are unusually low, rival producers, seeking to increase their share of the total areal market (and profits), will pay distribution costs. This practice results in uniform pricing throughout a market area. The distribution of watches and cameras follows this practice on a national basis.

For a spatial monopolistic competitive situation, the economic rationale for a uniform-pricing policy is an expected net increase in profits. Any change in profits means, of course, that demand or production costs or both have changed. In the case of a shift from an f.o.b. mill-pricing policy to a uniform-pricing policy, demand (and total revenue) is expected to increase along with an increase in total cost. The increase in production costs plus transportation costs must necessarily be lower than the increase in total revenue. Consequently, producers expect an increase in profits. This is a point that we now need to examine.

The position of the areal-demand curve in Figure 5-7 is based on an f.o.b. mill-pricing policy; thus, quantity demanded is affected by distance. However, under a uniform-pricing policy, the delivered price of an item is the same at all consumer locations, and quantity demanded is not affected by distance from the seller. As seen by the seller, the adoption of a uniform-pricing policy will cause his demand curve to become more price elastic, providing the major incentive for the adoption.

Demand curve DD of Figure 5-8 shows the equilibrium price and output for an f.o.b. mill-pricing system. This is the same equilibrium situation as shown in Figure 5-7. The adoption of a uniform-price policy will shift the area-demand curve to DD' (see Figure 5-8) because the outward swing of the area-demand curve indicates an increase in the geographic size of the market from a limited areal market to a national market.

Clearly, distribution costs under a uniform-price system must be paid; and clearly, too, all the consumers of the product share in paying the total distribution costs. As already indicated, distribution costs become a part of the total cost of doing business; consequently, the average-cost curve will shift upward in the amount of the distribution cost, as shown in Figure 5-8. (The problem of including distribution costs in total production costs in our analysis is simplified by assuming a linear relationship between distribution costs and quantity sold. The average shipping cost, then, is a constant, and accordingly, the average-cost curve, which now includes production and distribution costs, shifts upward by a constant amount for all levels of output.)

The monopolistic competitor's economic justification for adopting a uniform-price system is a simple one. If the anticipated

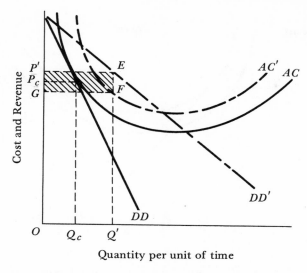

Figure 5-8 Expected profits from a uniform-pricing policy

increase in sales and revenue under the uniform-price policy is greater than the expected increase in cost, the seller's profits will increase.

Figure 5-8 shows the expected maximum-profit level of sales (output) to be Q' at a uniform price of P'.[2] Not only does the seller expect to maximize profits at this new level of sales but also, as shown by the shaded rectangle $P'EFG$, he expects to enjoy above-normal profits.

In reality, a uniform-pricing system seldom leads to excess profits. A seller in a monopolistic competitive market situation, assuming that his adoption of a uniform-price policy would not be noticed by his rival sellers, views his demand curve as being highly price-elastic, and hence, an incentive to offer a uniform-price policy. Unfortunately, rival sellers sense the same situation and also shift to a uniform-price policy. Each seller negates the actions of his rival sellers. In general terms, an industry-wide adoption of a uniform-pricing policy does not significantly alter the relative economic position of any one firm within the industry. The chances for excess profits are eliminated and, as shown in Figure 5-9, an average cost-price situation holds.

Unlike producers, however, consumers are affected by an industrywide uniform-pricing policy. Since distribution costs are

2. Although the marginal-revenue and marginal-cost schedules are not shown in Figure 5-8, the price P' represents the price at which marginal revenue equals marginal costs.

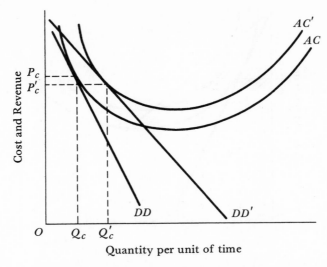

Figure 5-9 Equilibrium price after a uniform-pricing policy

averaged, distant consumers receive a price advantage over nearby ones. If the consumer is another producer, the input price does not affect his location decision since the price is the same throughout the country. (The possible locational effects of uniform pricing will be discussed in a later section of this chapter.)

The use of a uniform-pricing policy is also likely in a spatial oligopoly market situation. Whenever only a few rival firms exist, the individual oligopolist's keen awareness of the outcome of price competition makes him anxious to avoid a price war with his competitors. Because the relatively few sellers recognize that their actions will directly affect their rivals' markets, they will almost surely react to any adverse competitive measures; thus, certain subtle forms of competition are used, such as freight absorption and advertising.

In summary, uniform pricing is based on the competitive nature of the areal market and the relative significance of distribution costs to an item's price. A spatial oligopolist or a spatial monopolistic competitive producer who produces a high-value product with a low transport cost is likely to find the practice of uniform pricing essential in the competitive struggle for a share of the total areal market.

Basing-Point Pricing

A spatial-pricing policy well suited to bulky items is a basing-point pricing system. Basically, this pricing system operates in situations where distribution costs are figured from certain "agreed to" shipping points, certain base points. For instance, in the limited case of a single base point, all shipping charges of an item are figured from the base point regardless of the location of the seller. If Kansas City were selected as the base point by an industry group, a producer located at Omaha will charge his Chicago customers an artificial shipping cost from the Kansas City base point. The difference between the actual freight cost from Omaha to Chicago and the freight charged from Kansas City to Chicago, a phantom freight charge, is a windfall profit to the Omaha producer.

Since the establishment and selection of base points require the cooperation of all the major producers within the industry group, the basing-point pricing system is suited to a spatial-oligopoly (or duopoly) situation. In fact, because of the keen competitive rivalry among the producers of a spatial-oligopoly industry, they strongly prefer the basing-point system as a way to minimize the temptation toward independent pricing.

Such industries as steel, cement, and automobiles, to name a few, have at one time or another adopted a basing-point pricing policy.

The most striking example of the single basing-point system is the Pittsburgh-plus system that was used in the steel industry until 1924. A geographic point of production, Pittsburgh, was the industry's agreed upon basing point and all prices were quoted as the announced mill price at that point plus the freight charge to the final destination. This is illustrated in Figure 5-10 where the mill price is PB and the delivered prices are the Pittsburgh mill price plus freight, or line BT. Thus, a Chicago producer could quote a delivered price based upon the Pittsburgh-plus freight line BT. Buyers of steel in the Chicago area, consequently, were charged a price of CG when, in fact, the price from the Chicago mill (the Chicago mill price plus transport costs) was only CA. The difference of AG represents a windfall profit to the Chicago mill. As Figure 5-10 indicates, the Chicago mill could realize windfall profits on its sales beyond Dayton, Ohio, that is, to point X. Beyond point X, the mill price plus transportation costs were higher from the Chicago mill than the actual quoted Pittsburgh mill price plus freight.

At first glance, it appears that the Chicago mill gained from the Pittsburgh-plus system. However, it should be remembered that in the absence of the Pittsburgh-plus system, the Pittsburgh mill would have been cut off from Chicago buyers because of higher transportation costs relative to those of the Chicago mill. With the

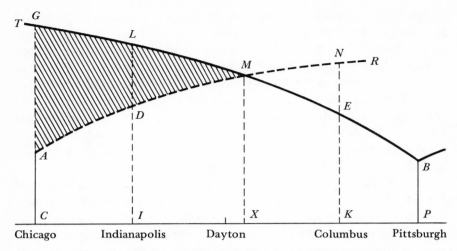

Figure 5-10 **Basing-point pricing.** (Reprinted from F. M. Scherer, *Industrial Market Structure and Economic Performance* © 1970 by Rand McNally and Company, Chicago, p. 266. Reprinted by permission of Rand McNally College Publishing Company.)

Pittsburgh-plus system, the Pittsburgh mill could penetrate the Chicago market since the delivered price of steel was the same from Pittsburgh as from Chicago.

The basing-point system of spatial pricing for the steel industry was later extended to include several base points—for example, Pittsburgh, Chicago, and Birmingham. The basing-point pricing system continued in use until a series of Supreme Court decisions during the 1940s outlawed it; however, there have been repeated efforts to resurrect the system. In many European countries, the practice is still legal.

Zone Pricing

A fourth form of spatial pricing is zone pricing. Simply put, under zone pricing a producer establishes price zones for his product and charges a different mill price in each of the zones. Zone pricing is spatial price discrimination. Superficially, as we shall see, it is similar to uniform pricing.

Though the use of zone pricing is more likely in a spatial monopolistic situation, its possible adoption by a spatial monopolistic competitive industry should not be ruled out. Since the necessary economic conditions for zone pricing are more usually found in a monopolistic situation, we will base our discussion on its use by a spatial monopolistic producer.

If three conditions exist, zone pricing becomes profitable for a spatial monopolist. First, it must be possible to divide the total areal market into submarkets. As long as the transportation cost between submarkets is greater than the difference between the established submarket prices, a producer can subdivide his areal market into submarkets and avoid the possibility that buyers in one submarket will resell in another submarket for a profit. Second, the price elasticities of demand (and the marginal-revenue schedules) must be different in each of the submarkets. This difference is necessary in order to make price discrimination profitable. Finally, as the third condition, the cost of dividing the market into submarkets must not be excessive. Too high a cost can wipe out any potential gains from zone pricing.

The economics of zone pricing are best seen in a simple diagram for a two-submarket situation. Panel A of Figure 5-11 shows the spatial-monopoly-demand and marginal-revenue curves before the areal market is divided into submarkets. The demand and marginal-revenue curves for the two submarkets are shown in panel B, in which the nearby submarket is labeled submarket one and the distant submarket is labeled submarket two. A comparison of the two submarket-demand curves shows that for all mill prices, the quantity demanded is greater in the nearby market. The rationale for this involves transportation costs. The vertical axis of panel B records mill prices, but the consumer pays the mill price plus delivery costs. For a given mill price, distant submarket consumers pay a higher delivered price than do consumers located in a nearby submarket. For a given mill price, then, economic logic argues that the quantity demanded in the distant submarket will be less than that demanded in the nearby submarket.

If, as panel A shows, the profit-maximizing output is $\bar{Q}$ before market differentiation, the problem for the producer is to divide the total output of $\bar{Q}$ between the two submarkets in order to increase profits. To do so, the producer will allocate the product by unit increments to the submarket with the highest marginal revenue. The total output of $\bar{Q}$ will be allocated to the two submarkets in order to equate marginal revenue in each submarket with the marginal revenue before market differentiation, which equaled marginal cost.

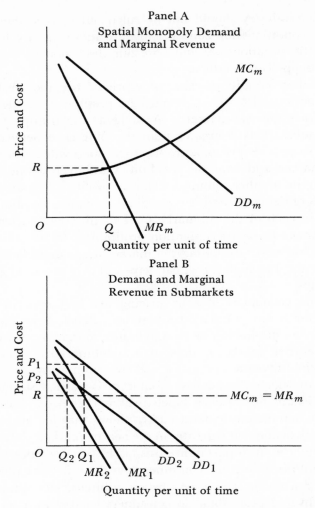

Figure 5-11   Zone pricing for a two-submarket case

At the marginal revenue R, the quantity allocated to and sold in submarket one is Q_1 and in submarket two, Q_2. Q_1 and Q_2 equal the total quantity produced, $\bar{Q}$.

In order to sell the quantities allocated to each of the submarkets, the spatial monopolist will charge different mill prices. As indicated in panel B, the nearby consumer pays a higher mill price P_1 than does the consumer located in the more distant submarket, P_2. The spatial monopolist has increased his revenues and profits by establishing price zones and, hence, by discriminating against the nearby consumers.

The effect of zone pricing is similar to that of uniform pricing, for it tends to develop uniform geographic pricing throughout the seller's market area. Its lower mill price offered to consumers located some distance from the seller frequently compensates for its added transportation costs and, resultingly, its delivered price to distant buyers tends to equal that offered to adjacent buyers. Zone pricing differs from uniform pricing, however, because it is usually limited to a particular geographic area within the total national economy. As was noted earlier, uniform pricing usually applies to the total national economy.

The economic rationale for adopting a zone-pricing policy is that it increases the spatial monopolist's profits. The same economic rationale may apply to a spatial monopolistic competitive situation, particularly when the spatial monopolistic competitive producer does not face significant competitive pressures in the market area adjacent to his plant.

SPATIAL PRICING AND INDUSTRY LOCATION

Thus far, we have discussed the various spatial-pricing situations which are characteristic of the several types of possible spatial-market situations—monopoly, oligopoly (and duopoly), and monopolistic competition. To continue, we now need to consider the general location pattern of industry groups for each of these spatial-pricing situations.

Uniform Pricing and Industry Location

Whenever uniform pricing is practiced, such market determinants as price considerations are not very important for location decisions. A uniform-spatial-pricing policy removes the influence of distance on demand (and its effects on receipts). Accordingly, the industrial-location pattern which develops among the producers who practice a uniform-pricing policy is based on the production-procurement differentials existing at all alternative locations.

A firm's physical proximity to its markets is not altogether ignored, however. Since each producer pays delivery costs, he attempts to minimize delivery costs throughout the market area.

Therefore, other things being equal, the initial producer will locate in the center of the market area. Since shipping charges are not a factor of demand, later-arriving producers will see no sales advantage through close physical proximity to a buyer; therefore, their chances of capturing a portion of the total market will be the same regardless of location. Still-later entrants who sell over the entire market area will be oblivious to the location of competitors. Logically, then, producers within an industry group will not be locationally inter-dependent and each will be primarily concerned to minimize production, procurement, and distribution costs independent of their competitors' locations.

Because producer market areas do not exist under a uniform-pricing policy, marketing demands do not influence producers to disperse. Indeed, each producer's attempt to minimize cost, all other things being equal, will lead to industry localization, a tendency reinforced by the agglomeration economies of concentrated areas (see Chapter 6).

Basing-Point Pricing and Industry Location

Although the basing-point pricing system has been outlawed in the United States since the 1940s, its influence in earlier industry location is worth consideration. Of particular significance are those recent geographic shifts in the location patterns of former basing-point-pricing industries which apparently reflect locational adjustments that followed the outlawed system. A striking example is the recent absolute and relative decline in the Pittsburgh steel industry since 1940.

A product group practicing base-point pricing tends to concentrate at the base point (or at several base points for a multiple basing-point system) because buyers of their products will relocate at the base point to take advantage of the lower price at the base point. Thus, some location and industrial organization specialists argue that a base-point pricing system misallocates industry location. For instance, industries heavily dependent upon the inputs supplied by these producers frequently concentrate too much of their capacity near base points and too little near their own customers, who are located away from base points. Such was the case under the early single-base-point pricing of steel products from Pittsburgh. A steel producer located in Chicago charged his Chicago buyers a shipping rate from Pittsburgh even though the steel was produced in Chicago; and as a result, the Chicago buyers were paying an artificially inflated price. Though the Chicago producer realized a phantom freight on sales near home, the Chicago buyers of steel were at a competitive disadvantage compared to rival firms located in the Pittsburgh area. This "unfair advantage" encouraged steel fabricators, typical buyers, to locate a disproportionate share of their steel-fabricating capacity in the Pittsburgh area, where the delivered price of steel was lower.

Zone Pricing and Industry Location

Though the earlier discussion of zone pricing was based on a monopoly situation, its industry-location effects also apply to other market situations—particularly a duopoly situation. Our earlier discussion suggested that the effect of zone pricing is that near buyers of an item pay a portion of distant buyers' delivery costs. The portion of the delivery costs that is shifted to the near buyers depends on the product's price elasticity of demand.

Obviously, the policy of shifting delivery costs from distant buyers to near buyers leads in the direction of equalizing final prices for all buyers. As mentioned earlier, to the extent that it creates uniform pricing throughout an area, it simulates a uniform-pricing system. It does differ from uniform pricing, however, by being generally limited to a particular geographic area, whereas uniform pricing usually applies to the total national economy.

Like f.o.b. mill pricing, zone pricing makes cost and price considerations important determinants of location. Where zone pricing is practiced by an industry group, the location of rival producers is important in a new entrant's location decision. Unless the cost savings from industry concentration are significant, he will avoid locating near rival producers.

An even more significant location effect of zone pricing, however, is its influence upon the location of those firms that purchase the output of a producer who practices zone pricing. Since a producer's location decision reflects all of his product's procurement and delivery costs, he is less influenced by the geographic source of an input sold under a zone-pricing policy than by the geographic sources of other inputs and his firm's physical proximity to final markets.

F.O.B. Mill Pricing and Industry Location

Because of spatial-competitive situations and the physical nature of most products, the most common spatial-pricing policy is the f.o.b. mill-pricing system. An industry group that practices f.o.b. mill pricing finds that plant-site location cannot be determined simply by reference to costs at alternative locations. Equally important to consider is the group's areal demand at alternative locations.

The latter consideration is seen in a firm's attempt to maximize its profits through advantageous location. A movement toward a major resource site and away from a major market area tends to reduce production and procurement costs at the expense of lower total receipts. Conversely, a movement toward a major market center and away from a major resource site will increase total receipts at the expense of higher production and procurement costs. Thus, a firm maximizes its profits by comparing production and procurement costs with receipts at each alternative site. The firm will locate at the site of most favorable comparative profits.

At the industry-group level, the oftentimes opposing locational forces of production-procurement costs, on the one hand, and market receipts on the other generally mean that industry groups practicing f.o.b. pricing can be classified as either resource-oriented or market-oriented. A moment's glance at the geographic pattern of industrial activity in the United States clearly indicates a general market-oriented industrial location pattern.

Though the nature of areal demand and market receipts has provided the pull toward market areas, the push has come from improved and more efficient methods of production, methods which have decreased the relative importance of most favorable resource areas as sites of location. In short, the major advances in technology in roughly the last half century have generally liberated much of industrial activity from resource areas. Increased input-substitution possibilities and agglomeration economies are both the result of such technological advances and the reason for our increasingly more market-oriented industrial economy.

Technological Change and Input Substitution. Historically, technological advancements in production have significantly increased the possibilities of resource-input substitution. A higher degree of input substitution allows a producer a wider choice of different types and combinations of inputs to yield the same amount of output. Oil and nuclear power–generated electricity, for instance, are significant substitutes for coal as major power sources for production.

As a general rule, a producer who enjoys a wide range of input substitutes also has the advantage of a consequently larger number of location possibilities. Clearly, the possibility of multiple input substitutes makes a producer less dependent upon any given resource site and allows him to place a correspondingly greater emphasis on the locational advantages of his market area. Such relative freedom is a locational-decision advantage.

SUMMARY

Although this chapter's presentation of industry-group geographic interdependence is highly simplified, it sheds some light on how spatial pricing and market areas are determined in the face of spatial competition. The analysis indicated that a firm must consider its competitors' locations as it makes a decision regarding its own location. Further, the analysis argued that the importance of comparative location sites is largely determined by the spatial-pricing policy practiced by the industry group. Less consideration is given to the location of competing firms where uniform pricing is practiced than in a situation where f.o.b. pricing is followed.

As a general observation, the theoretical analysis provides evidence that market areas, as contrasted to resource sites, are becoming increasingly influential in determining industrial-site location. Also, the existence of agglomeration economies in concentrated areas reinforces the importance of market areas as desirable places of location.

REFERENCES AND SUPPLEMENTAL READING

Martin Beckmann, *Location Theory* (New York: Random House, 1969).
Robert D. Dean, *et al.* (eds.), *Spatial Economic Theory* (New York: The Free Press, 1970).
Michael Goldberg, *Intrametropolitan Industrial Location: Plant Size and the Theory of Production*, The Center for Real Estate and Urban Economics, Institute of Urban and Regional Development, University of California at Berkeley, 1969.

M. L. Greenhut, *Microeconomics and the Space Economy* (Chicago: Scott, Foresman and Company, 1963).

V. G. Haines, *Business Relocation* (London: Business Books Limited, 1970).

Walter Isard, *Location and Space-Economy* (Cambridge: The M.I.T. Press, 1956).

Gerald Karaska and David F. Bramhall, (eds.), *Locational Analysis for Manufacturing* (Cambridge: The M.I.T. Press, 1969).

David L. McKee, *et al.* (eds.), *Regional Economics* (New York: The Free Press, 1970).

E. Willard Miller, *A Geography of Industrial Location* (Dubuque, Iowa: Wm. C. Brown Company Publishers, 1970).

Hugh O. Nourse, *Regional Economics* (New York: McGraw-Hill, Inc., 1968).

Harry W. Richardson, *Regional Economics* (New York: Praeger Publishers, 1969).

F. M. Scherer, *Industrial Market Structure and Economic Performance* (Chicago: Rand McNally and Company, 1970).

APPENDIX TO CHAPTER 5

Game Theory Approach to Location

Game theory analysis can be used as a pedagogical device to show that, under special conditions, industrial competition can lead to a common location site for rival sellers. The use of game theory will be demonstrated here with the application of a simple two-person zero-sum game model. To simplify the strategy (and the analysis), the following special conditions will be followed:

1. We will assume that there are two sellers of a homogeneous product each of whom is attempting to locate along a line in such a way as to maximize his profits.
2. The areal market is assumed to be a line (e.g., a street or highway) and consumers are distributed uniformly along the line.
3. Sellers quote delivered price as f.o.b. price plus transport cost.
4. Transport cost is proportional to distance from any location point along the line.
5. Demand is assumed to be moderately elastic, so that the pattern of delivered price becomes an important determinant of total sales.
6. Finally, it is assumed that there are no operating costs. Thus, revenue is equivalent to profit.

Figure 5-12 describes the simple linear market. Viewing it

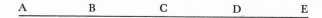

A   B   C   D   E

Figure 5-12 Simple linear market

as a street 40 blocks long, we will imagine that customers are distributed along the street in such a way that they are spaced at block intervals. Thus there are a total of 40 customers along the 40-block street. To further simplify the analysis, we will imagine that the two rival sellers are limited to five possible location sites: sites A, B, C, D, and E. We now need to state a price for the item and a transport rate. We will establish the price of the item at $1.00 and the transport rate at $.05 per unit item per block shipped. Finally, we need to specify the price elasticity of the item. We will assume that the price elasticity of demand is such that each consumer will buy three units if the delivered price is between $1.00 and $1.50, two units if

91

the delivered price is between $1.50 and $2.00, and no units if delivered price exceeds $2.00.

The task now is to construct a payoff matrix on the basis of the price and demand information. The payoff matrix of Table 5-1

TABLE 5-1. *Payoff Matrix*

		Seller II					
		A	B	C	D	E	Row Mini-mum
	A	0	−50	−50	−30	0	−50
	B	50	0	−20	0	30	−20
Seller I	C	50	20	0	10	50	0
	D	30	0	−20	0	50	−20
	E	0	−30	−50	−50	0	−50
Column Maximum		50	20	0	20	50	

is constructed in such a way that it shows the net payoff to seller I for all possible combinations of location sites for sellers I and II. Therefore, a positive value in the payoff matrix means that the profits of seller I exceed the profits of seller II by that amount. By the same analogy, a negative value means that the profits of seller II exceed the profits of seller I by that amount. To see how the values in the table are determined, consider, for example, the first row of Table 5-1. (We will ignore, for the moment, the last row and column of the table.) The reason that the first value in the first row is 0 is because both sellers locate at site A. In view of our earlier assumptions, both sellers are expected to earn the same amount of profits at site A. The next value of −50 can be easily explained by calculating the profits for both sellers based on the linear market of Figure 5-12. Seller I is located at site A and seller II is located at site B. The market area between A and B will be divided equally between seller I and seller II, as in Figure 5-13. This means that

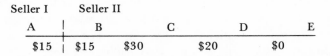

Figure 5-13 Profits with sellers at sites A and B

seller I's profits are fixed at $15, since there are only five consumers located to the left of the market boundary. Because of our assumption of demand, each consumer will buy three items when the delivered price is between $1.00 and $1.50. Seller II's market will extend all the way to point D. It will not extend beyond point D because the delivered price beyond point D exceeds $2.00. Consequently, seller II's total profits will be $65. The difference between the total profits of seller I and seller II is then $50 and is recorded in Table 5-1 as −50. The third entry in the first row of Table 5-1 is also −50. This is so because the profits of seller I are $30 and the profits of seller II are $80, as shown in Figure 5-14. Other figures in Table 5-1 were computed in a similar manner.

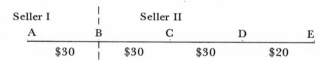

Figure 5-14   Profits with sellers at sites A and C

What strategy seems appropriate to determine the location pattern for both sellers? It seems appropriate to assume that the two sellers are actually contending over the same market. Consequently, a sale by one seller is considered as a lost sale by the other seller. This is exactly what Table 5-1 indicates; that is, the interests of seller I are diametrically opposed to the interests of seller II. In view of this situation, we can determine where the two sellers will locate. Starting with seller I, he has a choice of five possible location sites. If he should choose to locate at site A, he would then make it possible for seller II to exceed his profits by $50 if seller II would locate at either site B or site C. In short, by locating at site A, he would give a substantial portion of the total market to seller II. The best strategy for seller I is, then, to locate at site C. By locating at site C, he can at least return a profit equal to that of seller II. This is shown to be the case from the information shown in the last column of Table 5-1. What about seller II's location? Employing the same strategy, seller II will also locate at site C. A location at site C is the best location site because by locating at site C he concedes as little as possible to seller I. This is indicated in the last row of Table 5-1.

It turns out that the noncooperative contest between the two rival sellers leads to a common site of location. Their combined profits at site C are $100. It is interesting to note that both sellers could increase their profits with a B–D location pattern. But, as Table 5-1 indicates, a B–D location pattern is unstable. Such a location pattern would mean that both sellers have agreed to co-operate in order to maintain the pattern for an indefinite period of time. A final point of interest is that the B–D location pattern also minimizes the total transportation cost to consumers.

Further formulations of payoff matrices can conceivably be made by altering the f.o.b. price, transport rate, price elasticity of demand, number of sellers, production costs, and geographic distribution of consumers. The mathematical problems that would be encountered in the construction of a more general payoff matrix would make such an attempt impractical. Moreover, the use of game theory for a more general analysis of location would not add appreciably to our understanding of plant location. The discussion of plant location in Chapter 4, the text of this chapter, and the foregoing treatment of a special location problem are sufficient for a basic understanding of the economics of plant location.

6

City-Size Distribution
and the Economies
of Central Places

Chapter 5 was devoted, in part, to a discussion of market areas (or market nets). Under f.o.b. pricing, the total market plain subdivides into market areas equaling the number of firms within the industry group. The mapping of the market areas was illustrated as a net of hexagon-shaped areas. In connection with the discussion of market nets, it was indicated that the size of the hexagons varies from small to large and is dependent upon the demand and scale economies.

We now need to extend the idea of market nets by introducing the notion of a hierarchy of central places. Although the simplified assumptions used in our analysis of central-place hierarchy makes the discussion less complex than real experience would be, the discussion will clarify ideas concerning the dominance of the number, location, size, functions, and the spacing of urban areas in a free-market economy. In addition, the discussion will help explain the hierarchy of trading centers within an urban area.

In order to round out our understanding of central places and city-size distribution, the chapter ends with a discussion of agglomeration economies, those economic advantages that are realized by locating at central places.

SYSTEM OF CENTRAL PLACES

Central places are defined as centers where activities locate in order to serve a market area. Generally speaking, the larger the market area served, the larger and more functionally diversified will be the central place. Thus, central places will vary in size, from those performing few functions and serving a small-town market to those of very large and complex functions answering the needs of major market areas comprising a host of smaller centers. As a working hypothesis we propose that a hierarchy of central places exists: there are widely spaced, large cities with a full range of services; a greater number of medium-sized cities spaced closer together and having fewer functions; and, finally, a large number of relatively contiguous small towns with limited marketing functions.

Armed with an understanding of the economics of location and market-area determination (Chapters 4 and 5), we are now able to examine the validity of this hypothesis. We begin with an abstract model of market areas and central places. This is followed by examples of observed hierarchies of central places.

A Hypothetical Model

In order to simplify our analysis, Figure 6-1 has been drawn

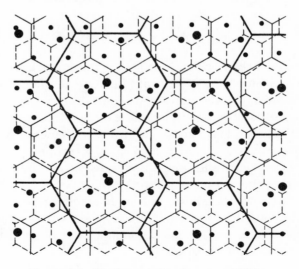

Figure 6-1 Market nets for three commodities

to show market nets for only three items (three seller groups). The market nets have deliberately been drawn to show the possibility of different-size market areas. The construction of Figure 6-1 actually involves the overlay of three market nets in a random fashion. The heavy solid lines represent the market-boundary areas for one seller group; the light solid lines represent the market-boundary areas for a second seller group; and the broken lines represent the market-boundary areas for a third seller group.

Implied in Figure 6-1 are the following assumptions made in our analysis in Chapter 5: (1) a geographic distribution of consumers who reveal identical product preferences; (2) uniform transportation costs; (3) uniform production costs; and (4) f.o.b. mill pricing. We shall discuss the realism of these assumptions later in this chapter.

Imagine that the market nets in Figure 6-1 have been placed randomly upon the market plain and that no two suppliers share a common place. Although there is no order to the arrangement of the three market nets, every consumer located on the market plain has access to every product.

A more economical arrangement of the three market nets is that of Figure 6-2. Because some suppliers share a common place of distribution, total distribution (transportation) costs are reduced. Notice that the rearrangement of the market nets in Figure 6-2 reveals a hierarchy of central places. The lowest or first order of central places is represented by a small circle. These first-order

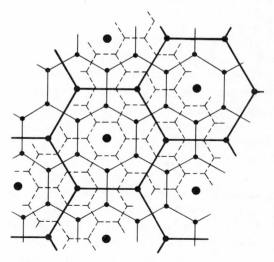

Figure 6-2 Central-place hierarchy

central places offer only one of the three items for distribution. Consumers must look to higher-ordered central places for additional goods and services. The second-order central places, represented by a larger circle, offer two of the three items for distribution. Accordingly, consumers must look to the third-order central places for all three items.

The third-order central places are shown in Figure 6-2 as the largest circles. In our simplified analysis, the third-order central places are the larger and more complex since they provide all three items. Additionally, the market area of a third-order center comprises the combined market areas of second-order and first-order centers.

We could extend our hypothetical example of a three-goods case to an n-goods case, but the general conclusion would be the same. That is, a size distribution of centers results from differences in the size of market areas for goods and services. As the analysis in Chapter 5 suggests, the size of a firm's market area represents, at least, a minimum level of population and income necessary to a firm's profitability. America's so-called "jerkwater" towns, the first-order centers, comprise only those activities with the smallest market areas. Examples of such activities are a bar and grill, a grocery store, a combination gas station and garage, and a church. Since even the lowest order of central places serves as a collection and distribution point, a combination grain elevator and feed store and a local post office would probably complete the list of goods and services offered at the first-order centers.

Each higher-order center provides a correspondingly greater variety of goods and services to a much wider market area. More specifically, each higher-order center offers all the goods and services provided by the next lower-order center plus some additional ones. For example, the second-order centers (small towns), in addition to the facilities of a first-order center, might have a bank, one or more dry-goods stores, a theater, a barber shop, and a farm-machinery store.

The Rank-Size Rule. Since the rank (or order) of a central place is based upon the number of functions provided, the population of each center will vary directly with the hierarchical order of central places. This relationship can be demonstrated by following Beckmann's early work[1] on the *rank-size rule* of central places. Along with

---

1. Martin J. Beckmann, "City Hierarchies and the Distribution of City Size," *Economic Development and Cultural Change*, vol. 6 (April, 1958), pp. 243–248. For a more recent

Beckmann, we will make the following assumptions. First, we will assume that the population of each central place is some proportion of the total population served by the central place. Suppose that the population of a central place is 2,000 and it serves a total population of 4,000. This means that the central place serves its own population of 2,000 plus an additional 2,000 persons who reside outside the central place under consideration. Thus, the ratio of the population of the central place to the total population served is 2,000/4,000 or 0.5. We will refer to this ratio as r. Next, we will assume that r is constant for all orders of central places. Accordingly, the total population served by a higher-order central place of 10,000 would be 20,000 (or 10,000/20,000 = 0.5). Mathematically, this means that

$$C_m = rP_m \qquad (1)$$

Where m = the rank order of the central place
C_m = the population of the central place of rank m
r = the ratio of the population of the central place to the total population served
P_m = the total population served by the central place of rank m

In a very general way, the r factor is an input-output coefficient. An r value of 0.5 means that each person who lives in a central place can provide services for himself plus one additional person.

A final assumption is that a central place of a given rank (or size) m can serve a certain number of central places of the next smallest size. We will refer to this number as s. Mathematically, this means that

$$P_m = C_m + sP_{m-1} \qquad (2)$$

Where P_m = total population served by central place of rank m
C_m = population of central place of rank m
s = number of central places that have a rank of m-1
P_{m-1} = total population served by central places of rank m-1

Substituting Equation (1) into Equation (2), we have

$$P_m = rP_m + sP_{m-1}$$
$$P_m - rP_m = sP_{m-1}$$
$$P_m(1 - r) = sP_{m-1}$$

and alternative approach to Beckmann's earlier work on rank size, see Martin J. Beckmann and John C. McPherson, "City Size Distribution in a Central Place Hierarchy: An Alternative Approach," *Journal of Regional Science*, vol. 10, no. 1 (1970), pp. 25–33.

99

or

$$P_m = \frac{s}{1 - r} P_{m-1} \qquad (3)$$

Equation (3) shows that the population of each order place is a multiple of $s/(1 - r)$ times the next smallest size.

As an illustration of one possible system of city-size distribution, suppose that $r = 0.5$ and $s = 2$. Suppose further that the population of the first-order city is 500 and that there are eight ranks of city size. With the use of this information and Equation (3), the figures in columns 2 and 3 of Table 6-1 can be determined.

TABLE 6-1. *Hypothetical System of Cities*

Rank Order m	Population of Central Place C_m	Population Served by Central Place P_m	Number of Central Places
1	500	1,000	128
2	2,000	4,000	64
3	8,000	16,000	32
4	32,000	64,000	16
5	128,000	256,000	8
6	512,000	1,024,000	4
7	2,048,000	4,096,000	2
8	8,192,000	16,384,000	1

The size of a city of the first order has been set at 500.[2] Therefore, the population served by a city of 500 is 1,000. The population served by a city of rank two is 4,000 ($2/[1 - .5] \times 1,000 = 4,000$). Since r is known, the population of a central place of rank two is 2,000. Other figures in columns 2 and 3 were figured in a similar way. The figures in column 4 of Table 6-1 can be determined by reference to s. When s is equal to 2, we know that the highest-order city (the city with the rank order of eight in our hypothetical case) serves two cities of the next smallest size. Thus, there are two cities with the rank order of seven. Each city with a rank order of seven serves two cities of the next smallest size; thus, there are four cities

2. You may have wondered how the size of a central place of the first order is determined. Basically, it is determined by the size of threshold markets. A threshold market refers to the minimum size of a market that is necessary for an activity to be profitable. In our hypothetical case, the minimum-size market for those activities located in the first-order central place is assumed to be 1,000.

with the rank size of six. More generally, if there are eight city-size ranks, the number of cities of rank m is equal to s^{8-m}.

A basic point of the rank-size rule is that the population of each order place is a multiple of the next smallest size (see Equation 3). Related to this point is the characteristic that the number of central places (cities) declines with order (see column 4 of Table 6-1). An additional characteristic of central-place hierarchy can be demonstrated with the use of a more refined model of rank order. Without developing such a model here, this characteristic is that the distance between centers of equal rank varies inversely with their rank. The distance between centers of a low-order rank, for instance, is less than the distance between two centers of the same higher-order rank.

The Theory of Central-Place Hierarchy and Reality. Does the theory of central places add to our understanding of the world of reality? More specifically, does the theory tell us anything about the nation's hierarchy of cities, population of cities, and distance separating cities? In response to this general query, we first need to reflect upon several of the assumptions which were incorporated into the theory of central-place hierarchy. Recall that in order to simplify the analysis of central places, several unrealistic assumptions were made (see page 97). In reality, we find that uniform production costs over a geographic plain are the exception and geographic variations in population density, demand, and production costs are the rule. In a later discussion of the rank-size rule, several additional assumptions were made. We would not expect to find, for example, a constant r factor, the same input-output coefficient for all city-size groups. What we would expect to find is some relation between city size and productivity. Because of the association of agglomeration economies with city size, it is conceivable that for many items larger cities can produce a greater output per unit of labor input than smaller cities. Finally, the astute reader may have detected that the rank-size rule nullifies an earlier assumption of a uniform distribution of population. Recall that the rank-size rule distinguishes between the population of a center and the total population served by that center. This distinction implies that the population density is greater at the center than for the rural area that surrounds the center.

Taken together, do these simplifying assumptions do violence to the analysis and lead us to invalid conclusions about city hierarchy, population of centers, and distance separating centers? This question

is partly answered by examining a map (Figure 6-3) detailing the
spatial configuration of towns and cities in southwest Iowa and
showing five distinct centers of hierarchy. The metropolitan area of
Omaha and Council Bluffs is the highest-order (fifth-order) center.
(Obviously, the market area for Omaha and Council Bluffs is much
larger than the area shown on the map.) The fourth-order centers,
nearly equidistant from each other, include Glenwood, Red Oak,
and Atlantic, Iowa. The areas found around the fourth-order centers
are also served by four third-order centers, seventeen second-order
centers, and ten first-order centers.

The frequency of centers at each rank shown in Figure 6-3
largely agrees with the theory of central places, for the frequency of
centers increases for each lower-order rank, with the exception of the
first-order rank. Furthermore, the spacing of centers on the map
agrees with the theory: the distance between lower-order centers is
less than the distance between higher-order centers.

To be sure, the area of southwest Iowa does not conclusively
prove the validity of the theory of central places. In fact, the physical
and economic features of southwest Iowa correspond more closely
to the theory's premises than many other areas in the United States.

The central-place hierarchy is more difficult to discern in an

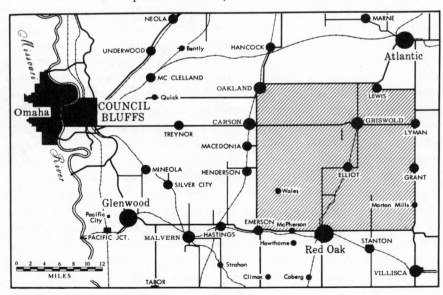

Figure 6-3 **Area map of southwest Iowa.** [Reprinted from Brian J. L.
Berry, *Geography of Market Centers and Retail Distribution* (Englewood Cliffs, N.J.: Prentice-Hall, Inc., 1967)
p. 13.]

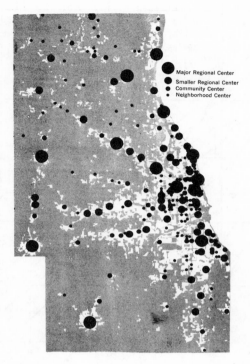

Figure 6-4 **The Chicago hierarchy.** [Reprinted from Brian J. L. Berry. *Geography of Market Centers and Retail Distribution* (Englewood Cliffs, N.J.: Prentice-Hall, Inc., 1967) p. 13.]

urbanized region. There, substantial distortions may exist that upset the regularities assumed in the theory. For instance, the location of harbor facilities, river crossings, and expressways are often anomalies distorting central-place regularity. Nonetheless, a hierarchy of business centers can be usually identified even in a highly urbanized region. A complete hierarchy of business centers has been identified for Chicago (Figure 6-4). That city's distinct types of centers range from "street corner clusters of convenience shops, through neighborhood, community, and regional shopping centers and culminating in the Loop, the metropolitan CBD (central business district)."[3]

Finally, Figure 6-5 shows that city-size distribution has been remarkably stable over time. Figure 6-5 shows for each census period a distribution of cities' population graphically ranked by size on a two-dimensional diagram. The horizontal axis of Figure 6-5

3. Brian J. L. Berry, *Geography of Market Centers and Retail Distribution* (Englewood Cliffs, N. J.: Prentice-Hall, Inc., 1967), p. 48.

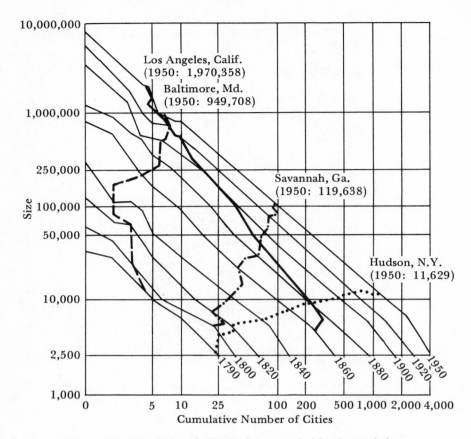

Figure 6-5 Population of urbanized areas ranked by size; and change in rank of four selected cities in ranking of cumulative number of places by size, 1790–1950. [Reprinted from Harvey S. Perloff and Lowdon Wingo, Jr., (eds.), *Issues in Urban Economics*, p. 127, published for Resources for the Future, Inc. by the Johns Hopkins Press.]

records the cumulative number of cities; its vertical axis indicates population. Ratio scales were used to make relative comparisons between the different time periods. That is, the axes have been scaled to reflect percentage changes. On the horizontal axis, for instance, the scaled distance between 5 and 10 is the same scaled distance as between 100 and 200, since in both cases the percentage increase in the cumulative number of cities is the same (i.e., a 100 percent increase). Similarly, for the vertical axis, the scaled distance between 2,500 and 10,000 is the same as the scaled distance between 250,000 and 1,000,000, since the scaled distances represent the same percentage increase in population (i.e., 300 percent increase).

As the city-size distribution line for 1790 shows, no city had 40,000 or more persons. Thus, the distribution line intersects the vertical axis at about 40,000. The other endpoint of the 1790 distribution line is positioned approximately at the intersection of the 2,500-population horizontal line and the vertical line of 25. (This endpoint can be verified from the data in Table 10-1 (i.e., there were 24 such cities in 1790). A downward movement along a distribution line shows the cumulative number of cities with a population of at least the size indicated on the vertical axis. In 1790, for example, there were five cities with at least 10,000 inhabitants.

The distribution lines for later periods are shown to be farther from the origin since there has been an increase in the total number of cities from 1790 to 1950. However, all the city-size distribution lines end at the 2,500 population scale since communities of less than 2,500 are not classified as cities.

If city-size distribution lines, for which each line represents a different time period, are parallel to each other, then there has been no relative change in the distribution of city size. As Figure 6-5 indicates, the city-size distribution lines for several time periods indicate that city-size distribution has, indeed, been relatively constant over time. It should be noted, however, that the evidenced stability of city-size distribution does not mean that all cities maintain their respective ranks over time. As Figure 6-5 shows, the selected cities of Los Angeles, Baltimore, Savannah (Georgia), and Hudson (New York) have all changed rank during the 1790–1950 period.

Although some selective empirical evidence has been presented here that seems to give some relevance to central-place theory, it would be unreasonable to expect to find a hierarchy of central places in the real world as perfectly ordered as the one depicted in the hypothetical rank-order illustration of Table 6-1. We would not expect to find, for instance, a uniform areal distribution of resources. Recall that one of the stated assumptions of central-place theory is the uniform areal distribution of resources. Reality shows that the areal distribution of resources is, at any point in time, quite unequal; that is, a few regions possess most of the nation's major resources. Extractive industries are necessarily attracted to these regions and this attraction effects the distribution of population. The irregular areal distribution of ports and navigable rivers is another example of how the assumptions of central-place theory are at odds with reality. In the early industrializing days of this country, nearness to ports and navigable rivers was essential to industry location, since water transportation offered the only reasonable form of transportation.

Consequently, industrial activity concentrated along these water routes. This geo-economic relationship is still evident today.

The real-world effects that brand-named products and patents have on the formation of market areas is a third example of how central-place theory is at odds with reality. Recall that product homogeneity was an important assumption in the development of the notion of central places. The existence of differentiated products (i.e., brand names) means that market areas for similar products will overlap, and therefore areal markets will not conform to the market-area configuration of central-place theory.

The practice of different spatial-pricing policies (Chapter 5) will also affect the size, spacing, and services of urban centers. The development of central-place theory was based upon a universal f.o.b. mill-pricing system.

Finally, the origination of location advantages from a concentration of economic activity and people (called agglomeration economies) will distort the regularity of the theoretical central-place hierarchy. For example, Detroit is the nation's leading city in total production of automobiles. Its market for automobiles is worldwide. Yet Detroit ranks only fifth in urban population size. New York City, the nation's largest city, produces no automobiles. Detroit's leading position in automobile production can be linked to the area's location advantages which relate to the simultaneous development of transportation equipment and related industries in the Detroit area. Because of the locational importance of agglomeration economies, the subject will be given special treatment in the next section.

As we have just seen, the application of central-place theory is limited by real-world conditions. While a perfect hierarchy of central places is not to be expected in the real world, the theory of central places is of value, for it gives us a basic understanding of the role that market forces play in the determination of central places. Equipped with this theoretical understanding, we can meaningfully broaden our comprehension of central-place formation by studying the effects of social, political, and geo-economic irregularities.

AGGLOMERATION ECONOMIES

The opening discussion of the theory of central places suggested that an economical arrangement of market areas (and the location of suppliers) is one in which suppliers share a common location because such an arrangement leads to savings in distribution costs. As important a reason as this is for business agglomeration, the economics of agglomeration clearly indicate that other determinants of location dynamics exist. Urban-regional specialists refer to these agglomerative influences as agglomeration economies. These influences are broader than those which are usually indicated as cost or price considerations (discussed in Chapters 4 and 5) and which include the usual locational factors such as low wage rates and proximity to raw materials.

Agglomeration economies cause and are caused by a geographic concentration of activity, though the extent to which these economies are a function of geographic concentration (city size) is not known. It is believed, however, that the "binding" effect of agglomeration economies is substantial in large cities. We can single out the New York City metropolitan region as an illustration of the importance of agglomeration factors.

> In some ways, the New York metropolitan region offers a paradox for anyone interested in the location of economic activity. Its raw materials are almost nonexistant; its splendid natural harbor, once a major advantage in competition with other areas, is no longer a factor of considerable importance; its location in relation to the nation's markets is hardly of the best; its wage structure is comparatively high. What is more, the region is not improving its competitive position in any of these respects. Yet its economic performance, measured in terms of employment, has not been much out of line with the growth of the country as a whole.[4]

We shall see shortly the impossibility of cataloging the various agglomeration factors into a concise classification system. For discussion purposes, however, we shall divide agglomeration economies into four classifications: transfer economies, scale economies, economies of labor specialization, and economies of professional interaction.

Transfer Economies

Transfer economies are those savings in transportation costs which accrue when firms locate at common places. Because a spatial

4. Raymond Vernon, *Metropolis 1985* (Garden City, New York: Doubleday & Co., Inc., 1963), p. 99.

arrangement of firms such as that in Figure 6-2 reduces total distribution (transportation) costs and ultimately lowers delivered prices to consumers, firms sharing common locations realize a commensurate sales increase, since consumers can now buy more goods for the same dollar outlay. A greater quantity of goods sold yields a higher level of total revenue for some or all businesses; therefore, transfer economies encourage businesses to cluster.

A reduction in procurement costs also yields transfer economies and is a further reason for highly interdependent buyers and sellers to locate near one another. Since this point is closely related to our second factor of agglomeration, its significance can best be understood by way of a discussion of this second factor, scale economies.

Scale Economies

Basically, two kinds of scale economies exist: *internal* and *external* scale economies. We shall first consider internal scale economies since such consideration is also pertinent to external scale economies.

For many production processes, general technological advancements have made large-scale production possible, and have reduced the average per-unit cost of production. This effect is referred to by economists and production-management specialists as *internal scale economies*. The downward-sloping portion of the long-run average-cost curve notes the range of internal scale economies. Most of the conditions that result in internal scale economies are familiar, but two of them are influential enough in their impact on external scale economies that they bear emphasis.

First, large complex plants make the specialization of labor possible in the production process. This greater efficiency results partly because workers are trained for specific production tasks and partly because specialization reduces the time that would be lost in moving from one task to another and from one machine or set of tools to another.

Second, large-scaled plants enable firms to use such cost-saving techniques of production as assembly lines and computerized machines. These techniques are not feasible for small-scaled plants with low levels of output.

Large-scale operations with high output levels necessarily require physical proximity to markets (i.e., concentrated industry areas) sufficient in size to consume a large volume of output. In general, then, volume production and internal scale economies both affect and are affected by location. Heavy population density leads to a geographic concentration of those industry groups where internal scale economies are significant; conversely, heavy industrial concentration leads to a greater geographic concentration of population. This mutual interdependence and influence is seemingly infinite.

A moment's reflection on the effect of labor specialization and large-scale production technological advantages on internal scale economies should reveal the notion that there is no economic reason why labor specialization and cost-savings techniques should be confined to the "inner walls" of a plant. In its broadest sense, specialization is applicable to industrial complexes, a grouping of plants that are spatially integrated by important production and marketing interrelations.[5] An excellent illustration of an industrial complex is the fabricated metals–iron ore industrial complex. The production of finished fabricated-steel products involves successive stages—from coal and iron ore through pig iron and steel ingots to the final fabricated-steel products.

Before spatial differentiation and specialization occurred in the metals industry, the successive stages of production were carried out largely in the same plant. Any cost savings via specialization were limited generally to the demand for (and output of) the firm's finished product.

The full benefits of specialization were realized when labor specialization and other cost-savings production techniques were applied to each stage of the production process, and moreover, were not limited to a single plant. For instance, a steel fabricator could adopt cost-savings production techniques in the early production stages of steel ingots. Cost savings could not occur, however, if the new techniques were efficient only at high levels of output—a level of output in excess of the plant's requirements of steel ingots. However, the greater efficiency of specialized production techniques for steel ingots could occur in a specialized-products plant if it produced steel ingots for several fabricated-steel producers. This potentially greater efficiency in the production of steel ingots ultimately led to lower production costs of fabricated-steel products, because a single plant specializing in production offered the product at lower costs than less specialized producers. The cost savings that result from

5. Walter Isard, *Methods of Regional Analysis* (Cambridge: The M.I.T. Press, 1960), p. 377.

the spatial differentiation and specialization of steel-ingot production is called an *external scale economy.*

An external scale economy can also be an internal scale economy. The duality can be clarified through a closer look at an example of the spatial-differentiation process in the steel-industry complex. In this example, technology made it possible to produce a larger quantity of steel ingots at a lower average per-unit cost. This cost-savings production technique is an internal scale economy in the production of steel ingots.

A finished-product manufacturer whose requirement for ingots is inadequate to justify the heavy expenditures that technical cost-savings equipment requires would find it profitable to "phase out" his own ingot production and purchase the materials from a firm that specializes in such production by using cost-savings techniques on large-volume production. We assume, of course, that the finished-product manufacturer's demands are not unique, that similar firms having the same requirements have created an overall demand great enough to satisfy the cost-savings needs of a special ingot-producing plant. Sufficient demand also requires that these several potential buyers of steel ingot are in proximity to each other. Assuming that there are several potential buyers of steel ingots and given the new cost-savings method of steel-ingot production, the workings of the market will create a spin-off of steel-ingot production from the initial unspecialized plant. Thus, when a "threshold" market, a profitable market, for steel ingots exists, the production of steel ingots will be differentiated out from the present unspecialized producers of final fabricated-steel products. Further, this specialization of steel-ingot production leads to a specialization in fabricated-steel production. The fabricated-steel producers will buy the steel ingots (a new input linkage) instead of producing them.

Lower production costs for steel ingots mean lower production costs for the final fabricated-steel products. Graphically, this means that the long-run average-cost curve for fabricated-steel products has moved closer to the horizontal axis, and the lowering of the average-cost curve because of lower input costs (due to internal scale economies on the part of suppliers) is an external scale economy for a fabricated-steel producer.

It is not difficult to cite many other examples of progressive spatial division and specialization of industrial activity that causes industry cost curves to slide downward, reflecting the increased efficiency of specialization. The textiles-apparels complex and the livestock production–livestock processing complex are examples of the spatial specialization of industry activity.

A crucial factor in cost savings associated with the spatial differentiation of production is the location of the separated but interdependent plants. It is obvious from our earlier location analysis (Chapter 4) that the location of many plants is directly linked to the location of other related plants. Simply put, the locating of interdependent activities in close proximity to one another reduces total transportation costs and offers greater returns for individual firms and the increased efficiency of total production. The savings in transportation costs generated by these economic advantages are transfer economies.

While the related processes of technological advancement and spatial differentiation and specialization usually lead to central location of interdependent activities, it is possible for some of the activities to disperse to other areas. An excellent example of this is seen in the livestock-processing business.

As recently as the early 1960s, livestock processing was concentrated in a few major midwest cities—Chicago, Omaha, St. Louis, Kansas City (Missouri), and St. Joseph (Missouri). Livestock was shipped from the farms to these major livestock-processing centers and the fully processed meat products were shipped to distribution centers. Indeed, the giants of the livestock-processing business— Armour and Swift—carried out the entire processing operation within a single plant. In some cases, this also included the processing of meat scraps for livestock feed and the production of fertilizer from waste materials.

These early livestock-processing plants were multistory structures in which the different stages of processing were carried out on different floor levels. Given the technology of the time, the centralized "full-line" processing plant seemed to be the most economical arrangement for the livestock-processing industry. However, because of sweeping changes in livestock production, in livestock processing, and in retail distribution and transportation, the onetime bustling activities of these plants and of the livestock-exchange terminals are now mostly history.

The recent trend in livestock feeding, particularly of cattle, has been the development of large, commercial feedlot operations that handle thousands of animals annually. The specialized feedlot's competitive advantage over the traditional, diversified farm unit of livestock and crop production has been enormous and has resulted in the geographic concentration of the feedlot industry.

Technological changes in livestock processing and the rapid growth in the large, retail food-store industry have placed the early stages of livestock processing near the large feedlots and the final stages of processing in or near the large food stores in metropolitan areas. The slaughtering operations, once handled solely by the now obsolete full-line processing plants, have been taken over by the small-scaled, highly specialized slaughtering plants located near areas of concentrated livestock production. Final processing has shifted to the major market areas, and to a large extent, has become a part of the operations of the large, retail food chains. Finally, major technological changes in transportation (e.g., the refrigerated motor truck) have been most instrumental in the spatial dislodgement of the onetime highly concentrated livestock-processing industry.

Today's geographic allocation of the livestock-processing operations typifies the way in which production and market forces continually rearrange the geographic distribution of economic activity. But even with the livestock production–livestock processing complex, much of the activity has remained in the urban areas.

Generally, increased specialization leads to increased interdependence among units in an industrial complex. The location of individual manufacturing plants which are highly interdependent is, in a sense, determined simultaneously—final-goods producers must have easy access to both the intermediate goods needed as inputs and to markets for the final product; intermediate-goods producers must have easy access to volume markets sufficient to realize economies of large-scale production. The solution for both groups is obvious. By locating close to one another they create an economic structure which provides both inputs and markets in sufficient scale and variety to meet their total needs. The cost saving (and additional revenue) from agglomeration is repeated at other points in the total spatial economy.

Economies of Labor Specialization

The economic reasons for the agglomeration of economic activities are reinforced by agglomeration's consequent labor-cost advantages. The location of different economic activities at a common place creates a large and diversified labor pool with a wide range in specialized skills.

One unobvious effect of the spatial concentration of different labor skills is that such concentration may lead to the development of a complementary labor pool. For instance, an industry that largely employs married male workers will bring to a community a potential supply of female workers. This means that businesses with heavy demands for female workers, such as garment plants, are attracted to the same community.

Economies of Professional Interaction

Our discussion of agglomeration economies has thus far considered agglomerative factors which are statistically verifiable. The fourth factor of agglomeration, the advantages of professional interaction, is less susceptible to such proof. One can nevertheless argue that the important role which professional interaction plays in creating products and improved industrial processes does much to encourage economic agglomerations. The personal contacts necessary to professional interaction take place best in large cities.

A crude yardstick of the degree of professional interaction found in a central place is the speed at which new information and new ideas are transformed into new production processes and new products. Frequently, such interaction can mean the difference between success and failure. This is particularly true for those businesses plagued with highly unstable markets. Consequently, the importance of professional interaction is directly related to the degree of uncertainty involved in the production of a good or service.

Businesses faced with high degrees of uncertainty must fit their operations to that uncertainty. In the words of Raymond Vernon: "They cannot commit themselves to specialized machinery; for specialized machinery, though well able to turn out long runs at low cost, usually is not easily adapted to swiftly changing products. The dressmakers dare not commit their capital to button-making machinery; the printers dare not stock all kinds of type faces nor all sorts of presses . . . . Instead, each must rely on outside specialists who can fill his needs as the needs arise."[6]

6. Raymond Vernon, *op. cit.* p. 102.

SUMMARY

Central-place theory partially explains the spatial distribution of cities and their difference in size and function. Supply and demand forces create a hierarchical development of central places, a development which includes a few very large cities spaced far apart and having a full range of services, a greater number of medium-sized cities with fewer functions and spaced closer together, and many small, limited-service towns spaced close together.

The theory of central places seems to reflect economic reality well. The spatial configuration of both rural and urban areas shows evidence of a central-place hierarchy of functions. In urban areas, this hierarchy is evident in the development of a network of many business districts, ranging from the small, neighborhood shopping area to the major central business district. Indeed, in many ways the hierarchical order of business centers found in an urban area is similar to a corresponding order of villages, towns, cities, and "super" cities that dot the nation's economic landscape. In each case, functional centers serve a fairly defined market area. The substantial difference between the two orders lies in the spacing of the centers. In an urban area, one functional center seemingly merges with the next, for urban functional centers are not defined by the green farmland belts that separate the functional centers in a predominately rural region (e.g., southwest Iowa). The key factor that determines the distance separating functional centers is population density. Since a firm's market area is, in large part, determined by population and income level, the market area of an urban business will be substantially smaller than the market area for a similar business located in a rural area.

The hierarchical order of business centers has policy implications. Cities of 50,000 to 200,000 people must decide on the relative merits of a single-core city (one central business center) versus a multicore city (many business centers). The theory of central places implies the emergence of a multicore configuration if market determining factors are free to operate. More will be said about this point in a later chapter.

A general explanation of central places and their locational importance required a general discussion of agglomeration economies. As mentioned, agglomeration economies result, in part, from the proximity of interdependent firms and the concentration of population. The extent of agglomeration economies in concentrated areas frequently offsets such competitive disadvantages as wage rates and proximity to raw materials.

REFERENCES AND SUPPLEMENTAL READING

Brian J. L. Berry, *Geography of Market Centers and Retail Distribution* (Englewood Cliffs, N.J.: Prentice-Hall, Inc., 1967), Chapters 1–3.

Walter Isard, *Methods of Regional Analysis* (Cambridge: The M.I.T. Press, 1960), pp. 375–78.

William H. Leahy, *et al.* (eds.), *Urban Economics* (New York: The Free Press, 1970), pp. 105–55.

Harvey S. Perloff and Lowdon Wingo, Jr. (eds.), *Issues in Urban Economics*, Resources for the Future, Inc. (Baltimore: The Johns Hopkins Press, 1968), pp. 81–138.

A. J. Rose, *Patterns of Cities* (Camden, N.J.: Thomas Nelson (Australia) Ltd., 1967), Chapters 4 and 5.

Raymond Vernon, *Metropolis 1985* (Garden City, New York: Doubleday and Company, Inc., 1963), Chapters 1–5.

7

Regional Structure
and Growth

The determinants of firm and industry location patterns, discussed in the previous three chapters, provide a basic understanding of spatial specialization and urban-regional economic structure. But this discussion of the location of economic activity has been based primarily on static analysis and cannot provide the total picture.

We have examined two questions in the previous chapters: (1) Given a particular economic landscape, where will an individual firm best be located? (2) Given a particular economic landscape, how do entire industries tend to locate? But the economic landscape is hardly unchanging, for a variety of forces continually cause shifts in the location of economic activity, including those changes in the landscape which occur *because of* the location of firms.

Reflecting a century of shifts of population and economic activity, Table 7-1 indicates the distribution of population among the major regions of the nation at ten-year intervals. The time interval represented by Table 7-1 begins after the Civil War, with the industrial revolution reshaping the spatial economic structure. In 1870, 82 percent of the people lived in the New England, Middle Atlantic, East Central, North Central, South Central, and South Atlantic regions. By 1970 this share had declined to 65 percent. At the same time, the share of the population living in the Pacific region jumped from 1.8 percent to 13.1 percent. Dramatic shifts in people and economic activity are continuing. As indicated by Table 7-2, state

TABLE 7-1. *Geographic Distribution of Population*

Year	United States (thousands of persons)	Percentage								
		New England	Middle Atlantic	East North Central	West North Central	South Atlantic	East South Central	West South Central	Mountain	Pacific
1870	38,558	9.0	22.9	23.7	10.0	15.2	11.4	5.3	0.8	1.8
1880	50,156	8.0	20.9	22.3	12.3	15.1	11.1	6.6	1.3	2.2
1890	62,948	7.5	20.2	21.4	14.2	14.1	10.2	7.5	1.9	3.0
1900	76,094	7.3	20.3	21.0	13.6	13.7	9.9	8.6	2.2	3.2
1910	92,407	7.1	21.0	19.9	12.6	13.3	9.1	9.6	2.9	4.6
1920	106,466	7.0	20.9	20.5	11.8	13.2	8.4	9.7	3.1	5.4
1930	123,077	6.6	21.4	20.6	10.8	12.9	8.0	9.9	3.0	6.7
1940	131,954	6.4	20.9	20.3	10.2	13.6	8.2	9.9	3.1	7.4
1950	151,235	6.2	20.0	20.2	9.3	14.1	7.6	9.7	3.4	9.7
1960	179,992	5.9	19.1	20.2	8.6	14.5	6.7	9.5	3.8	11.9
1970	203,212	5.8	18.3	19.8	8.0	15.1	6.3	9.5	4.1	13.1

SOURCE: U.S. Census of Population

TABLE 7-2. *State and Region Population, 1970, and Percent Change, 1960–1970*

Area	1970 Population (in thousands)	1960–70 Percent Change
New England	11,842	12.7
Maine	992	2.5
New Hampshire	738	21.5
Vermont	444	14.1
Massachusetts	5,689	10.5
Rhode Island	947	10.5
Connecticut	3,032	19.6
Middle Atlantic	37,199	8.9
New York	18,237	8.7
New Jersey	7,168	18.2
Pennsylvania	11,794	4.2
East North Central	40,252	11.1
Ohio	10,652	9.7
Indiana	5,194	11.4
Illinois	11,114	10.2
Michigan	8,875	13.4
Wisconsin	4,418	11.8
West North Central	16,319	6.0
Minnesota	3,805	11.5
Iowa	2,825	2.4
Missouri	4,677	8.3
North Dakota	618	−2.3
South Dakota	666	−2.1
Nebraska	1,483	5.1
Kansas	2,247	3.2
South Atlantic	30,671	18.1
Delaware	548	22.8
Maryland	3,922	26.5
D. C.	757	−1.0
Virginia	4,648	17.2
West Virginia	1,744	−6.2
North Carolina	5,082	11.5
South Carolina	2,591	8.7
Georgia	4,590	16.4
Florida	6,789	37.1
East South Central	12,803	6.3
Kentucky	3,219	6.0

Table 7-2.   (*Continued*)

Area	1970 Population (in thousands)	1960–70 Percent Change
Tennessee	3,924	10.0
Alabama	3,444	5.4
Mississippi	2,217	1.8
West South Central	19,321	14.0
Arkansas	1,923	7.7
Louisiana	3,641	11.9
Oklahoma	2,559	9.9
Texas	11,197	16.9
Mountain	8,282	20.8
Montana	694	2.9
Idaho	713	6.9
Wyoming	332	0.7
Colorado	2,207	25.8
New Mexico	1,016	6.8
Arizona	1,771	36.1
Utah	1,059	18.9
Nevada	489	71.3
Pacific	26,523	25.1
Washington	3,409	19.5
Oregon	2,091	18.2
California	19,953	27.0
Alaska	300	33.6
Hawaii	769	21.7

Source: Department of Commerce, Bureau of the Census, *General Characteristics of the Population, 1970.*

population growth rates between 1960 and 1970 ranged from a decline of 6.2 percent in West Virginia to an increase of 37.1 percent in Florida.

How does a region grow? The dynamics of a regional economy are a complex of economic, social, and political forces. In this chapter we will begin to examine factors associated with regional economic change and sketch the major shifts which have occurred. We will focus on the relationships between a regional economy's *internal* characteristics and its growth rate. External relationships and regional growth will be considered in the next two chapters.

A PRODUCTION-FUNCTION FRAMEWORK

A multitude of economic, social, and political factors within a region influence its growth and change, among them its natural resources, physical capital, human capital, social environment, and political leadership. A detailed list of items within a region that influence its economic performance would not only be lengthy but also unwieldy from an analytical viewpoint. Consequently, we turn to economic theory to reduce such a diverse, protracted list to few key relationships. Curiously, the "supply side" of regional-growth theory is less well developed than the demand side. The relatively meager theory on the relationship between internal regional factors and growth stems from the diversity of internal factors, not from their lesser importance.

A useful theoretical base from which to launch a discussion of internal growth factors is a production function. Its use as a framework in analyzing national growth suggests that it may also be a useful conceptual framework for urban-regional growth. Basically, the production function relates changes in aggregate inputs to changes in aggregate output. An example is the classic Cobb-Douglas production function, a simple case of which is

$$\frac{\Delta O}{O} = \frac{\Delta A}{A} + b\frac{\Delta L}{L} + (1 - b)\frac{\Delta K}{K}$$

which says that the rate of change in output ($\Delta O/O$) is determined by the rate of change in productivity ($\Delta A/A$), the rate of change in labor input ($\Delta L/L$), and the rate of change in capital input ($\Delta K/K$). The b and 1-b parameters are the elasticities of output with respect to labor and capital. In the Cobb-Douglas formulation, these parameters sum to 1, but this condition may not apply to an urban-regional economy. Ordinarily, parameters are estimated from times-series data. However, relatively little work has been done on urban or regional production functions. This deficiency is partly attributable to a lack of data on urban-regional output and partly to conceptual problems.

Because there has been little conclusive work done on estimating an urban or regional production function, we will settle for a more general form as a discussion framework of internal growth factors:

Growth in regional output $= f_1$ (natural resources) $+ f_2$ (technology)
$+ f_3$ (labor) $+ f_4$ (capital) $+ f_5$ (institutional change)

Natural Resources

Access to raw materials has been an important locational determinant in the development and evolution of many regional economies.

During the early formation of the United States economy, agricultural production coupled with transportation access dominated the location and growth of economic activity. The transportation and communications network developed for an agriculturally based economy became an important framework for future development. Likewise, when minerals became important inputs into economic processes, substantial infrastructure was developed to facilitate this type of economic development.

Although it is becoming increasingly less important, an industry's access to raw materials still has a significant influence on economic change in some regions and forms the initial basis for change in many.

The influence of resource accessibility on the location of industries and the growth of regional economies can be divided into three periods during the development of the United States economy.[1] The first, the *agricultural period*, was dominant until about 1840. During the early settlement of the country, fertile and accessible land was the dominant location factor. The developing and improving of transportation and establishing of market centers formed the spatial structure for subsequent growth. The influence of this early orientation is evident in our current economic growth and change.

About 1840 the *minerals period* began to influence the spatial growth of the economy. The economy of the period required different inputs which, in turn, placed increasing importance on minerals in the production process. Because of new resource requirements, a new location orientation occurred, for the manufacturing era saw the growth of industries that were closely tied to minerals. The development dramatically shifted the geographic distribution of economic activity.

1. H. S. Perloff, E. S. Dunn, E. E. Lampard, and R. F. Muth. *Regions, Resources, and Economic Growth* (Baltimore: Johns Hopkins Press, 1960).

Beginning about 1950, another set of resources began to influence regional growth. Climate, cultural and recreational potential, and similar characteristics associated with pleasant living conditions began to influence regional economic growth. This new orientation was labeled the *amenities and services period.*

This latter period signaled a diminished effect of the traditional resource orientation of earlier growth patterns.

However, resource orientation continues to influence many regional growth rates. The importance of resources depends on technology and demand, both of which change over time. The depletion of resources may precipitate decline unless a self-sustaining size or other countervailing forces are attained. In recent years energy shortages and sources have become important growth factors. Shifts in energy sources are likely to exert a strong effect on the spatial distribution of economic activity just as past resource orientations have done.

Technology

At any point in time, available inputs can be combined only in certain known ways to produce goods and services. This general knowledge about production processes is called technology. An increase in such knowledge is an increase in technology and can result in economic growth, because it means more output with the same quantity of inputs or the same output with fewer inputs.

But technological change is more likely to occur in some regions than others. In order to understand this phenomenon, we must examine some of the determinants of technological change which are related to regional differences.

Technological change may be thought of as invention followed by innovation, and invention has been thought to be at least partly a matter of chance. If so, regional size, density, and wealth may be important determinants of the number of inventions occurring in a region. Further, both invention and innovation are a function of a systematic investigation which requires research expenditures. Since such expenditures are, in part, a function of regional output or income, the larger urban regions are more likely to generate more technological advances, not only because of their large expenditures for research to produce inventions, but also because they have the investment potential necessary to translate the inventions into innovations. Both immobile technological information flows and the patent system tend to inhibit technology exchange, and this results in a further advantage to the large urban region.

Labor

A primary resource of any region is its people. Since the economic welfare of people is the paramount goal, labor resources are probably the most important of all regional resources. To refer to a regional labor supply is, of course, misleading. Numerous labor supplies and markets exist on the basis of skill levels and geographic location, all of which are interrelated.

The supply of labor in a region has a quantity and quality component. The internally generated quantity of labor available within a region depends on the region's population growth rate, the wage rate, and commuting patterns. The quality of labor is a function of the investment in human capital, namely education and training. (Migration, which can affect both the quantity and quality of the labor supply, is discussed in Chapter 9.)

Regional differences in natural population growth were substantial in the earlier history of the country. Both birth and death rates showed spatial variation: the agricultural areas have had high birth rates; mining regions have had higher mortality rates; certain urban areas exhibited relatively high mortality rates. These differences have tended to disappear as the nation has become more urban. Currently, the most substantial differences in population growth rates reflect regional differences in the age structure of the population.

A rise in the wage rate can also affect the supply of labor by inducing persons not in the workforce to enter and by offering an incentive for those already employed to work more. The entry of women into the labor market has been an important variable in the labor-supply function. Of course, an extensive increase in the wage rate may result in no further increases (or even a decrease) in the labor supply if workers choose more leisure over more income.

The commuting patterns of workers present an interesting spatial aspect of the behavior of the region's labor-supply function. In fact, as Chapter 1 mentioned, regions may be defined on the basis of commuting patterns. Labor supply (as well as other spatial characteristics of the economy) encounters the friction of distance.

As this is reduced, primarily through improved transportation, the labor supply may increase. The effect of commuting distance on a region's labor supply is seen in many central business districts in large metropolitan areas. Firms must often pay higher wages or require fewer hours to induce employees to travel from the suburbs. Thus, growth in the labor supply tends to be conditioned by the spatial structure of the region.

The development of the interstate highway system and urban freeways continues to alter the access to jobs and, conversely, to labor markets. The opening of a new urban freeway provides new links to parts of an urban region. An urban freeway system coupled with commuter trains can link more than a half-dozen counties in a labor market.

The labor supply in nonmetropolitan regions has also been altered by improved transportation. Many farm operators now hold off-farm jobs made possible by easier commuting. Likewise, the entry of women into the labor force has increased rapidly in rural areas.

Increases in the labor supply will bring increases in output, but at a declining rate if all other factors remain unchanged. If there is no increase in capital, the marginal physical product of labor will decline as the labor supply increases (K/L will decline). This relationship is seen in Figure 7-1. The capital-labor ratio K/L is a useful measure of the productive potential of an economy. The higher the K/L ratio, the greater the relative marginal physical product of labor. Under these conditions, which assume constant returns, wages will decline if they are reflective of the marginal productivity of labor. However, changes in the region's capital stock can affect the capital/labor ratio and its wage rate.

The quality of labor in a region depends on the human capital embodied in the workforce. Human capital consists of the skill, education, and other earning potential which the worker carries with him into the workforce. Striking differences exist among regions with regard to investment in human capital. For instance, public school expenditures per pupil in 1971 ranged from $1,370 for New York to $489 for Alabama.

Capital

Both private and public capital are critical to the growth process. Increases in the private-capital stock of a region depend

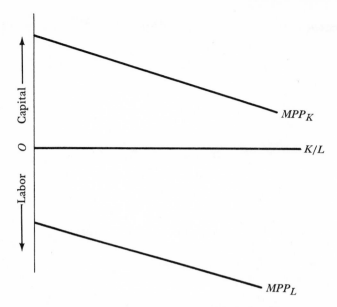

Figure 7-1　The relationship between the marginal physical product
of labor, the marginal physical product of capital, and the
capital/labor ratio

both on the supply of and demand for investment funds. The quantity of savings is the key component of supply, since the total amount of investment in any given period equals the quantity of savings in the same period. In turn, the amount of regional savings is a function of regional income, because savings originates from profits and wages and both depend on the level of income and its distribution. The rate of technological change, variations in demand relative to productive capacity, expectations, and the rate of interest are the major determinants of investment among a host of complex, interrelated factors.

Public capital may be thought of as being either economic-overhead capital or social-overhead capital. The former is that public capital which supports the economic activity of an area and the latter is that which supports the area's population. Some have argued that economic-overhead capital precedes economic growth in that it provides the preconditions for private capital and that social-overhead capital follows growth by providing the public facilities for the population.

The general impact of additional capital on the regional economy is worth noting. Usually regional output increases with an

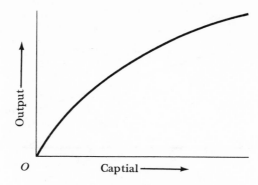

Figure 7-2   Capital-output relationship

increase in capital, but it does so at a declining rate.   In other words, the marginal physical productivity of capital declines.   This is illustrated in Figure 7-2.   If there is a constant output price, then the real rate of return will behave as does the marginal physical product of capital.   The rate of return will fall as the capital stock increases.

The process of capital accumulation is illustrated in Figure 7-3.   If a region has an initial capital stock A which yields a rate of return B, this rate will bring about net investment C.   This new net investment will add to the existing capital stock A an amount AD, which is equal to C, thereby yielding a total new capital stock of D. The new capital stock D results in a lower rate of return and in a subsequent reduction in new investment for the next period.

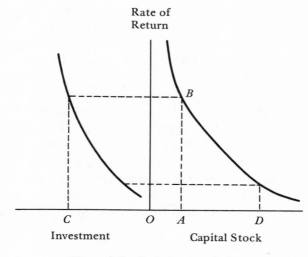

Figure 7-3   Capital accumulation

Institutional Change

In any region, various institutional structures influence regional growth. These institutions have evolved over time to enable the region to conduct its business in an orderly fashion. As the nature of the regional economy changes, however, these institutional structures may not respond quickly enough to prevent their having a negative impact on the region's growth rate. Three examples may illustrate the effects of institutional rigidities.

One of the most publicized institutional problems is political fragmentation. Within a region, dozens of political units may exist with overlapping and conflicting geographic and functional lines. In addition to the difficulties of providing public services (see Chapter 14), such fragmentation may retard the region's growth rate by failing to support efficiency in the private sector. Any improvement in such an institutional arrangement can foster economic growth.

Zoning laws may be another factor which can affect the region's growth rate. Principles governing land use are often archaic and inhibit the orderly development of the region's economy.

Banking laws may also inhibit economic growth. Spatial banking structure differs widely from state to state. Branch banking is the most noticeable difference. Studies have indicated that a favorable structure of the banking system can exert a positive effect on a state's growth rate.

Production-Function Models

As indicated earlier, relatively few production-function models of urban or regional growth exist. Although it is possible to identify the general theoretical components, modeling efforts have been stymied by a lack of reliable data and a maze of potential functional forms. However, there have been a few noteworthy efforts.

Perhaps the most common regional-growth model launched from a production-function base is the regional derivative of the neoclassical growth model. The usual production function is the following general form:

$$Y = f(K, L, T)$$

Where Y = regional income
                  K = capital stock

L = supply of labor

T = time with technological change embodied

If it is assumed that factors of production receive their marginal net products and that there are constant returns to scale, then a regional-growth model may be written as:

$$y = ak + (1 - a)\,l + t$$

where the lowercase letters represent rates of growth of the corresponding values in the above production function and a and $(1 - a)$ are elasticities with respect to capital and labor.

Such a neoclassical growth model has been employed by Borts and Stein[2] to examine interstate growth-rate differences in per capita income.

Regional-production functions have been estimated by Mera[3] for Japan to determine the role of social capital in production. Included as variables in Mera's model were various measures of land, labor, and capital inputs. By disaggregating capital into seven sub-categories of private and social capital, the model could focus on the role of various mixes of private and social capital in the regional-growth process.

Production functions have been employed to estimate part of the urban-growth process. Usually such modeling efforts have been restricted to one urban characteristic such as housing. Muth's[4] modeling of urban housing is one such example.

SOME SIMPLE THEORIES

Despite a mushrooming volume of empirical studies, the formation of urban-regional growth theory has been frustrated by the complex maze of interactions which thwart satisfying generalizations. Instead, numerous partial theories have gained and retained appeal. Even though they lack theoretical or analytical rigor, each offers some insight into the growth process. Three of the more popular of

2. G. H. Borts and J. L. Stein, *Economic Growth in a Free Market* (New York: Columbia University Press, 1964).

3. Koichi Mera, "Regional Production Functions and Social Overhead Capital: An Analysis of the Japanese Case," *Regional and Urban Economics*, Vol. 3, No. 2, (1973) pp. 157–186.

4. Richard F. Muth, *Cities and Housing* (Chicago: The University of Chicago Press, 1969).

these "theories"—economic-base theory, sector theory, and stages-of-growth theory—will be considered in this section.

Economic-Base Theory

The most popular theory of regional economic growth has been economic-base theory; indeed, in the embryonic stages of regional-growth theory it was dominant. This popularity may stem more from its simplicity than its veracity, but it does represent a reasonable first entry into the maze of regional growth.

Economic-base theory emphasizes the importance of a region's economic specialties. A dichotomy is established between those activities in which a region specializes and those activities which are not unique to it. The economic specialties are called *basic activities*, and their consequential activities are referred to as *nonbasic activities*.

Alternatively stated, a local economy may be divided into two components: economic activity serving markets outside the region and economic activity serving markets within the region. For instance, steel production is part of the economic base of Gary, Indiana, while a retail food store in Gary is not. According to economic-base theory, the growth of Gary depends on the growth of its steel industry and other economic specialties which are distinguishable by their out-of-region markets. The nonbasic activity such as the retail food store depends on the activity levels of the basic industries.

Two different sets of labels have been used when referring to this dichotomy. The basic activity may be viewed as that for which the demand is *exogenous* (independent of the region's level of activity), while the nonbasic activity is *endogenous* (dependent primarily on the region's level of basic activity). Slightly different nomenclature divides the activities of an urban area into *city-forming* and *city-formed* activities.

An explanation of the growth process via economic-base theory occurs at two levels. Of initial concern are the factors which cause basic industries to locate in a region; thus, economic-base theory may be viewed as an extension of location theory. The second stage is an investigation of the effect which the basic sectors have on the total activity of the regional economy.

An increase in the external demand for a basic industry's product results in an increase in the activity of the nonbasic industries as well. The internal expansion of the economy stemming from the increase in demand for the product of a basic industry can be estimated with a "base multiplier" of the following form:

$$\begin{bmatrix} \text{Increase in} \\ \text{regional income} \end{bmatrix} = \begin{bmatrix} \text{increase in} \\ \text{basic income} \end{bmatrix} \times \begin{bmatrix} \dfrac{1}{1 - \left(\dfrac{\text{nonbasic income}}{\text{total income}}\right)} \end{bmatrix}$$

In addition, employment, value added, or output could be used to measure the region's activity. A more rigorous model will be presented in the next chapter when we discuss regional-trade models.

Economic-base theory, as an extension of location theory, emphasizes the role of the economic base in attracting capital. Capital flows to these regional specialties which offer higher rates of return. Also, externally supplied capital not only increases the productive capacity of the region, but it also improves its economic environment for future growth.

Thousands of economic-base studies of varying degrees of sophistication have been completed for regions and localities. Frequently, the economic-base study divides the activity in the region into basic and nonbasic activities simply by industry type. For instance, all manufacturing activity is considered basic and all services, retail trade, and local-government activities are nonbasic. Crude as this may appear, the technique has been used to provide economic-base studies for hundreds of areas in the United States.

A somewhat more precise measure of a region's economic base is the location quotient. This technique uses the national economy as a measure of self-sufficiency. If a region has a greater ratio of its total activity in a particular industry than does the nation as a whole, that industry is considered the region's specialty. Using employment as a measure of activity, the location quotient for an industry in a region is calculated as follows:

$$\frac{R_A/R}{N_A/N}$$

Where R_A = regional employment in industry A
R = total regional employment
N_A = national employment in industry A
N = total national employment

If the ratio is greater than 1, regional industry A is an exporter. If the ratio is less than 1, it is an importer. And, if the ratio is equal to 1, the quantity produced by industry A is exactly equal to the amount necessary to satisfy regional consumption of that product.

Three assumptions are needed to use a location quotient to estimate export activity: no spatial variation in consumption patterns, no spatial variation in labor productivity, and each industry produces a single, homogeneous product.

The location quotient is used to estimate export employment in industry A (X_A) as follows:

$$X_A = \left(\frac{R_A}{R} - \frac{N_A}{N} \right) R$$

Although an improvement over the categorization approach, the location quotient technique has several drawbacks. First, exports are easily underestimated because of the degree of industry disaggregation to which the technique is applied. For any industry group, some products are imported and others are exported. The location quotient measures only net exports for any industry group and, consequently, may substantially underestimate the total exports in the industry group.

A more satisfactory approach to measuring a region's economic base is to obtain actual data on the movement of goods and services out of the region. This approach involves great effort and expense since little data exist on these flows other than from individual firms. Some data exist for multistate regions in the United States in the Census of Transportation data, but as yet these are of limited value for base studies.

Once the economic base has been identified, projections of the basic activities are made. Usually these are tied to some national-growth projections which are possibly adjusted for anticipated changes in the region's competitive position, but the primary focus is on the *external* demand for the region's goods and services. We will return to this notion in the next chapter.

After projections of the basic sectors have been made, the nonbasic sectors are projected by using multiplier relationships. The "base multiplier" is the simplest of these. If the value added in the basic industries is one-half of the total regional value added, and if we assume that the proportion remains the same as the base expands, then if value added in the basic industries increases by $1 million, value added in the nonbasic industries will increase by $1 million. But the assumption of a constant base multiplier is tenuous at best.

Studies have indicated that the size of the multiplier varies over time.[5]

The basic theoretical difficulty of the economic-base approach is its overemphasis on exports as the determinant of regional growth. While identification of a region's economic specialties has merit, economic-base theory omits more than it considers. In fact, some theorists argue that the nonbasic rather than the basic sectors provide the basis for growth.[6] The base industries often stagnate, often die. A region's ability to replace these basic industries depends on the viability of the local service sector. Thus, the argument continues, the large cities are particularly equipped to grow because of their large service sectors.

A pragmatic test of the theory might be how well it works in forecasting growth. Pfouts examined the relationship between urban growth and basic activity for several urban areas and found a clearer relationship between the nonbasic activities and growth than between the basic activities and growth.

Despite these criticisms, economic-base theory does focus on some important growth relationships. Change in the structure and output of a region's economy is related to national and even international phenomena. Spatial specialization is recognized in the basic-industry identification and, in a highly aggregated manner, both external and internal interdependence are considered.

Sector Theory

Sector theory views regional economic growth as an internal evolution of specialization and the division of labor. Like economic-base theory, sector theory has numerous deficiencies as a satisfactory theory of regional growth, but it is worth considering because of its relationship to more satisfying regional-growth theories.

The origin of sector theory is the Clark-Fisher hypothesis that economic growth (per capita income) depends on how rapidly resources are shifted out of agriculture (primary activity) and into manufacturing (secondary) and service (tertiary) activities. Resource shifts occur because of both supply and demand pressures. Differential rates of productivity in the sectors result in shifts of labor

---

5. Ralph Pfouts, "An Empirical Testing of the Economic Base Theory," *Journal of the American Institute of Planners*, Vol. 23, 1957.
6. H. Blumenfeld, "The Economic Base of the Metropolis," *Journal of the American Institute of Planners*, Vol. 21, 1955.

and capital. Also, higher income elasticities of demand are associated with the products and services of secondary and tertiary sectors.

Initially, sizeable sector shifts out of agriculture gave validation to sector theory; indeed, early sector theory relied heavily upon empirical studies of these shifts. The demand for food was income inelastic, and manufacturing production was growing rapidly.

Among the numerous problems offered by sector theory in its purest form are its high level of aggregation and its assumed correspondence between the income-elasticity-of-demand sectors and the high-productivity-growth sectors. Dividing the economy into only three sectors blurs many important relationships, and such aggregation is particularly inadequate now that the agricultural transition has slowed. Although structural evolution may be important, sector theory is too highly aggregated to identify significant changes. Of importance, too, is the fact that a sector with a high income elasticity of demand need not have high productivity growth.

Stages-of-Growth Theory

Sector theory and location theory have been combined to form a theory of development stages. Although these stages are primarily descriptive, they provide an insight into the structural evolution which accompanies the growth of a regional economy. Several stages-of-growth labels have been developed, but they all have the same substance. Theoretically, a fully developed regional economy has had to move historically through each consequent stage.

1. *Self-sufficient subsistence economy*. A regional economy which is basically self-contained has little specialization and little export trade. In developed nations, such economies are virtually non-existent. With no significant export trade, such regions have few interregional transportation links.
2. *Specialization in primary activity*. Historically, regional growth stems from such primary-activity specialization as agriculture or mining. The expanding interregional trade resulting from this specialization encourages and is encouraged by an improvement in transportation. Better transportation improves access both to markets and supplies.
3. *Development of secondary industries*. As primary activity expands, population and supporting (secondary) activities also grow. Establishments providing services to the primary processing activ-

133

ity and to the regional population develop and grow. There are also important increases in social-overhead capital.

4. *Industrial diversification.* The initial stages of growth stimulate rising incomes and the formation of simple industrial linkages. These effects provide the basis for diversification. The social-overhead capital and service establishments and the larger labor force and expanding market attract still other firms.

5. *Specialization in tertiary activities.* The final stage of structural evolution occurs when the region becomes an exporter of services. In the early stages of development, the meager industrial structure necessitated importing many services. As the region grew it became more self-sufficient in these services, and, if growth continues, it eventually becomes an exporter of services.

These stages of growth are a reasonable description of the historical growth process; however, they do not provide an understanding of the complexities of current regional growth.

STRUCTURAL ANALYSIS

The principles influencing the location of economic activity which we examined in Chapters 4 and 5 indicated that a highly differentiated economic landscape is a natural outgrowth of market forces. The resulting spatial specialization means that each regional economy has a unique industrial structure. These structural differences are helpful in explaining differences in both potential and actual growth performance among regions. The dynamics of a region's industrial structure is considered the main engine of economic growth by several important theoretical and empirical investigations of regional growth. Thompson bluntly states, "Tell me your industry mix and I will tell your fortune."[7]

Growth Impact and Industrial Structure

One way to investigate regional growth is to examine the hypothetical impact of a new industry in an existing economy. What, for instance, will be its impact on the growth of the Simcity economy?

7. W. R. Thompson, "The Economic Base of Urban Problems," in Neil Chamberlain (ed.), *Contemporary Economic Issues* (Homewood, Illinois: Richard D. Irwin, 1969), p. 1.

The input-output characteristics of the new firm, the existing industrial structure of Simcity, and the time horizon are all important to an analysis of the growth impact. To begin, let us distinguish among the three different time periods.

1. *The preproduction capital-expenditure phase.* Prior to beginning production, the firm must acquire plant and equipment to produce its product, and these capital expenditures will increase production in those local industries from which the firm buys its plant and equipment. Though a large portion of these purchases may come from outside the region, income and employment will increase to the extent that the purchases are regional. These income and employment effects will be significant only for the period required to produce the new plant and equipment.

2. *The short-run phase.* In the period immediately following the start of production, income and employment in the region increase both in the new plant and in industries selling to the new plant. But, in the short run, no additional structural change occurs.

3. *Long-run dynamics.* The new firm may provide the stimulus to further expansion in the economy. Other new firms may locate in the region to produce goods which use the outputs of the initial plant as their inputs, or firms may locate in the region to sell goods and services to the new firm and other firms in the region. Also, transportation rates may fall because of the new firm and additional firms may be attracted to the area because of the region's increased competitiveness in transportation rates. These are but a few of the possible paths of long-run structural change and growth.

Preproduction Impact. Although acquisition of plant and equipment has but a temporary impact on the regional economy, that impact may be great if the regional economy has the industries which supply a large portion of the inputs for the new plant and equipment.

The potential immediate impact on Simcity of the new firm's capital outlays is shown in Table 7-3, which indicates the amounts being supplied within the region. Income, employment, and output in these three industries, as well as those indirectly linked to them, will increase temporarily as a result of the capital spending.

The time sequence of the impact of the preproduction expenditures can be illustrated by Figure 7-4, where t indicates the time period in which production begins. Path B illustrates the behavior

TABLE 7-3. *New Firm Preproduction Capital Requirements*

Type	Total	Within Region
Contract construction	$3,000,000	$2,000,000
Machinery	1,500,000	500,000
Office furniture	200,000	25,000

of industries supplying capital goods directly to the new firm. Their production will increase until the capital requirements of the simulated activity are met; then a decline occurs after the demand for capital has been satisfied. But, as we learned in Chapter 3, increased output in one industry results in output increases in industries which supply inputs to the first industry. Path A represents an output path of an industry supplying inputs to the capital-supplying sector described by Path B. Its stimulus and decline occur prior to that of the industry represented by Path B. Finally, Path C represents a typical industry supplying inputs to the firm for normal production.

An important determinant of the regional impact of the capital expenditures is the region's industrial structure. If the region has a relatively undeveloped industrial structure, relatively insig-

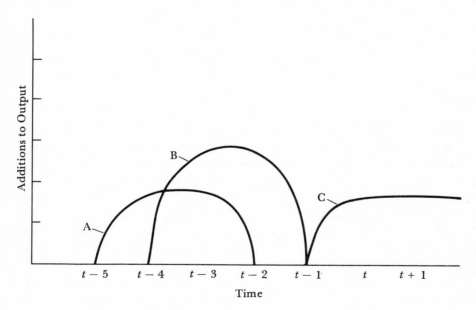

Figure 7-4   Impact of a new plant on industries in the region

nificant capital spending will take place in the region and regional economic impact will be minor.

Postproduction Short-Run.   Once the plant starts producing, its effect on the region's output and income is relatively rapid, for in order to produce its output, the plant purchases a variety of inputs which have a direct, indirect, and induced effect on the regional economy. These were the impacts discussed in Chapter 3, and they can be measured with input-output analysis.

The extent of the impact will vary among regions according to the region's industrial structure, itself closely related to population size.   This can be simply illustrated by Figures 7-5 and 7-6.   For a mature industrial structure such as represented in Figure 7-5, the $10 million annual sales in the first round will result in $3.42 million local income, $4.91 million expenditures on local goods and services, and $1.67 million imports.   The sum of all rounds of spending will yield total local income of $6.84 million, twice the first round income. But for an immature economic structure, the income multiplier is considerably less, as indicated in Figure 7-6.   The smaller the region, the fewer the linkages are among industries and the greater the potential *leakage* through imports.

Total employment effects accrue to the region in a similar way.   If, to produce $10 million in goods, the new plant employs 100 workers, other firms in the region must increase their output by 75 more workers.   The total regional employment increase is 175.

Long-Run Dynamics.   The growth of one industry in a region not only has immediate impacts on other industries in the region but it may also generate long-run structural changes in the local economy which alter the growth potential of the economy.

To illustrate this structural evolution and location-linkage process, let us sketch a plausible growth sequence along the lines of the stages of growth presented earlier in this chapter.

Suppose we begin with a region in its embryonic stage of development, specializing in a product (e.g., cattle) or a service (e.g., railroading), of which part is exported.   After the internal processes of specialization are set in motion, the next step in the growth process will likely be tied to the first.   For instance, the initial resource will be further exploited by processors who will locate at the raw-material source.   In these early stages of production, industries tend to locate at raw-material sites since early production processes are frequently

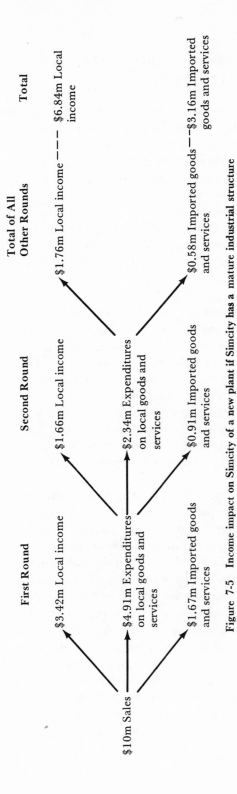

Figure 7-5   Income impact on Simcity of a new plant if Simcity has a mature industrial structure

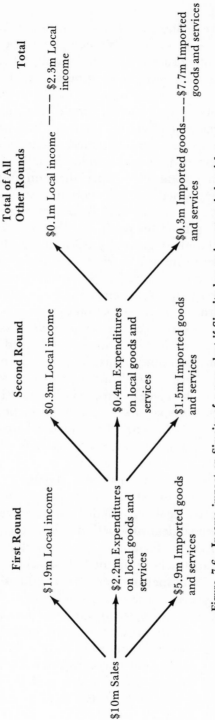

First Round

$1.9m Local income

$2.2m Expenditures on local goods and services

$5.9m Imported goods and services

$10m Sales

Second Round

$0.3m Local income

$0.4m Expenditures on local goods and services

$1.5m Imported goods and services

Total of All Other Rounds

$0.1m Local income

$0.3m Imported goods and services

Total

$2.3m Local income

$7.7m Imported goods and services

Figure 7-6 Income impact on Simcity of a new plant if Simcity has an immature industrial structure

139

weight or bulk reducing, which lower transportation costs. As the region continues to grow, its basic energy will be derived from new firms either becoming suppliers to the initial processors or functioning as firms utilizing their outputs as inputs. In this manner linkages are established between firms' inputs or supply requirements and their output or markets. Consequently, one of the unique characteristics of regional development is the tendency for firms to develop in "families" which are structurally related, a tendency which encourages the growth of certain industries while virtually discouraging others.

This evolving nature of specialization and growth both nurtures and is constrained by the economic structure of the region. Disregarding for the moment that the process may arrive at a plateau for any region at a level below "total development," the next phase of regional development generally exhibited is that of complexes of economic activity forming a more diversified economic base for the region. This stage results from and contributes to the concentration of economic activity in a large city or metropolitan area.

As the raw-material-processing industry expands and the initial satellite firms succeed, a cumulative process begins. Area expansion takes place as new firms are attracted by the advantages of locating in an expanding industrial area. Simply stated, existing firms attract new firms. Industries provide markets for other industries, or conversely, serve as suppliers for other industries. Because of these linkages, transportation costs tend to be minimized by adjacent locations and, in turn, help further area expansion. The resulting concentration of economic activity is what we have called an agglomeration.

Certain internal and external economies of scale are associated with this agglomeration which transform it into a "growth pole." The internal scale economies of an individual firm are often such that its technological production characteristics require a large-scale plant to produce efficiently. For a market-oriented firm, such a condition requires a large immediate market of the sort which is most accessible in a metropolitan area. These characteristics of individual firms are also true of agglomerations.

External economies result from a concentration of firms in one geographic area to provide the specialized services that are needed to serve a growing number of firms. These, in turn, reduce costs for the basic firms and encourage the location of other firms to take advantage of these external economies. Large pools of specialized labor, more-favorable transportation rates, the availability and maintenance of business machines, and highly developed utility, communication, transportation, and governmental services are but a few examples of the external cost-saving features accruing even to unrelated firms in a concentration. Such activities are self-generating, and the resulting major economic concentrations have been referred to as "growth poles" to convey the idea that they are the areas within broader regions to which the bulk of economic activity gravitates.

Backward and Forward Linkages

The above illustration is not intended to be a general description of the growth process but rather a way of illustrating the influence of linkages in the growth process. Three types of linkages were apparent: supply linkages, market linkages, and agglomeration linkages.

Supply and market linkages, also called forward and backward linkages, are illustrated in Figure 7-7. Cattle feedlots represent a forward linkage to the meat-packing plant, and coal mining is a forward linkage to glassmaking. The leather-tanning firm which uses the hides from the meat-packing plant forms a backward linkage to the meat-packing plant, just as the window manufacturer forms a backward linkage to the glass manufacturer.

The relationship between interindustry linkages and regional

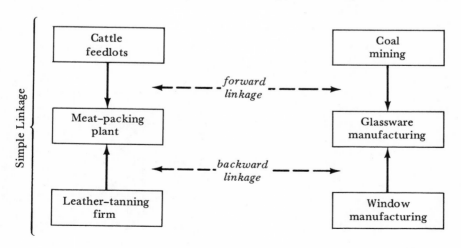

Figure 7-7 Spatial linkages in a regional economy

growth can be visually depicted by examining an adaptation of input-coefficient matrices described in Chapter 2. If we rearrange the rows and columns so that the industries in the upper rows make relatively few significant inputs to other industries while the lower rows make increasingly more significant inputs to other industries, we have *triangularized* the input-output table. The triangulation arranges the industries in a transactional hierarchy. For any sector, the sectors above or to the left of it are its customers; those below or to the right of it are its suppliers.

The triangulation allows a visual comparison of economic structures. Figure 7-8 indicates four triangularized matrices representing different levels of development. The upper-left matrix represents an economy with little interdependence and a low level

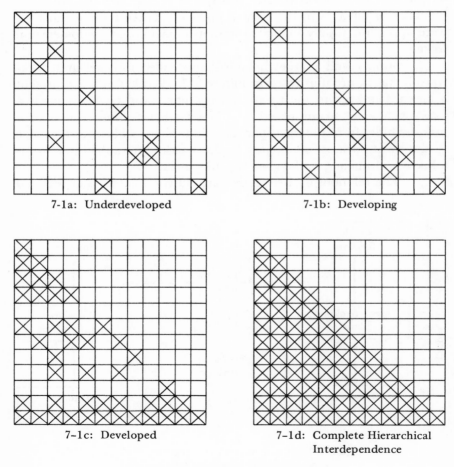

7-1a: Underdeveloped   7-1b: Developing

7-1c: Developed   7-1d: Complete Hierarchical
                                          Interdependence

Figure 7-8   Regional development structures

of development. The number of economic specialties and the inter-dependence is greater in each subsequent matrix. The lower-left matrix represents a mature regional economy with a high level of interdependence.

Since each region has a unique economic structure, growth expectations are not the same. Each industry is influenced by demand conditions unique to that industry. Since demand does not change at the same rate for each industry, differences in industry mix will result in different growth rates. A regional economy containing industries which are either new or have a high income-elastic demand for their product will tend to have above-average growth.

Shift-Share Analysis

A technique called shift-share analysis has been devised to measure regional-growth differentials based on the differences in regional industrial structure. If employment is used as a measure of growth, share analysis determines the hypothetical growth between two periods in a region if each industry in the region had grown at the same rate as that industry has nationally. To the extent that the actual differs from the hypothetical, a competitive shift has occurred; if the hypothetical growth rate exceeds the actual, the region has experienced negative shifts.

A region can have a faster or slower growth rate than the nation because of either its industrial mix or its competitive share. If a region has a high proportion of fast-growing industries and if each of these grows at the national rate for that industry, then the region will, because of its industrial mix, experience a more rapid rate of growth than will the nation. The competitive component takes into account the difference between the actual performance and the hypothetical growth.

Suppose that we have the employment data for the nation and for Simcity indicated in Table 7-4. Between 1960 and 1970, total employment for the nation expanded 19.45 percent. If Simcity had grown at the same rate as the nation, its 1970 employment would have been 508,000. Instead, its employment was 545,000, or 37,000 higher than if the Simcity economy had grown at the same rate as the nation. Shift-share analysis divides this above-average growth into two components: industrial mix and competitive shift. The industrial-mix component can be measured by comparing the growth

TABLE 7-4. *Employment in the Nation and Simcity, 1960 and 1970 (in thousands)*

	Nation		Simcity	
	1960	1970	1960	1970
All industries	65,800	78,600	425	545
Manufacturing	16,800	19,400	140	170
Nonmanufacturing	49,000	59,200	285	375

in each sector with the national growth in that sector. Had the manufacturing sector in Simcity grown at the same rate as the nation, its 1970 manufacturing employment would have been 162,000 (140,000 × 1.155). Similarly, nonmanufacturing employment would have been 344,000 (285,000 × 1.208). The sum of these two hypothetical sector growth rates indicates that the Simcity economy would have had 506,000 employees in 1970 had both sectors grown at the same rate as their national counterparts. This is 2,000 less (506,000 − 508,000) than had the Simcity economy grown at the national rate for all industries. This 2,000 difference is the mix effect and indicates that the Simcity economy has a slightly unfavorable industrial mix. The remainder of the increase is attributed to positive competitive shifts. The results are summarized in Table 7-5.

TABLE 7-5. *Shift-Share Analysis of Simcity Employment Growth (in thousands)*

	All Industries	Manufacturing	Non-manufacturing
Total change	120	30	90
National growth	83	22	59
Competitive shift	39	8	31
Industrial mix	−2	—	—

Input-Output Access

A useful idea in considering the relationship between spatial position and regional growth is "input-output access."[8] This approach derives from location theory to the extent that access to inputs coupled with access to markets is the primary focus of profit-maximizing location theory. The region's cumulative advantages—such as natural resources, labor quality, markets, and its cultural advantages—are what is reflected in the idea of input-output access. A classification scheme such as that of Table 7-6, which reflects market

8. H. S. Perloff *et al., op. cit.*

TABLE 7-6. *Input-Output Access*

		Good access to basic inputs from external regional and national sources		Poor access to basic inputs from external regional and national sources	
		Good access to basic inputs in home region	Poor access to basic inputs in home region	Good access to basic inputs in home region	Poor access to basic inputs in home region
Poor access to external regional and national markets	Poor access to markets in home region	Region 1 2	Region 2 1	Region 3 1	Region 4 0
	Good access to markets in home region	Region 5 3	Region 6 2	Region 7 2	Region 8 1
Good access to external regional and national markets	Poor access to markets in home region	Region 9 3	Region 10 2	Region 11 2	Region 12 1
	Good access to markets in home region	Region 13 4	Region 14 3	Region 15 3	Region 16 2

NOTE: The number in the lower-right-hand corner indicates the number of "good" access dimensions.

SOURCE: Harvey S. Perloff, Edgar S. Dunn, Jr., Eric E. Lampard, and Richard F. Muth, *Regions, Resources, and Economic Growth* (Baltimore: Johns Hopkins Press, 1960), p. 91.

and supply access, is helpful in considering relative potential growth. Region 4, lacking ready access to all inputs and markets, has the least potential. At the other extreme, Region 13 has the greatest potential for growth because of its good access to all inputs and markets. The remaining regions lie somewhere in between.

As discussed in the previous chapter, the growth prospects of urban areas depended upon their locations. A small town adjacent to a large urban center has strong growth potential. The same-size town located 80 miles from the large urban center has a lower growth potential. But the same-size town located 150 miles from the large urban center may have a greater growth potential than the town 80 miles away. Thus, although these towns are the same size, their location determines that they will have different economic structures.

Thresholds

Regional economic development is not a smooth, continuous process; rather it is more a series of sporadic jumps in the growth curve. An important reason for this discontinuity in the growth process is the existence of thresholds which reflect the indivisibility of investment and have both demand and supply characteristics.

A threshold "denotes a limitation within which a variable does not change under the influence of a gradually increasing factor.[9] A demand threshold refers to some minimum level of aggregate demand that is necessary to support an activity. A supply threshold is reached when the existing capital structure cannot support any additional activity and when a large input of investment is required for further expansion.

The demand threshold can be considered the minimum sales necessary for a firm to make normal profits and is usually measured by income or population. Each economic activity has a unique threshold, which helps explain why many kinds of economic activity exist only in larger areas. Grocery stores and service stations require only a small population to thrive; and with such low thresholds, they exist even in small villages. A full-line department store has a larger threshold, as does a data processing firm. Demand thresholds can be illustrated by Figure 7-9, which indicates that aggregate demand may increase considerably before a threshold for

9. B. Malisz, "Implications of Threshold Theory for Urban and Regional Planning," *Journal of the Town Planning Institute*, LV, 1969, p. 108.

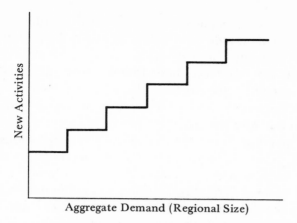

Figure 7-9 Demand thresholds and regional growth

new activity is reached. Subsequent new activity starts up only after the next threshold is reached.

Supply thresholds act similarly on regional growth; technology requires that investment be a "lumpy" rather than a continuous process.

Urban-Size Ratchet. A related view of the interaction between urban-regional size and growth is what has been labeled the urban-size ratchet effect, the effect by which past agglomerations tend to lock in future growth. This view of urban growth holds that, because they do not generate the agglomeration effects necessary for a self-sustaining growth mechanism, only the smaller towns are likely to decline. Larger urban places, once they reach a certain size, will not normally decline. The critical size is determined by the spatial position of the urban place, cultural factors, and the overall level of industrial development. Several factors tend to lock in growth, including industrial diversification, the development of a mature service sector, political power, and entrepreneurial and innovative abundance.

SUMMARY

Differential rates of regional growth have occurred throughout the history of the United States. Major structural changes in the economy have been associated with interregional, rural-urban, and interurban shifts in economic activity and population. Natural resources were dominant in location patterns as recently as 1950. But markets, amenities, and services have been the chief orientations.

Some simple theories have been set forth to explain regional and urban growth. Export-base theory is the most common and perhaps the simplest. Numerous techniques have been developed to identify and measure the economic base.

An investigation of the dynamics of regional industrial structure ranges from short-run impacts to long-run dynamics. The structural evolution is clearly identifiable from a historical viewpoint, but the task of forecasting this evolution is considerably more difficult. Techniques like shift-share analysis have focused on ferreting out the contribution of industrial structure to growth.

Finally, the industrial structure works in tandem with spatial structure in influencing growth rates. The notion of input-output access captures this relationship.

REFERENCES AND SUPPLEMENTAL READING

Brian J. L. Berry, "City Size Distributions and Economic Development" *Economic Development and Cultural Change*, Vol. 9 (July, 1961).

Edgar M. Hoover, *An Introduction to Regional Economics* (New York: Alfred A. Knopf, 1971).

Edgar M. Hoover and Raymond Vernon, *Anatomy of a Metropolis* (Cambridge, Mass.: The M.I.T. Press, 1956).

Wassily Leontief, "The Structure of Development" *Scientific American*, September, 1963.

Hugh O. Nourse, *Regional Economics* (New York: McGraw-Hill, 1968).

Harvey S. Perloff, Edgar S. Dunn, Eric E. Lampard, and Richard F. Muth, *Regions, Resources, and Economic Growth*, (Baltimore: Johns Hopkins, 1960).

Allen R. Pred, *The Spatial Dynamics of U.S. Urban-Industrial Growth, 1800–1914* (Cambridge, Mass.: The M.I.T. Press, 1966).

Harry W. Richardson, *Regional Economics* (New York: Praeger, 1969).

Horst Siebert, *Regional Economic Growth: Theory and Policy*, (Scranton, Pa.: International Textbook Co., 1969).

Wilbur R. Thompson, "The Economic Base of Urban Problems," in Neil Chamberlain (ed.), *Contemporary Economic Issues*, Richard D. Irwin, 1969.

8

Interregional Trade

Chicago may now have a different economic base than that suggested by Carl Sandburg's poems. But now as then, certain economic specialties pump economic vitality into the region and do so because of economic ties with other regions. A few years ago the economic base and interregional linkages of the Seattle area were front-page news because of the precipitous decline of its aircraft manufacturing. Every region has certain economic specialties in which it engages and which result in trade with other regions. This interregional trade is an important mechanism for determining the performance of a regional economy and the transmission of economic growth between regions.

Our purpose in this chapter is to explore the importance of a region's external economic relationships to its overall economic performance. We are interested in why regions trade and how trade and changes in trade affect growth.

WHY REGIONS TRADE

Explanations of interregional trade vary from gravity models of the social-physics approach to relative-price-differential models of traditional trade theory. The rudiments of each of the approaches provide a useful starting point in our discussion of the role of interregional trade in regional economic growth.

Gravity Models

Social physics views the behavior of members of a social group, a social mass, as analogous to the interaction between physical masses. Developed by the astronomer John Q. Stewart,[1] three demographic concepts are the core of the social-physics models and are included in gravity models of social phenomena—gravitational force, gravitational energy, and gravitational potential. Stewart's basic model follows the formula of gravitational force as a constant times the product of the two masses, divided by the square of the distance separating them.

The idea of demographic force F can be expressed as

$$F = G \, \frac{P_i P_j}{d_{ij}^2}$$

Where   i and j represent two regions
   P_i = population of region i
   P_j = population of region j
   d_{ij} = distance between region i and region j
   G = constant

Demographic energy E can be stated as

$$E = G \, \frac{P_i P_j}{d_{ij}}$$

And demographic potential V at region i produced by the population of j is

$$_iV_j = G \, \frac{P_j}{d_{ij}}$$

The total demographic potential at i produced by all relevant regions is

$$_iV = G \sum_{j=1}^{h} \frac{P_j}{d_{ij}}$$

Gravity-Trade Models

The gravity-trade models explain trade on the basis of the relative economic size of trading regions and the distance separating them. In general form

1. John Q. Stewart, "Suggested Principles of 'Social Physics'," *Science*, Vol. 106, 1947, pp. 179–180.

$$T_{ij} = G \frac{Y_i{}^a \, Y_j{}^b}{d_{ij}{}^c}$$

Where T_{ij} = value exports from region i to region j
      G = export parameter
      Y_i = regional income of region i
      Y_j = regional income of region j
      d_{ij} = distance between region i and region j
      a, b, and c = exponents to be determined

The above equation indicates that the amount of trade between two regions depends on: (1) the size of the exporting region's income, which is indicative of its ability to supply exports, (2) the size of the importing region's income, which represents the size of the potential market, and (3) the distance between the two regions, which reflects transportation costs.

Several variations of this model have been developed for international and interregional trade models.[2] Among these is Linnemann's embellishment of the basic gravity-trade model. The rationale for his approach is that nations or regions trade because their domestic patterns of production are not the same as their domestic patterns of demand. The comparative advantages of regions, which make trade profitable, result primarily from differences in economies of scale and technology. Technological differences result from a time lag in the diffusion of innovations.

Linnemann's model views trade as a function of regional income and population. Trade resistance is a function of distance. Population size is inversely related to the value of trade because larger populations increase the possibility that efficient market size (demand threshold) will be reached for more commodities.

Price-Differential Models

Although social physics has been successfully employed in empirical trade studies, the approach lacks a rigorous theoretical

2. P. Pöyhönen, "A Tentative Model for the Volume of Trade Between Countries," *Weltwirtschafliches Archiv*, Vol. 90, 1963, pp. 93–100.

J. Tinbergen, *Shaping the World Economy*, Twentieth Century Fund, 1962, Appendix VI: "An Analysis of World Trade Flows," pp. 262–293.

H. Linnemann, *An Econometric Study of International Trade Flows*, (Amsterdam: North-Holland, 1966).

W. Leontief and A. Strout, "Multiregional and Input-Output Analysis," in T. Barna (ed.) *Structural Interdependence and Economic Development*, (New York: St. Martin's Press, 1963).

K. R. Polenske, "Empirical Implentation of a Multiregional Input-Output Gravity Type Trade Model" in A. P. Carter and A. Brody (eds.), *Contributions to Input-Output Analysis* (Amsterdam: North-Holland, 1969).

basis for understanding the reasons for and the growth consequences of trade. We now turn to the rich legacy of international- and interregional-trade theory which is capable of shedding more light on the basis for trade and the mechanism by which trade affects the transmission of economic growth from region to region.

Gains from Trade. One of the fundamental ideas in economics is the principle of comparative advantage. Although the principle is a familiar one, we will sketch its basic premises as a background for a discussion of the role of trade in regional growth.

Let us suppose that two regions produce two commodities but with different production functions. In addition, let us suppose that the two regions do not trade with each other because they have poorly developed transport facilities and consequently high transport costs.

The production possibilities for one man/day of labor in each region appear in Table 8-1. The data show that region 1 can

TABLE 8-1. *Production Possibilities of Regions 1 and 2 with One Man/Day of Labor*

Item	Region 1	Region 2
Food	8	2
Clothing	6	3

produce both more clothing and more food with one man/day of labor than can region 2, for its clothing-food price ratio is 8/6, whereas that of region 2 is 2/3. In other words, in order for region 1 to get eight units of food, it must give up six units of clothing. These production possibilities are also illustrated in Figure 8-1.

Now let us suppose that our assumption of prohibitively high transport costs is replaced by one of zero transport costs. Regardless of region 1's production advantage, trade will now be beneficial to both because the comparative costs are different in the two regions. Region 1 has a comparative advantage in the production of food, and region 2 has a comparative advantage (least comparative disadvantage) in the production of clothing. Region 1 is twice as productive as region 2 in clothing, and four times more productive in food. If region 1 can produce eight units of food and trade them for *more than* six units of clothing, region 1 will produce food to trade for clothing,

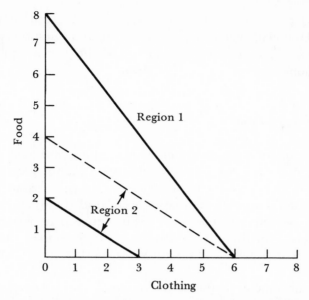

Figure 8-1   Production-possibility curves of food and clothing for regions 1 and 2

since the cost of six clothing is eight food.   Similarly, region 2 would gain by receiving *more than* two units of food for three of clothing.

One mutually beneficial trading ratio would be six units of clothing for six units of food.   Region 1 gains because it requires less than one day of labor to produce the six food units to be traded for the six units of clothing, which require a full day's labor if regionally produced.   Region 2 would also gain by producing six units of clothing and trading them for six units of food, because regionally produced six food units require more labor than do six units of clothing.

The terms of trade could vary from four food for six clothing to eight food for six clothing, depending on the relative supply and demand factors in the two regions.   We will consider the behavior of the terms of trade in greater detail.

The notion of comparative advantage establishes the basis for specialization and trade between regions, but it is a static framework which we now translate into a dynamic setting.

TRADE DYNAMICS AND GROWTH

The principles of comparative advantage are based on a static set of conditions of unchanging tastes, income, factor endowments, and technology. But what if one or more of these factors change? How will regions be affected? Such a question requires an examination of the processes by which trade helps transmit economic growth among regions.

Terms of Trade

The relative price differences of clothing and food in the two regions in our previous example indicate that interregional trade would result in a gain for both regions. But each region's share of the gain depends on the resulting terms of trade between them. The terms of trade refers to the relationship between import prices and export prices. In quantity terms as in our example, the terms of trade may be expressed as a quantity of exports traded for a quantity of imports.

A movement in the terms of trade can either positively or negatively affect the growth of a trading region. In our example, let us suppose that the demand for clothing increases more than the demand for food, so that the terms of trade shift from six units of clothing for six units of food to six units of clothing for seven units of food. Region 1 would now have to trade one more unit of food to get the same amount of clothing, but trade would still be advantageous to region 1 as well as region 2.

Several approaches to the measurement of the terms of trade have been used. In a study of the terms of trade for the Pacific Northwest, Pfister[3] used the net-barter terms of trade and the gross-barter terms of trade. The net-barter terms of trade is the ratio of export prices to import prices in one period compared with the same ratio for a different period. The gross-barter terms of trade is the ratio of import quantities to export quantities in physical terms, such as tons.

The results of Pfister's study appear in Table 8-2. Focusing only on the net-barter terms of trade, a substantial improvement in the terms of trade occurred for the region in the post–World War II period compared with earlier years.

But price changes are generally accompanied by volume changes. This is illustrated by the gross barter terms of trade in the second column. A favorable improvement in the net barter terms of

---

3. Richard L. Pfister, "The Terms of Trade as a Tool of Regional Analysis," *Journal of Regional Science*, Vol. 3, No. 2, 1961, pp. 57–65.

TABLE 8-2. *Net-Barter and Gross-Barter Terms of Trade and Ratio of Exports to Imports, Pacific Northwest, Selected Years 1929–1955.*

Year	Net Barter Terms of Trade†	Gross Barter Terms of Trade*	Value of Exports / Value of Imports
1929	100	100	100
1934	84	97	86
1935	99	120	81
1936	105	116	91
1937	110	121	91
1938	101	99	102
1939	114	80	142
1948	169	188	90
1949	146	149	98
1950	168	186	91
1951	176	182	97
1952	168	167	101
1953	145	145	101
1954	147	136	108
1955	153	145	104

†Price index of exports divided by price index of imports.
*Quantity index of imports divided by the quantity index of exports.
SOURCE: Richard L. Pfister, "The Terms of Trade as a Tool of Regional Analysis" *Journal of Regional Science*, Vol. 3, No. 2, 1961, p. 60.

trade may be accompanied by large increases in imports relative to exports, resulting in a jump in the ratio of the value of exports to value of imports.

These data suggest that a discussion of the terms of trade can be misleading unless subsequent effects are considered, because the terms of trade represent a partial analysis. This is true of many analytical devices.

Transport Rates and Trade

Transport rates affect not only the terms of trade but also the extent of price equalization of the traded goods. As discussed above, the relative price differences in the two regions stimulated trade. Although trade *per se* will tend to equalize the price of the traded goods in both regions, transport costs alter this equilibrium.

The effect of transport costs can be illustrated with partial-equilibrium analysis that does not account for changes in the prices of other goods, changes in income, or other factors affecting the demand and supply for the single commodity in the two regions.

The demand and supply of clothing and the equilibrium price in regions 1 and 2 are depicted in Figure 8-2 for a situation with no transport costs. Note that the demand and supply curves for region 2 have been "flip-flopped" in order to get both regions on the same diagram. The equilibrium price *ad* exists where the excess supply *ab* in region 2 is equal to the excess demand *cd* in region 1. The diagram also indicates that region 2 produces *ax* clothing but consumes only *bx* while exporting *ab*. Region 1 consumes *xd* but produces only *xc* of that total.

With the more realistic inclusion of transport costs, the equilibrium price differs between the two regions by the amount of the transport cost. As illustrated in Figure 8-3, the equilibrium prices equalize imports and exports, *ab* equals *cd*, but trade is reduced from what it would have been without transport costs. The price in the exporting country is lower than it would have been (assuming constant returns), and the price in the importing country is higher.

Over the long run, the regional development process can be partially viewed as a lowering of transport rates. Initially, rates may be so prohibitively high as to prevent commodity movement. The transport cost per unit would, in this case, be equal to or greater than

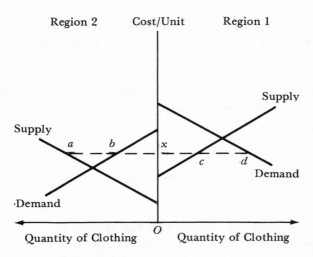

Figure 8-2 Partial-equilibrium price of clothing in regions 1 and 2 with no transport costs

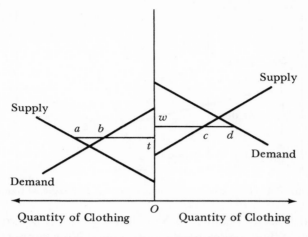

Figure 8-3 **Partial-equilibrium price of clothing in regions 1 and 2 with transport costs**

the difference between the prices in the two regions. Lower transport rates widen competitive-price ranges and increase trade. Previous intraregional commodities may become interregional as transport facilities improve and transport rates decrease.

As a result of transport costs, we can view regional specialization with the following relationships:

Region i will tend to specialize in those activities for which

$$P_i + T_i < P_j + T_j$$
or
$$P_i < P_j + T_j - T_i$$
or
$$P_i - P_j < T_j - T_i$$

Where P_i and P_j = costs of production in regions i and j

T_i and T_j = transport costs from i and j to the market

Transport costs impede trade and a transportation differential $(T_j - T_i)$ can reinforce, neutralize, or reverse a production-cost advantage $(P_i - P_j)$.

A simple example can illustrate the results of transport-cost reductions on interregional trade. Let us suppose that there are three regions, two which produce peanuts and the third which consumes them. Peanuts are grown in region 1 at A and in region 2 at B. Figure 8-4 illustrates the spatial arrangement. Production costs per bushel of peanuts are $4.00 and $3.00 at A and B respectively. The transport costs per bushel are $T_A = \$1.00$ from A to M and $T_B = \$3.00$ from B to M. As a result, A will produce the peanuts because

157

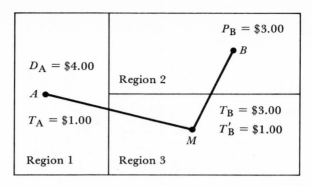

Figure 8-4 Transport costs, production costs, and regional trade

its delivered price of peanuts to M is lower than B's delivered price, even though A has higher production costs. Now suppose that the transport technology between B and M is improved to such an extent that transport costs drop from $3.00 per bushel to $1.00 per bushel ($T_B$). If there is no change in the transport rates from A to M, B will become the production site for the peanuts.

We could consider other changes which would alter the pattern of trade, but this simple example permits some general observations about the relationship between transport costs and interregional trade patterns.

Differential rates of improvement in transportation will alter regional cost advantages; however, a general decrease in transport costs gives greater influence to production-cost differentials among regions. In fact, generally improved transport may work to the disadvantage of poorer regions if they lack other competitive capacities. The depressed areas of Appalachia, which will be discussed later, may be an example of such a situation.

Besides transport costs, other barriers to interregional trade may exist. International trade restrictions, essentially tariffs and quotas, significantly affect regional trade. The most striking example is the major shift in regional trade occurring within the European Economic Community after trade barriers were reduced.

External Demand and Growth

In the previous chapter we discussed economic-base theory, which is the same concept as export-base theory but with a slightly different emphasis. We will now reconsider this simple theory and emphasize exports instead of the dichotomy of the region's internal structure.

Export-Base Theory

Export-base theory views the growth of a regional economy as dependent on the increase in external demand for the output of its industries, namely, its exports. An increase in exports induces other regional industries' expansion to support the growth of the export industry. This multiplier reaction can be measured by the ratio of total regional output to total regional exports.

Export-base theory derives its orientation from Keynesian income theory, but it focuses on exports rather than investment as the volatile component of final demand. Even the accelerator concept is adopted, with the full expansion process occurring when export expansion adds to aggregate spending in the region. Thus, income increases induce new investment and accelerate growth.

Exports and Regional-Income Theory

The export-base concept can be formulated in an income-analysis framework. The fundamental relationship in the base theory is the income relationship:

[Regional income] = [regional expenditures] + [regional exports]

or

$$Y_R = (E_R - M_R) + X$$

Where Y_R = regional income
   E_R = regional spending on regionally produced goods and services
   M_R = imports, out-of-region purchases
   X = exports

E_R and M_R are assumed to be linear functions of regional income, but X is autonomous. If we let $C_R = (E_R - M_R)$, then Figure 8-5 represents the basic relationships. The equilibrium level of income is Y_{R1}, where total effective demand equals total output.

To identify the region's current account balance B, let

$$B = X - M_R$$

Now suppose that exports increase by ΔX, as illustrated in Figure 8-6. The new equilibrium level of income is now Y_{R2}. The increase in income, $\Delta Y_R = Y_{R2} - Y_{R1}$, is a multiple of ΔX. The export-base multiplier is determined by the leakages from the regional-income stream, imports and out-of-region lending. If both of these

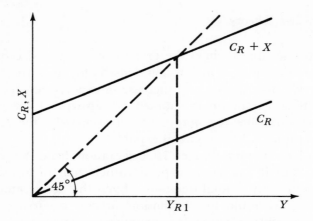

Figure 8-5   Regional expenditure-income function

are linear functions of regional income, then their corresponding marginal propensities are m and b where $m = \Delta M_R / \Delta Y_R$ and $b = \Delta B / \Delta Y_R$.

Then the export-base multiplier e can be stated as

$$e = \frac{1}{m_R + b}$$

Then the increase in the equilibrium level of income is

$$\Delta Y_R = e \, \Delta X$$

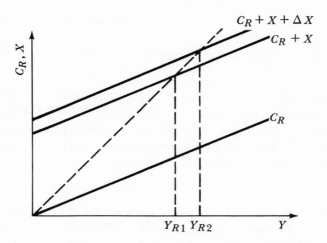

Figure 8-6   Regional expenditure-income function after an increase in exports

This relationship assumes that m and b are constants and that there are negligible feedback effects from the increase in exports. Feedback effects will be discussed later.

Implied Assumptions

Implied in the export-base model is the assumption of a disequilibrium, an unemployment equilibrium, or a marginal propensity to consume that is greater than unity. If the increase in total regional income resulting from an autonomous increase in exports does not result in an increase in imports at least equal to the increased exports, the increased exports will have a dampening effect on the equilibrium rate of growth. This occurs because an import surplus represents a supplement to internally generated capital. Thus, the regional growth rate is greater when $M > X$.

Interindustry Effects

The input-output model discussed in Chapter 3 allows a more detailed look at the consequences of increased exports and shows them as a part of final demand and as having direct and indirect effects on regional industries. In the previous chapter we illustrated how the internal industrial structure influenced the amount of interaction, or multiplier effect, stemming from increased demand. These same principles apply to export increases, one component of final demand. The more immature the industrial structure, the greater the "leakages" and the lower the multiplier effect. Conversely, the more mature the industrial structure, the less the leakage, and the greater the multiplier effect.

The industrial composition of an increase in exports also can have a differential effect on the impact of an increase in exports. For instance, suppose that each of the three processing sectors of the Simcity economy (Table 2-1) experiences a $3 million increase in autonomous exports. Each will have a different magnitude of impact on the Simcity economy, as indicated in Table 8-3, which shows the direct and indirect requirements necessary for each sector to deliver the additional $3 million exports. The column totals show the output increases in all industries as a result of $3 million more exports by the column industry. The row totals show the total output in-

TABLE 8-3. *Output Effects of a $3 Million Increase in Autonomous Exports in Each Industry*

	Manufacturing	Trade	Services	Total
Manufacturing	3.68	.87	.67	5.22
Trade	.41	3.69	.76	4.86
Services	.46	.58	3.80	4.84
TOTAL	4.55	5.14	5.23	

creases of each industry in order for all industries to deliver an additional $3 million of exports.

Feedback Effects

A more realistic but more complex approach is the consideration of feedback effects. The exports of one region are the imports of another. Thus imports and exports transmit income changes back and forth among regions. These feedback effects can be captured with the following model:

$$O_R - A_R O_R = T_X O_W + F_R$$
$$O_W - A_W O_W = T_M O_R + F_W$$

or

$$(1 - A_R) O_R - T_X O_W = F_R$$
$$- T_M O_R + (1 - A_W) O_W = F_W$$

Where O_R = total regional output
F_R = regional final demand other than product account exports
O_W = total rest-of-the-world output
F_W = total rest-of-the-world demand
A_R = matrix of regional input coefficients
A_W = rest-of-the-world input coefficients
T_X = matrix of export coefficients showing per units of rest-of-the-world inputs supplied by the region
T_M = matrix of per unit supplied by the rest of the world to the region

The model shows, for instance, that an increase in the final demand for a region's products resulting in more exports to the rest of the world will require more imports by the region from the rest of the world in order to produce the additional exports. For the rest of the world to produce the additional imports, more inputs are required, including more exports from the region.

Technology Diffusion and Trade

Technology is the general state of production-process knowledge. Innovations change the ways in which available inputs are combined to produce goods and services and, as previously indicated, these changes in technology are not spatially uniform. First, we will examine technological innovation and its spatial diffusion and then the role of technological change in regional trade.

Technological change can affect regional trade in three possible ways. First, the innovation may be neutral in its effect on trade. Figure 7-1 in the previous chapter represents this neutral effect. The production-possibilities curve merely shifts further out without changing shape. Second, an export-biased innovation results in a productivity gain in the export good. This situation is graphically represented in Figure 8-7. The terms of trade tend to worsen because the export commodity is now cheaper to produce. Third, an import-biased innovation results in a reduction in the cost of import-competing commodities and improves the terms of trade because either less expensive regional goods replace imports or import prices fall in order to compete with more efficient regional production.

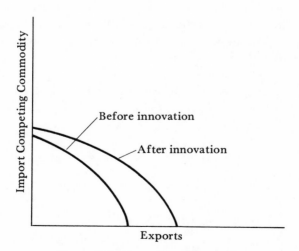

Figure 8-7   Export-biased innovation

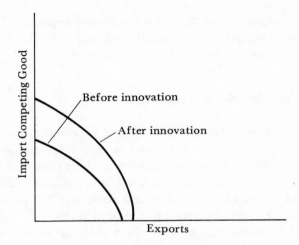

Figure 8-8 Import-biased innovation

Such a case is illustrated in Figure 8-8. Unless demand strongly favors the export good, neutral innovation also worsens the terms of trade. Thus, these shifts in the terms of trade resulting from technological change are critical to the interregional transmission of economic growth benefits.

Trade and Factor Prices

Our previous discussion has concentrated on changes in the terms of trade without explicitly examining the effect of trade on factor prices. We now extend our discussion to factor flows and factor prices in the following chapter.

For summary and selected readings, see the end of the next chapter.

9

Interregional
Factor Flows

In the preceding chapter we examined interregional commodity movements; in this chapter we will consider interregional factor movements. The factors of production, with the obvious exception of land, are more mobile within an interregional setting than they are in an international one. We will examine the determinants of labor and capital flows from one region to another and the interrelationship between the two.

INTERREGIONAL CAPITAL FLOWS

From our discussion of the process of capital formation in Chapter 8, we determined part of the process by which a regional economy adds to its productive capacity. But, because of the openness of a regional economy, interregional capital flows may amplify or retard the internal capital-formation process.

Capital Flows Defined

The flow of capital between regions is measured by a region's net exports—the difference between total exports and total imports. For instance, if a region's exports exceed imports, the region accumulates claims on other regions which represent the extent of that region's investments in other regions. Conversely, if a region has a net import surplus (imports exceed exports), the surplus indicates the amount which the region is borrowing from other regions—its capital inflow.

The relationship between net exports and gross regional income is

$$\text{Gross regional income} = \text{regional spending} + \text{net exports}$$

and since

$$\text{Gross regional income} = \text{consumption} + \text{gross savings} + \text{taxes}$$
$$\text{(excluding transfer payments)}$$

and

$$\text{Regional spending} = \text{consumption} + \text{gross investment} +$$
$$\text{government purchases}$$

then

$$\text{Net exports} = (\text{consumption} + \text{gross savings} + \text{taxes}) -$$
$$(\text{consumption} + \text{gross investment} +$$
$$\text{government purchases})$$

becomes simplified as:

$$\text{Net exports} = \text{gross savings} + \text{taxes} -$$
$$(\text{gross investment} + \text{government}$$
$$\text{purchases})$$

If net exports are positive, the region is exporting capital by the amount of the net exports. If net exports are negative, the region is importing capital by that amount.

Net current exports consist of three main components: (1) Net exports of goods and services is by far the largest and generally the most important. (2) Net unilateral transfers are private- or public-income payments other than those for the recipient's production of goods and services. (3) Income or investment from regionally owned resources located outside the region may be an important source of current regional income if past lending was sizable. We will return to these three components when we consider long-run capital flows later in the chapter.

Determinants of Capital Flows

The demand and supply of investment funds determines the flow of capital among regions. Theoretically, capital flows toward areas offering high returns and away from areas offering low returns, tending to ultimately equalize rates of return. But market imperfections, transportation costs, and uncertainties modify these tendencies. Savings, a supply of capital, is generated both in different rates and volume from region to region, and is absorbed by differences in regional investment demand.

Existing capital stock and capital indivisibilities are two important factors which retard capital flows. The existing plant and equipment are generally tied to their current location. Thus, subsequent increases in capacity may be tied to existing capital stock. Because of certain types of large-scale technologies, capital must flow in large quantities or not at all. These indivisibilities tend to retard capital flows because of their large minimum requirements.

Uncertainties may most significantly impede interregional capital flows. If a region has had characteristically unstable past rates of return, a present high rate of return may not attract sufficient capital. Some regions may have had policies (tax and other) which reduce expected future rates of return. Some evidence suggests that the cost of obtaining capital increases with the distance from major financial centers, a reflection at least in part of increased uncertainty.

Rate-of-return equalization and the effect of uncertainty can be illustrated in Figure 9-1. The marginal efficiency of investment schedules (MEI) for regions 1 and 2 illustrate a situation where the

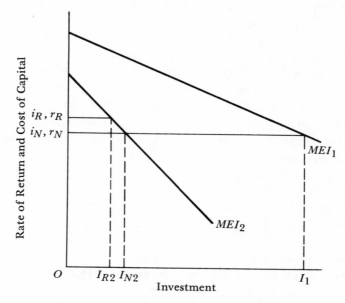

Figure 9-1 Capital-rate-of-return equalization

expected rate of return in region 2 on investment opportunities is generally less than in region 1. If both regions have equal access to capital at a national interest rate, i_N, then capital will move between regions until the marginal efficiency in each region is equal to i_N. In the diagram, the levels of investment for region 1 and region 2 are I_1 and I_2, respectively.

Suppose that the cost of available funds is greater in region 2 than in region 1 because previous lower rates of return cause lenders to add a risk premium to the normal national rate of interest. The added premium raises the rate of interest (cost of capital) to region 2 to i_R and this lowers investment in region 2 because rates of return are now equated to the otherwise different capital costs in the two regions.

Long-Run Capital Flows

As indicated earlier, a region may be either a debtor (capital importer) or creditor (capital exporter). But there may be several situations characteristic of each, and a region may move from one position to another and back again through a long-run development path. Table 9-1 is indicative of several possible debtor and creditor positions for a regional economy.

A region initiating a growth trend by importing capital from other regions will be a net importer and considered an immature debtor. Over a period of time, if this import surplus continues, the continuous borrowing will raise the interest burden on the rising debt to other regions until the income required to meet periodic interest payments exceeds net new borrowing, or alternatively, until the interest payments exceed the region's deficit on current account. The region is now a mature debtor and finds that its annual borrowing is not sufficient to meet even the interest on past loans. The added productive capacity as a result of the capital inflow will eventually result in an export surplus and make the region a new creditor. This situation will allow the region to repay its loans and possibly become a lender. Eventually this will result in the region becoming a net receiver of interest from other regions rather than a net payer, and thus, an immature creditor. Finally, if the region continues to be a net exporter, its net interest income will become larger than its export surplus on current account (net exports from domestically employed resources will become negative). The region will then become a mature creditor. Of course, once a region ceases to have

TABLE 9-1. *Possible Debtor and Creditor Positions of Regions*

	Net Exports	Net Income on Investments	New Exports from Domestically Employed Resources
New debtor	−	+	−
Immature debtor	−	−	−
Mature debtor	−	−	+
New creditor	+	−	+
Immature creditor	+	+	+
Mature creditor	+	+	−

Each group can be defined as follows:

New debtor: A state which is running a net import surplus on current account but is also (because of a past creditor position) a net receiver of income on investments. Its new net borrowing is thus greater than the deficit indicated on current account.

Immature debtor: A state which is running a net import surplus on current account which is greater than its income payments for past borrowings. Its new borrowings are thus less than are indicated on current account.

Mature debtor: A state which is running a net import surplus on current account which is smaller than income payments for past borrowings.

The creditor classifications are the reverse of the debtor:

New creditor: A state which is running a net export surplus on current account but is also (because of a past debtor position) a net payer of income in investments. Its new net lending is thus greater than the credit surplus indicated on current account.

Immature creditor: A state which is running a net export surplus on current account which is greater than its income on past investments. Its new lending is thus less than is indicated on current account.

Mature creditor: A state which is running an export surplus on current account which is smaller than its income receipts from foreign investments.

a net export surplus, it becomes a new debtor and the cycle may start again.

Net exports, or capital flows, were estimated for regions of the United States for several time periods by Romans.[1] A sample of his results is presented in Table 9-2, which shows capital flows for 1953. Private net exports and total net exports both measure capital flows but the former excludes exports and imports (in kind), though the federal government and the latter includes them. The largest exporters of capital in the study period were the New England and Mideast regions.

MIGRATION

Population Shift

As a result of nearly 40 million persons moving each year, one person out of every five has a different address at the end of the year than he had at the beginning. During the 1960s, about one-half of the counties in the United States lost population, and for the first time since the Civil War, the South experienced net immigration during the 1960s. About one-third of all migrants are in their twenties.

Patterns of Migration

While the settlement of the continent was seemingly a migration phenomenon, the evolving pattern of urbanization is similarly associated with labor mobility. A profile of the nature of the moves made by migrants is revealed in Figure 9-2. Moves are classified on a distance scale beginning with those within a county and continuing to those between noncontiguous states. Intercounty shifts within metropolitan areas generally imply a change of residence within commuting distance of a given job; intercounty moves outside of metropolitan areas usually involve a change of job. The Bureau of the Census defines the latter move as migration, or, specifically,

---

1. J. T. Romans, *Capital Exports and Growth Among U.S. Regions* (Middletown, Connecticut: Wesleyan University Press, 1965).

TABLE 9-2. *Net Exports, Income on Foreign Investments, and Net Exports from Domestically Employed Resources, by Regions, 1953*

(in millions of dollars)

Area	Total Net Exports	Private Net Exports	Net Income on Foreign Investments	Total Net Exports from Dom. Empl. Res.	Private Net Exports from Dom. Empl. Res.
New England	2,237	1,469	1,761	476	− 292
Mideast	8,444	6,362	1,741	6,703	4,621
Great Lakes	1,206	− 377	−2,692	3,898	2,315
Plains	− 699	479	75	− 774	404
Southeast	−9,424	−4,157	−1,251	−8,173	−2,906
Southwest	−3,502	−2,165	− 558	−2,944	−1,605
Rocky Mt.	− 938	− 115	27	− 965	− 142
Far West	1,126	− 412	1,949	− 823	−2,361
Cont. U.S.	−1,550	1,090	1,052	−2,602	38

SOURCE: Copyright © 1965 by Wesleyan University. Reprinted from *Capital Exports and Growth Among U.S. Regions*, by J. Thomas Romans, by permission of Wesleyan University Press.

171

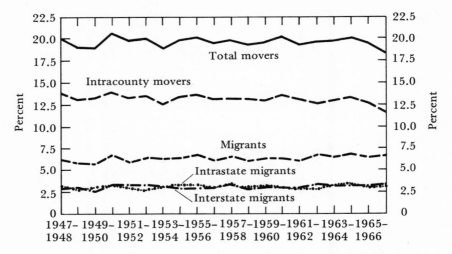

Figure 9-2   Movers by type of mobility as percent of population one
year old and over, for the United States: April 1948–
March 1967

intrastate migration.   As indicated by Figure 9-2, there has been surprising stability in the rates of these different types of moves. About two-thirds of the moves are within the same county; less than one-sixth are to another county in the same state; and less than one-sixth are to another state.

Several geographic patterns of mobility have also emerged during the past decades.   A consistent trend of net migration into the West has diminished only recently.   Between 1960 and 1964, the net migration rate into the West was about 500,000 annually, but this had decreased to 15,000 between 1964 and 1966.   During the 1960s there was a net movement of whites to the South and West and of blacks from the South to the North and West.

Rural-to-urban migration trends have been prevalent for several decades.   In 1900, 60 percent of the population was rural, and by 1970, 26 percent.   Since 1940 the farm population has dropped from 32 million to less than 10 million.   Today, farmers, farm workers, and their families are only 5 percent of the nation's population.

The evidence on migration suggests that certain types of persons have a greater tendency to move.   Men are somewhat more mobile than women.   Nonwhites are more mobile over short distances than whites, while the reverse is true for longer distance moves. Persons with some college training and professional persons tend to have greater mobility. High mobility is also observed among un-employed males.

Age also plays an important role in the decision to move. Young adults (18–34 years) have a substantially higher mobility rate than the older population. A recent study found that young adults had a mobility rate of 34 percent compared with the older group's 12 percent.

Data limitations obscure migration flows over time, but a study by the Survey Research Center at the University of Michigan provides some interesting insight into the movements of individuals and families. Nearly seven out of ten family heads now live in a labor market other than that in which they were born, but only 21 percent of them lived more than 1,000 miles away. About 20 percent of all moves were to a place where the family had once lived.

Of the 21 central cities with a 1960 population of one-half million or more, 15 had lost population by 1970. Indeed, the de-clining central cities lost more population in the 1960s than did declining rural counties. Thus, by 1970 over one-half of the metro-politan population lived outside the central city.

The recent past has been characterized by three types of migration: (1) the rural-to-urban movement (out of economically depressed areas to improved economic conditions), (2) the intra-urban movement (the suburban shift to gain better housing and more open space), and (3) interurban migration (to gain better economic and environmental conditions).

Where Do People Want to Live?

We have sketched the distribution of population and its movements. But do these patterns indicate where people want to live?

Surveys of public attitudes indicate that many do not live where they would like, particularly with respect to town size. The results of a typical opinion survey, presented in Table 9-3, indicate that a strong preference for small towns and rural areas is expressed. Of the people surveyed, 34 percent said they would prefer to live in open country, but only 12 percent actually live there now. Only 14 percent indicated that they would prefer to live in a large city or suburb, compared with the 27 percent who do.

TABLE 9-3. *Survey of Residential Preference by Size of Place*

Place	Where do you live now? (percent)	Where would you prefer to live? (percent)
Open country	12	34
Small town or city	33	30
Medium-sized city or suburb	28	22
Larger city or suburb	27	14
TOTAL	100	100

SOURCE: *Population and the American Future*, The Report of the Commission on Population Growth and the American Future (Washington D.C.: U.S. Government Printing Office, 1972), p. 34.

Does this mean that the location of people is incongruous with their preferences? Other studies indicate that this is not necessarily so. Apparently, people would prefer to live in open country that is close to a large metropolitan center. They would like to have the best of both situations—the pleasant, clean environments of rural areas and the range of opportunities of the large urban center.

Another interesting outcome of these opinion polls is that over one-half of the population expressed the view that the federal government should "discourage further growth of large metropolitan areas" or should "try to encourage people and industry to move to smaller cities and towns." We will consider policies toward population distribution in Chapter 18.

Migration Theory

The mobility which we have surveyed occurs for both economic and noneconomic reasons. Although economic incentives may not be a sufficient condition to induce migration, they would appear to be necessary. In this section, we examine the economics of labor movements in a spatial setting.

If interregional differentials in real wages exist, neoclassical general-equilibrium theory indicates that labor will move from the low-wage region to the high-wage region. This relationship is a useful starting point for an investigation of migration theory, not because of its obvious validity but because of the assumptions upon which it rests. An examination of these assumptions can meaningfully explain migration.

The pure neoclassical explanation of migration rests on the following assumptions: (1) a homogeneous labor supply, (2) the constant returns to scale, (3) no migration costs, (4) perfectly competitive labor markets, and (5) migrants responding solely to wage differentials.

Labor is hardly homogeneous. Unions and institutional rigidities modify the assumptions of homogeneous labor supply and perfectly competitive labor markets. In addition, skill levels vary substantially and, consequently, their migration potential and migration impact vary. We have already noted that mobility is greater for those with some college or professional training. Further, an unemployed migrant creates a different economic effect than an employed one. The departure of an unemployed person should have less impact on the wage level of the sending region than that of an employed one.

The assumption of zero migration costs is also untenable. Both the economic and noneconomic costs of moving may be great. Movement involves a comparison of increased monetary gains associated with a new location and the costs associated with the move. Because a major cost of migration is transportation, the greater these costs are, the larger will be the required income differential to induce a move. Distance also increases the uncertainty to the potential migrant.

Interregional migration is retarded by locational inertia. Most individuals have socio-cultural ties to a region that they weigh against greater income and other attractions in making a decision to migrate. Such factors defy quantifiable terms, yet they are an important aspect of the migration decision-making process. This locational inertia will prevent the interregional equalization of wage rates through migration even if the other assumptions of neoclassical theory were true.

Risk and uncertainty have both origin and destination characteristics. A person may decide to move because of employment uncertainty in his region. This has influenced rural-urban migration whenever the overall decline in job opportunities in rural areas increases the uncertainty of future employment in the region. However, uncertainty and risk in the region of residence is generally considered to be less because conditions in the region are more familiar. The potential destination region may represent either a higher or lower level of risk and uncertainty. Even though the potential destination region may be unfamiliar, the prospective migration may have greater expectations of future employment opportunities.

Information about better employment opportunities in other regions can alter migration. The existence of better opportunities elsewhere does not mean that prospective migrants have this information. How does a potential migrant receive information about better alternatives? Government agencies, trade associations, and similar organized bodies facilitate the flow of job information. Not to be underestimated is the information flow from recent migrants who relay information about opportunities to friends and relatives in the region from which they migrated, for such information flows reinforce existing migration flows.

An increasingly important migration factor has been the general environment—importantly, cultural amenities and climate. Amenities have been important for industries as well as for people. The South and West have experienced above-average population growth rates partly because of their warmer climate.

Impact of Migration

When labor migrates, both the sending and receiving regions are affected. Wage rates, returns to capital, and land values tend to shift and with them a variety of economic adjustments are initiated.

The impact of labor migration on both the sending and receiving regions can be illustrated by an Edgeworth-box diagram. Suppose that two regions have the same stock of capital but that region 2 has a larger supply of labor, as is illustrated in Figure 9-3. The lines O_1O' and O_2O' are contract curves based on production functions which are characterized by decreasing marginal productivities. Because of the larger supply of labor in region 2, its wage rate will be lower. Assume that this difference is large enough to induce migration. The reduction in the labor supply in region 2 is identical to the increase in the labor supply in region 1. The contract curve of region 1 is shifted outward because of the increase in its total productive capacity; the shift is opposite for region 2 from which the labor has migrated. If there are no interregional transportation costs, migration will equalize wages in the two regions (contract curves O_1O'' and O_2O''), since the marginal productivity of labor in

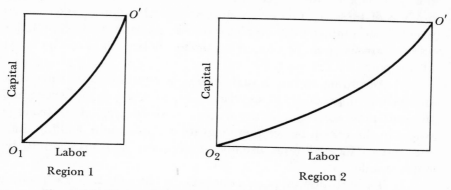

Figure 9-3 **Two regions with identical capital stock but dissimilar labor supplies**

region 1 decreases and that in region 2 increases. The resulting shifts are represented in Figure 9-4.

An important shift has also occurred in the capital/labor ratios for the regions. The K/L ratio in region 1 declined with the movement of new labor into the region. Conversely, the K/L in region 2 increased as labor moved out of the region.

Private and Social Costs and Returns

Until now we have implicitly assumed that the migrant bears all the costs and receives all of the returns for migrating. But, evidence and logic indicate that this is not the case. Usually migra-

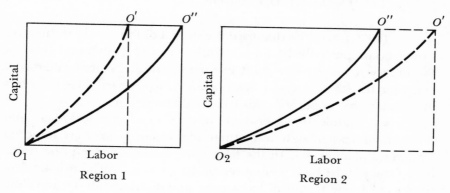

Figure 9-4 Two regions after migration

tion will involve costs and returns to nonmigrants as well. A thorough analysis of these interactions requires a consideration of externalities which is both sufficiently complicated and important to deserve major attention in Chapter 12. Nonetheless, a few observations can be made at this point.

According to our initial theory, a region experiencing substantial out-migration will experience an increase in the wage rate, but this may not occur if the migrants are earning above-average wages in the region before they migrate. This is quite feasible since the better-educated (and usually higher-paid) persons tend to be more mobile.

The out-migrant region may also be left with an infrastructure designed for a larger population, an infrastructure which must still be supported. In rural areas, where population declines have been persistent, costs of maintaining an obsolete infrastructure have become burdensome on the nonmigrants.

Evidence suggests, too, that in rapidly growing areas, in-migrants impose cost burdens on the region exceeding any contribution they pay in taxes. The new residents require public services and public capital which may fall heavily on the original residents. Increases in congestion and pollution also occur to affect the well-being of the original population.

At this point, we will not evaluate these criticisms of in-migration or out-migration; we simply note their presence. We shall return to these and related questions in Chapter 18.

TECHNOLOGY DIFFUSION

In Chapter 7 we discussed the spatial differences in technology which occur partially because of differences in population density. We observed that at any point in time significant spatial differences existed in the stock of technical knowledge. Now we will look at factors influencing the mobility of this technical knowledge.

Communication is essential to the flow of technical ideas, and the communication system for these ideas may be severely impeded by several phenomena. In the first place, for knowledge to be transferred there must be a willing sender and receiver. The private-firm producer of new technical knowledge may be particularly unwilling to part with the information which provides him with an advantage over competitors. But even if the firm is willing and actively engaged in attempting to do so, there must be a willing recipient. A major determinant of this situation is the existing spatial industrial structure. The number of firms that can make use of a particular flow of new technical knowledge will vary considerably among regions.

In addition to communication problems which impede the spatial diffusion of technical knowledge, differences also exist with regard to transforming an idea into a feasible production process The availability of funds for investment is variable among regions. Since the sources of these funds are retained earnings, other savings, and depreciation, regions with a large concentration of economic

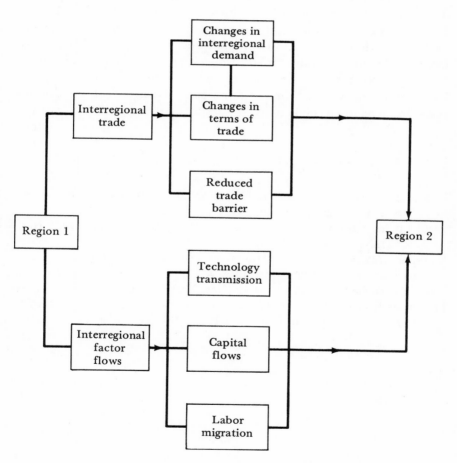

Figure 9-5 Interregional interaction channels—simplified one-way flow

activity will have a greater potential to innovate. Also, because these highly industrialized regions have a larger existing-capital stock, replacement investment is more likely to occur there.

SUMMARY

In this chapter and the previous one we have examined the mechanisms of interregional interaction through interregional trade and factor flows, a simplified visual summary of which appears in Figure 9-5.

The basis for an extent of interregional trade was explained in terms of social-physics principles and comparative advantage. Changes in interregional trade relations are affected by the reduction of trade barriers, increases in demand, and variations in the terms of trade. The improvement in transportation technology can reduce the friction of distance between points and thereby increase trade. Increases in the demand for a region's exports will set off a multiplier reaction in regional income.

REFERENCES AND SUPPLEMENTAL READING

George H. Borts and Jerome L. Stein, *Economic Growth in a Free Market* (New York: Columbia University Press, 1964).

Bertil Ohlin, *Interregional and International Trade* (Cambridge, Mass.: Harvard University Press, 1957).

E. Olsen, *International Trade Theory and Regional Income Differences* (Amsterdam: North-Holland, 1971).

Harry Richardson, *Regional Economics* (New York: Praeger, 1969).

J. Thomas Romans, *Capital Exports and Growth Among U.S. Regions* (Middletown, Conn.: Wesleyan University Press, 1965).

10

Urban Structure: Descriptive Analysis

The study of urban-regional growth, of the formation of central places (including the economics of location), and of urban structure is vital to an understanding of the problems of urban transportation, poverty, housing, population, and urban public finance, because each of these problems has spatial characteristics. Urban-regional growth analysis, the theory of central places, and the economics of location have been treated in earlier chapters of this text. This discussion, however, generally treated cities as points in space. This was largely intentional in order to devote major attention to the conceptual analysis of interindustry relations, spatial competition, and regional growth. These topics are important for a complete understanding of the economies of cities. But we must now recognize that cities occupy space and, therefore, we need to begin to deal with intra-urban spatial relationships. This will round out our understanding of the economies of cities and will prepare us with the necessary economic concepts to investigate urban problems of later chapters.

The objectives of the present chapter are threefold. To set the stage for what follows in the next several chapters, we first need to sketch urban growth briefly. Second, after having reviewed the past and the expected future growth in urban areas, we will move to a descriptive analysis of urban structure. Several descriptive time-period models of urban structure are summarized to indicate the growth and development of our nation's cities. Third, we shall discuss the major reasons why certain businesses and households are leaving the inner cities. The earlier chapters on location, particularly Chapter 4, are basic here.

The following chapter, Chapter 11, will rigorously analyze urban structure. The model of that structure developed in Chapter 11 builds on the location analysis of earlier chapters.

URBAN GROWTH

Urban Area Defined

Before discussing urban growth, we need to define *urban area*. The Census Bureau considers an urban area to be an incorporated place of at least 2,500 inhabitants. Additionally, densely settled or heavily populated unincorporated areas are also regarded as urban by the Census Bureau. Throughout this and following chapters, we shall use the terms "urban" and "city" interchangeably.

Urbanization of Population

In 1790, when the newly formed national government instituted a comprehensive census system, 95 percent of the 3.9 million Americans lived in rural areas and some 85 percent were engaged in agricultural activities. By 1920, the nation had become predominantly urban: the urban population numbered 54.1 million, and the rural, 51.5 million. From 1920 to 1940 the urban population increased by 38 percent, while rural population increased 11 percent. During World War II and the years immediately following, urban growth more than doubled, while the overall rural population increased by a scant 3.7 million. By 1970, more than 70 percent of the nation's population was urban.[1]

The first column of Table 10-1 shows the increase in the number of cities since 1790. In the second column, the proportion of urban to total population is given for each census year. Finally, columns 3, 4, 5, and 6 show the total number of cities in each different

1. U.S. Census Data

TABLE 10-1. *Number of U.S. Cities by Size Group, 1790–1970*

Year	All Cities	Percent of Urban to Total Population	2,500–24,999	25,000–249,999	250,000–999,999	1,000,000+
1790	24	5.1	22	2	—	—
1800	33	6.1	30	3	—	—
1810	46	7.3	42	4	—	—
1820	61	7.2	56	5	—	—
1830	90	8.8	83	7	—	—
1840	131	10.8	119	11	1	—
1850	236	15.3	210	25	1	—
1860	392	19.8	357	32	3	—
1870	663	25.7	611	45	7	—
1880	939	28.2	862	69	8	1
1890	1,348	35.1	1,224	113	11	3
1900	1,737	39.7	1,577	145	15	3
1910	2,262	45.7	2,034	209	16	3
1920	2,722	51.2	2,435	262	22	3
1930	3,165	56.2	2,789	339	32	5
1940	3,464	56.5	3,052	375	32	5
1950*	4,741	64.0	3,800	474	36	5
1960*	6,041	69.9	4,680	714	46	5
1970*	7,061	73.5	5,520	859	50	6

*The figures for the census years 1950, 1960, and 1970 are calculated on the basis of the current urban definition.
SOURCE: U.S. Census Data.

city-size group as classified by population and indicated in the column headings.

The largest increase in city size is in the 2,500–25,000 size group. But what is not revealed here is the continuing concentration of the nation's population in cities larger than 25,000. This becomes plain when we focus on the actual increase in urban population, Table 10-2. A more refined city-size classification system than the one used in Table 10-1, Table 10-2 indicates that between 1950 and 1960, the average population increase for cities of one million or more was 16,000. This jumped to an average of 210,000 for the period 1960 to 1970. The average change in population for the next two city-size groups is equally impressive.

The increases in population for the different city-size groups indicate an obvious pattern of increasing concentration. However, this does not mean that the future will produce a few "super-sized" cities. This is unlikely for at least two reasons. First, the total population of the United States will not support many such cities. Second, and most importantly, the central-place theory of city distribution suggests a continuation of a hierarchical distribution of city size.

Future Growth of Urban Areas

According to Urban Land Institute projections,[2] 131 million persons (55 percent of the nation's population) will live in four major urban fields by 1980. By 2000, over 187 million persons (60 percent of the country's projected population) will live in these four urban regions. Thus, most of the population growth from now until 2000 will be absorbed in these four regions. Where will these urban fields be located?

The Urban Land Institute projections suggest that the largest urban field will be the 500-mile corridor from Boston to Washington, D.C. This Atlantic-seaboard urban region will contain a projected population of 67.9 million by 2000. The second urban field will comprise a chain of cities extending the nearly 1,000 miles from Utica, New York to Green Bay, Wisconsin, and by 2000 it will contain 60.8 million people. The third urban field will be that of the West Coast from San Francisco to San Diego. It will have 44.5 million people by

2. Jerome P. Pickard, *Dimensions of Metropolitanism*, Urban Land Institute Research Monograph 14 (Washington, D.C.: 1967), pp. 21–23.

TABLE 10-2. *Average Net Change in Population, by Size Group, 1950–60 and 1960–70*

Size Group	Actual Change in Population 1950–60	Number of Cities 1960	Average Change Per City*	Actual Change in Population 1960–70	Number of Cities 1970	Average Change Per City*
1,000,000+	80,000	5	16,000	1,258,000	6	210,000
500,000–1,000,000	1,923,000	16	120,000	1,856,000	20	93,000
250,000–500,000	2,524,000	30	84,000	−324,000	30	11,000
100,000–250,000	2,173,000	81	27,000	2,633,000	100	−26,000
50,000–100,000	4,905,000	201	24,000	2,888,000	240	12,000
25,000–50,000	6,143,000	432	14,000	2,869,000	519	6,000
10,000–25,000	5,701,000	1,134	5,000	3,846,000	1,384	3,000
5,000–10,000	1,641,000	1,394	1,000	3,156,000	1,840	2,000
2,500–5,000	1,090,000	2,152	less than 1,000	461,000	2,296	less than 500

*Rounded to the nearest thousand.
SOURCE: U.S. Census Data.

2000. Finally, the fourth major urban field will be in Florida, between Jacksonville and Miami westward to the Tampa–St. Petersburg metropolitan areas and its population will be 13.8 million by 2000.

In addition, the Urban Land Institute projects that by 2000 another 52 million will be living in 14 smaller urban regions and five metropolitan areas. These smaller urban areas and the four large urban fields show a projected population of 241 million persons (77 percent of the nation's population) for 2000, an increase of 37 million over the 1970 population. The most striking point of these projections is that this 241-million urban population will occupy only 11 percent of the nation's continental land area.

EARLY DESCRIPTIVE MODELS OF URBAN STRUCTURE

Concentric-Zone Hypothesis

The earliest theoretical model of urban structure was the concentric-zone hypothesis proposed by Ernest W. Burgess in 1923.[3] From an empirical investigation of several large cities, Burgess concluded that a city expands radially from its center to form a series of concentric zones (or bands). Using Chicago as an example, Burgess identified five different concentric zones of activity.

The Central Business District (Zone I). Burgess' first zone was the city's core, the central business district. This district contained such diverse sites as department stores, specialty shops, office buildings, clubs, banks, hotels, theaters, museums, and organizational head-quarters. In essence, Burgess found that the core of the city was the "hub" of the major retail and service activities of the city. Burgess also included wholesale activities in zone I, since he found that the wholesale establishments were generally adjacent to the hub of retail and service activities. He noted, also, that transportation terminals (rail terminals) in or near the city's hub also caused wholesale establishments to locate near the central business district.

The Zone of Transition (Zone II). Burgess was careful to note that the physical growth of the central business district would result in its

3. T. V. Smith and L. D. White (ed.), *Chicago: An Experiment in Social Science Research* (Chicago: University of Chicago Press, 1929), pp. 114–23.

encroaching upon the surrounding occupied space and that this continuing threat of expansion would create a highly unstable land-use pattern around the central business district. Burgess rightly referred to this zone as the zone of transition. He found it to consist of an inner belt of light manufacturing and an outer belt of generally blighted living units—rooming houses, multistory apartment buildings, and single-dwelling rental units. It was in this zone that Burgess placed the city's poverty, vice, and crime.

The Zone of Independent Workingman's Homes (Zone III). Burgess defined the third concentric zone as a relative stable land-use zone since zone II absorbed most of the expansion of the central business district. He observed that displaced manufacturing establishments usually located somewhere at the periphery of the city, leaving zone III largely untouched.

The Zone of Better Residents (Zone IV). Beyond zone III was an area described by Burgess as a zone of better residents. Here lived the middle-class Americans in single-family residences or apartments. Within this area, at strategic places, were located local business centers similar, Burgess thought, to miniature central business districts. Burgess noted that as families and individuals prospered, they tended to move from zone II to zone III, and from zone III to zone IV. Burgess observed that some are fortunate enough to make it all the way to the fifth zone of upper-income residents.

Zone of Upper-Income Residents (Zone V). This was the area of the better residences, and it consisted of a ring of encircling small cities, towns, and hamlets. They were mainly dormitory suburbs whose residents worked in the central business district.

Manifest in Burgess' concentric-zone model is a growth pattern extending outward from the central business district. Although the concentric-zone pattern of development best described the empirical evidence, Burgess did recognize certain "distorting" factors, such as natural and artificial barriers. For instance, his close study of the Chicago area showed how a natural barrier—Lake Michigan—can affect the concentric-zone pattern of development. Finally, his recognition of the miniature (or satellite) central business districts in zone IV gives evidence of central-place development in urban areas.

Sector Theory

After an extensive study of 64 American cities for 1934, Homer Hoyt proposed the sector theory of urban structure development as a more accurate description of how the structure of an urban area is formed.[4]

Basically, Hoyt's sector theory argues that if a sector of the city first develops as a high-, medium-, or low-rental residential area, it will tend to retain that character for long distances as the sector is extended outward by the city's growth.

Although Hoyt did not formulate any specific geometric pattern of sector growth, he did note some general observations about sector location. Hoyt noted, for instance, that bands of commercial activity will generally string out along the main thoroughfares, indicating the importance of access. He noted that the highest-income residential areas tend to be on high ground, or alongside a lake, river, or ocean shore, and close, but not adjacent, to major transportation lines. He also found proximity to country clubs and parks as desirable for high-income families. Low-income families tend to live in areas situated farthest from high-rent areas and normally dwell on the least desirable land alongside railroad, industrial, or commercial areas. Finally, Hoyt's findings show that medium-income families live in the residential area between the high-income and the low-income areas.

The Multiple-Nuclei Theory

A third model of urban structure, the multiple-nuclei model, was formulated by Chauncy Harris and Edward Ullman in 1945, as a modification of the concentric zone and the sector model.[5] The basic thesis of the Harris and Ullman model is that the land-use pattern of a city does not reflect a development from a single center, but rather, the pattern indicates that cities develop about several distinct nuclei. The model also indicates that the number of nuclei increases with the growth of the city.

4. Homer Hoyt, *The Structure and Growth of Residential Neighborhoods in American Cities*, Federal Housing Administration (Washington, D.C.: U.S. Government Printing Office, 1939).

5. Chauncy D. Harris and Edward L. Ullman, "The Nature of Cities," *Annals* of the American Academy of Political and Social Science, CCXLII (November 1945), pp. 7–17.

Harris and Ullman identified a number of districts that had developed around certain nuclei activities such as original retail districts, ports, railroad yards, and factory areas. For example, they noted that a city's central business district usually includes, or is adjacent to, the original retail area. The wholesale district, as a second example, is usually located next to a railroad terminal or a port.

The Harris and Ullman model of residential-area location is similar to Hoyt's model. Both note that high-income residential districts develop in those areas that provide certain advantages— picturesqueness, quiet, cleanliness, and distance from low-class districts.

Harris and Ullman suggested that the development of a nucleated urban structure resulted from a combination of four factors:

1. Certain activities cannot afford the high rents of the most desirable sites; thus, low-class housing is seldom built on lots next to the highest-priced houses in the city.
2. Certain activities require specialized facilities, e.g., financial institutions require intracity access to law firms. A spatial juxtaposition of these activities usually occurs.
3. Certain similar activities group together because they profit from proximity, e.g., retail activities may cluster to facilitate comparison shopping.
4. Certain dissimilar activities are detrimental to each other. The pungent odor of an oil refinery is not compatible with a retail district's concern for a clean and odor-free environment.

THE CHANGING STRUCTURE OF TODAY'S CITIES

Probably the most significant change occurring in our cities is the decline in the relative importance of the central business district. City officials, small inner-city businesses, and inner-city dwellers stand forlorn as businesses and medium- and high-income households move to the periphery of the city. City officials fear the economic and political repercussions of an eroding tax base; small inner-city business proprietors fear the growing likelihood of an early retirement; and inner-city dwellers fear the loss of jobs as businesses relocate in suburban areas.

These groups seek the reasons for the persistent decline in the relative importance of the inner city as a place in which to work, live, and operate a business.

A number of conditions have contributed to the relative (and often absolute) decline of people and businesses in the inner city, but the most important reason has been the rapid expansion in the use of the passenger car and the motor carrier over the last several decades. Today, approximately 80 percent of all intracity freight is carried by the motor carrier, and approximately 90 percent of all intracity passenger miles involve the passenger car.

Suburban Population Growth

America is a young and urbanized nation. Although it was not until the late 1920s that this nation had a majority of its population living in the urbanized areas, today urban residents comprise over 70 percent of our population. This very rapid rural-to-urban migration process has led some scholars to point out that even though we are an urbanized nation, our urban areas show very strong rural characteristics. Most Americans still prefer ample space, as shown by the popularity of the single-family home with its attached, fenced-in yard. Also, America's development of the automobile and urban growth's consequent high-income levels have allowed the population's propensity for suburban living to be technically and economically possible.

Fifteen of the 21 cities with a 1960 population of at least 500,000 experienced an absolute decline in central-city population by 1970.[6] Over one-half of the 1970 metropolitan population lived outside the central city, where almost all metropolitan growth occurred during the decade.

Intra-Urban Location of Retail and Service Trades

The movement of the higher-income families to the suburbs has been a major factor in the relative relocation of retail and consumer-related services in the suburbs. Just as it has played a major role in the growth and development of suburban residential areas, the automobile has also played a major role in determining the

6. U.S. Department of Commerce, Bureau of the Census, *General Demographic Trends for Metropolitan Areas, 1960 to 1970*, PHC (2)-1 (Washington: U.S. Government Printing Office, October 1971), p. 33.

suburban-retail and service-establishment patterns. The automobile gave the suburban housewife mobility, but it consequently created intracity traffic congestion and burdensome parking problems. The two difficulties have made the downtown shopping districts inconvenient for most suburban dwellers and have led to the development of suburban shopping centers characterized by ease of access and commodious parking areas.

One reason for the inadequate downtown parking facilities is relatively high costs. In an early 1960 study of urban transportation problems, Professors Meyer, Kain, and Wohl[7] estimated that the land-cost difference per parking space between a central-city, multistoried parking site and a suburban, ground-level parking site was about $1,400 to $1,500. In addition to the land-cost difference, the early-1960 cost estimates indicated that construction costs per space were as low as $400 for paved, open lots in suburban locations to over $3,000 per space for downtown garages. Annual maintenance and operating costs are additionally higher.

In light of suburbia's growing dependence on the automobile and the substantial parking-cost differentials which exist between a downtown location and a suburban location, it is not difficult to understand why retail and service establishments are moving to locations where they can better serve the "drive-up" customer. To nobody's surprise, shopping centers with acres of ground-level parking dot the urban landscape of today's metropolitan areas.

The rise of the suburban shopping center also reflects substantial changes in technology merchandising. Merchandisers have long recognized the cost savings that can be realized with high-volume mass merchandising in a one- or two-story plant layout. Thus, both the high central-city land costs and the increase in suburban high-income families have helped attract high-volume mass-merchandising operations to suburban areas.

Although many retail and service establishments prefer suburban locations, other businesses still seek a central-city location. In most large American cities, for example, the downtown area is still the center of entertainment. Traffic congestion and inadequate parking are less bothersome in the evenings, and those large cities that are convention centers encourage a downtown location for most kinds of entertainment.

Similarly, specialty shops are still attracted to the downtown

7. J. R. Meyer, J. F. Kain, and M. Wohl, *The Urban Transportation Problem* (Cambridge: Harvard University Press, 1965), pp. 213–18.

areas. The area usually provides a central location for the outer residential ring of high-income families. Furthermore, a downtown location places the specialty shops near the high-income, white-collar workers employed in finance, business services, and central-office operations.

We would be remiss if we did not note here that downtown shopping activities in large American cities have always accounted for a smaller proportion of retail activity than they do in smaller cities. This implies that commercial decentralization accompanies urban growth. It also implies the importance of central places.

Intra-Urban Location of Industry

In 1923, Burgess observed that there was a tendency for manufacturing plants to locate on the periphery of large cities. Since then manufacturing activity has grown more rapidly in the outlying areas than in the inner cities. Several reasons can be cited for this.

Technology of Mass Production. Assembly-line production, because it requires large horizontal work areas, has made the multi-story plant structure obsolete. This technological fact has forced manu- facturing firms to acquire additional space for sprawling one-story plants. Because of a lack of unused space in the inner-city areas and the high cost of tearing down existing structures, the firm's location choice is limited to the outlying, undeveloped areas.

Modern Transportation and Communication Facilities. The congestion and deterioration of the inner city make it economically advan- tageous for manufacturing firms to locate on a city's periphery; modern transportation and communication facilities make it possible. The versatility of the motor carrier has lessened industry's dependence on inner-city rail terminals. Now trucks find it practical to load at rail terminals and move goods directly to plants. In fact, for short hauls, the net economies of the motor carrier encourage a peripheral location of the plant, since such a location avoids the problems of traffic congestion and inadequate parking and loading space at inner-city locations.

Although transportation technology has encouraged the movement of plants away from the inner city, communication facilities have allowed manufacturing firms to realize the advantages which accrue to inner-city location of central-office functions. Most manufacturers find it desirable to locate the sales and executive offices of the business in the central city where face-to-face contacts with buyers, advertising specialists, lawyers, and financial experts can be maintained.

Professors Meyer, Kain, and Wohl comment on the spatial separation of the sales and executive offices from the production plant:

(The communications revolution has reduced the) need for locating all the functional activities of a given industrial firm or type of business in close proximity. Rather, it is becoming increasingly feasible to locate different functions about the city at points of maximum locational advantage. For example, such industries as women's apparel, clothing accessories, costume jewelry, and others producing specialized high-fashion goods seem to have a very real need to locate their showrooms and selling activities in reasonably central locations, thus minimizing the need for visiting buyers to travel to see the various wares. In essence, sellers in these industries strongly desire to be located in a central market so as to ensure the maximum possibility of wares being seen by important buyers. Once the marketing pattern is set, strong reasons thus exist for staying close to the central group.

Traditionally, at least in New York, these industries have also tended to perform their manufacturing functions very close to their showrooms; but with improved communications and transportation there may no longer be any great advantage in doing so. If not, showrooms may stay where they are while the manufacturing operations relocate over time at the periphery of the city or other locations with cost advantages. It also seems possible that the market place itself may move to a less central location. When most business travel is by airplane, a cluster of showrooms close to the airport would seem to be as logical as one near the rail terminal. Indeed, the recent growth of hotel and exposition facilities near big-city airports suggests that this development is already underway.[8]

One wonders, however, why communication advances have not lessened the need for face-to-face personal contacts. Conceivably, the intercommunications between business executives and business specialists could be handled through closed-circuit television or video-telephone systems in the same way that the business executives now manage processing-plant operations from downtown locations. A possible answer is that the innovation of advanced technology may

8. *Ibid.*, p. 16.

be slower in specialized business-service fields than it is in the standardized processes of production. If this is correct, then the full impact of the communications revolution upon central-city structure has not yet been realized. It may be that the general adoption of new communications devices could exert a decentralizing influence on the downtown core of insurance offices, financial institutions, law firms, and advertising agencies—organizations whose more logical location may be near the city air terminals.

Some manufacturing activities may still require an inner-city location, however. For example, the production and distribution functions of new, untested consumer items are generally found near the complex of special production and marketing services. These specialized services, as already noted, are still located in the core of the large cities. To a large extent, this urban-core complex of specialized services acts as an incubator for new consumer items. If the product proves marketable on a large scale, the eventual standardization of the production and marketing processes will lead to a decentralized location.

Finally, large manufacturing activities that are dependent upon rail transportation services for the movement of large, bulky materials may still find that a central location close to established rail terminals and industrial siding facilities is best. This may be true of such industries as the primary steel industries, the fabricated-metals industries, or others that are large users of coal.

Warehouse Activities and Intra-Urban Location

The Burgess description of the historical development of urban areas shows the warehouse district to be part of the first ring in the concentric-zone pattern of urban development. This central location clearly notes its early importance in the growth and development of the urban area. Today, however, the importance of the warehousing industry has so declined that for several reasons the warehouse districts of large American cities are deteriorating. The use of the motor carrier has made it possible for businesses to locate away from the established inner-city warehouse district. Materials and supplies can be easily moved from rail cars on which an increasing proportion of items are being shipped in "piggyback" containers to motor carriers for final shipment. In most cases, the retail and service establishments provide their own trucking. Also, the move to large-volume, mass merchandising has reduced the need for the traditional warehouse facility. To a large extent, the seemingly endless rows of counter space found in large merchandising stores provide the "warehouse" space for goods that eventually will be sold. Finally, modern production, transportation, and communication means have reduced the need to accumulate large stocks of items, since the time period between the date of order and the date of delivery has been sharply reduced.

Travel-Related Services and Intra-Urban Location

With the increased use of the automobile and the shift from the rails to the airplane as the major public mode for long-distance travel, the hotels, restaurants, and allied services are moving to locations near air terminals and interstate highway interchanges. Although the need for hotel and restaurant services has not altogether disappeared in downtown areas, the relative proportion of travel-related personal services in central locations is declining. For the large cities, the future for the downtown complex of hotels, restaurants, entertainment places, and other allied services is not as uncertain. The well-established hotels at the heart of the large cities are becoming year-round convention centers, and nearby theaters, restaurants, and entertainment establishments provide necessary services for convention delegates.

SUMMARY

The structure of an urban area is constantly changing. The three descriptive models of urban structure presented in this chapter reflect this change in their differing emphasis on certain structural changes that occurred during the time periods that separate the models. The Burgess model, for example, emphasizes the central business district as the single most important growth center. Contrastingly, later empirical investigations by Harris and Ullman show that growth occurs around several distinct nuclei which form business and residential districts.

The most glaring changes in urban structure occurred as a consequence of the increased use of the motor vehicle. The automobile made way for middle- and upper-income households to escape the congested, high-density areas of the inner city. The motor carrier freed most businesses from places of location near inner-city rail terminals. The net result of the impact of the motor vehicle has been a decline in the relative importance of the inner city. Suburban areas are growing at its expense. But inner cities are not without growth. Unfortunately, their growth seems most spectacular in their high rates of unemployment, inadequate housing, and poverty. These problems will be discussed in a later chapter.

REFERENCES AND SUPPLEMENTAL READING

Advisory Commission on Intergovernmental Relations, *Urban and Rural America: Policies for Future Growth* (Washington, D.C.: U.S. Government Printing Office, April 1968), Chapter 1.

John C. Bollins and Henry J. Schmandt, *The Metropolis*, 2d ed. (New York: Harper & Row Publishers, 1970), Chapters 1 and 4.

Larry S. Bourne (ed.), *Internal Structure of the City* (New York: Oxford University Press, 1971), pp. 67–128.

J. R. Meyer, J. F. Kain, and M. Wohl, *The Urban Transportation Problem* (Cambridge: Harvard University Press, 1965), Chapters 2 and 3.

Anselm L. Strauss (ed.), *The American City* (Chicago: Aldine Publishing Company, 1968), Chapters 6, 7, 12, 13, and 14.

11

Urban Structure: Theoretical Analysis

The previous chapter treated early descriptive models of urban structure. Basically, these models described observable land-use regularities for a sampled number of urban areas at a particular time. However, changes in time result in changes in land-use regularities; consequently, an examination of the theory of land-use patterns is fundamental to an understanding of these changes. More specifically, our task is to develop a theoretical model of urban land use based upon the notion of access. The earlier discussion of plant location (Chapter 4) and central-place theory (Chapter 6) will be quite useful here.

ACCESS

Many different businesses locate near one another because of markets and input needs. Indeed, input-output relations, as described in a transactions table (Chapter 2), reflect the importance of access. Suppliers require access to buyers of goods and services and, conversely, buyers of goods and services require access to suppliers. Workers are concerned with access to places of work and employers are concerned with the availability of a sufficient, local labor supply.

This geographic business concentration means a concentration of people who work and reside in the area. Such a population concentration affects the household sector of an urban area by creating interhousehold access linkages (i.e., social activities) and various household-to-shopping, household-to-school, household-to-church, and household-to-entertainment access linkages.

In order to analyze the importance of access in the development of an urban land-use model, we need a yardstick to measure the locational significance of an access linkage—a yardstick indicating the *time* and *transport cost* associated with the movement of persons (or things) between two points. We shall assume that the distance between two points can be measured as a straight-line distance, where time and transport cost are directly proportional to distance. As a further simplification of our measurement of access, we shall equate time with cost. Suppose, for the sake of illustration, that a person journeys 30 minutes from origin to destination. If the person is on a business trip and the individual generally earns $6.00 an hour, the trip-time cost to the business is $3.00. Accordingly, for businesses where face-to-face contact is a major part of their operations, business travel time is a major cost consideration of location.

The origin-to-destination time intervals also can be equated with goods and materials cost since the trip-time interval causes a delay in the consumption (or use) of items being shipped. It also seems reasonable to assume that household units intuitively attach some cost factor to resident trip-time patterns, since household units seek proximity to places of shopping, schools, church, and friends. Edwin Mills suggests that a commuter values his travel time somewhere "between one-third and one-half of the wage rate, the fraction increasing with the wage rate."[1] To the commuter, quick access to work is important. This affects not only his choice of residence, but also his choice of a transport mode—a topic for later discussion (Chapter 13).

Total access cost can be defined as the trip-time cost plus the actual transport outlay, where total access cost varies with the type of access linkage—highest for face-to-face business contacts and, probably, lowest for household-to-entertainment travel patterns.

Access-Cost Minimization

Since a decision to invest additional resources (time and dollars) in transportation means that these resources are no longer

1. Edwin S. Mills, *Urban Economics* (Glenview, Illinois: Scott, Foresman & Company, 1972), p. 201.

available for use in the production or consumption of other items, businesses and households will logically attempt to keep total access cost for the combined, relevant access linkages to a minimum. The general assumption of access-cost minimization does not rule out the possibility for an access/site trade-off. In fact, spatial residential patterns clearly indicate that higher-income families do substitute low-density sites for access, and hence access cost is not at a minimum. More will be said about the matter of an access/site trade-off later.

URBAN LAND-USE MODEL

Let us suppose that the geography of an urban area is basically circular, a uniform geographic plain where development extends equally in all directions from the central point. Such a model simplifies analysis without invalidating our conclusions.

The central area is the point of maximum, overall area accessibility and, since businesses and households seek to reduce total access costs, the location of businesses and households will tend to gravitate toward this central core. Not all the individual businesses and households can locate at the core; however, the problem of overconcentration is somewhat alleviated by the fact that different businesses and households attach different degrees of importance to access costs.

Rent-Bid Line

Firm Location. Leaving the matter of household location aside for the moment, we will focus on a theoretical analysis of the intra-urban location of business firms through a discussion of a *rent-bid line*, a collection of alternative points (location sites) where firms can maximize profits.[2] Chapter 4 asserted that a maximum-profit site is one that yields the greatest difference between total costs and total revenue (or where marginal cost equals marginal revenue). When total costs and total revenue vary from site to site, profits can be maximized at any one of several sites. This is the basic premise

2. Rent-bid arguments are expressed in this chapter as linear functions. The rent-bid function for a business (or household) is more likely convex to the origin. In order to simplify the analysis, a linear relationship has been applied.

199

which underlies the notion of a rent-bid line. We will examine that premise in a moment.

Graphically, a firm's rent-bid line can be shown as in Figure 11-1. The origin of the two-dimensional diagram is the center of the urban area and distance from that center is measured along the horizontal axis. The amount of rent the firm is willing to pay at varying sites in the urban area is recorded on the vertical axis. Figure 11-1 should be viewed as representing every direction from the center of the urban area. Thus, the rent-bid line is actually a rent-bid cone, which is generated by revolving the RD line on the vertical axis. For discussion purposes, however, we shall confine our comments to the RD line, since it represents every direction from the urban center.

As shown in Figure 11-1, the amount of rent the firm is willing to bid for a site varies inversely with its distance from the urban center. The highest rent bid for a site is at the center, since the center affords the firm maximum access to the entire urban area. At some distance from the urban center, D in Figure 11-1, the firm is unwilling to bid any price for a site since areas beyond this point are not maximum-profit sites of location.

More than one site of maximum profits exists because access costs differ for various location sites under consideration. At the center, the firm has its greatest access to buyers and suppliers of inputs located in the urban area; consequently, all other things being equal, the firm's total revenue (and rent) will be highest at the urban center.

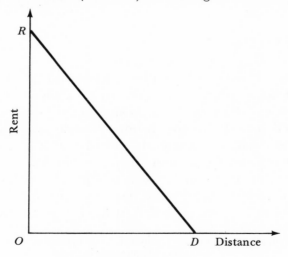

Figure 11-1 Rent-bid curve

But rent is a cost factor similar to others such as labor and material costs in making up total costs. When a firm considers an off-center location, it will bid a lower rent for the site since its total site revenue will be below that for the urban center. It is also possible that other production costs will be higher (or lower) at some off-center site than at the urban center. Generally, the amount of rent a firm is willing to bid for an off-center site just offsets any difference in total revenue and production costs between the off-center site and the urban center. In such a case, the maximum profit for the off-center site is the same as for the urban center. Since more than one maximum-profit site exists, a firm can indifferently choose any one of the maximum-profit sites.

Each firm (or industry group) has a particular rent-bid line. Figure 11-2 illustrates the rent-bid line for three different industry groups (i.e., similar firms with the same rent-bid line). Notice in Figure 11-2 that the rent-bid line for industry group A is quite steep, indicating that the industry group finds the urban center a most desirable location. Imagine that industry group A represents a group of businesses where face-to-face contact is necessary. In order to make off-center sites as profitable as the urban center, land rent must be close to zero, as indicated by the amount of rent offered for

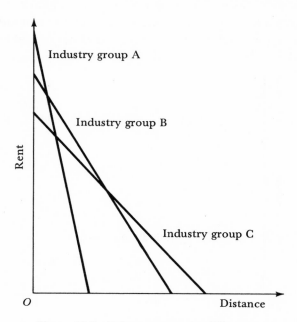

Figure 11-2   Industry-group rent-bid curves

201

off-center sites (Figure 11-2). The rent-bid line for industry group B also indicates a desire for a central location, but this desire is not as great as for industry group A. Finally, the rent-bid line for industry group C indicates that access is less important to this industry group than for either industry group A or industry group B.

Where will the industry groups actually locate? The answer lies in the assumption that land owners want the largest return possible from their land holdings and rent their land to the industry group that offers the highest rent. Returning to Figure 11-2, this means that industry group A will locate at the urban center, industry group B will locate next to the urban center, and industry group C will locate somewhere in the outer fringes of the urban area.

Residential Location. The notion of a rent-bid line also explains the general location of household groups in an urban area. Households fall into three groups: the low-, middle-, and high-income groups. A rent-bid line for each group is illustrated in Figure 11-3, and the steepness of each group's rent-bid line differs because of income level.

The general nature of a household rent-bid line is downward-sloping, indicating that the amount the household will bid for land will decrease with distance from the center. This decrease is at a rate just sufficient to produce an income effect which will offset the increase in access costs. Thus, the household rent-bid line is a

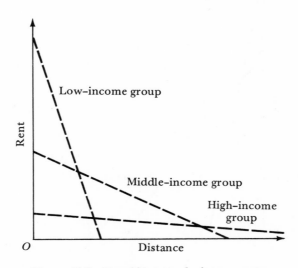

Figure 11-3 Rent-bid curves by income group

mapping of locations where the household will be equally satisfied at the price of land indicated on the vertical axis.

The rent-bid line for the low-income group is quite steep because the poor cannot afford expensive sites; therefore, changes in the price of land are not as important for the low-income group as the cost of access. Viewed another way, the rent offered for land by the low-income group will fall sharply with distance from the center in order to offset any increase in access costs. The rent-bid line for the high-income group is fairly flat, since this group desires and can afford expensive sites. As a result, the high-income group is generally unwilling to offer a high rent for a central location. The lower price for land in distant suburbs and the amenities of suburban living offset any dissatisfaction from commuting long distances (access cost). It should be added, however, that the marginal dissatisfaction of commuting depends on income. Since the commuter values his travel time as some fraction of his income, the very-high-income individual may find the total access cost in commuting from some distant suburb great enough that he finds it more desirable to locate nearer the urban center. Finally, though middle-income households usually cannot afford to buy sites in the distant suburbs, they can afford to live in the low-density suburban fringes of the urban area. The line for the middle-income group slopes less than that for the low-income group but greater than that for the high-income group.

Urban Structure

We may now join the household rent-bid lines and the industry-group rent-bid lines to depict land allocation in an urban area. The solid lines in Figure 11-4 are the rent-bid lines for the industry groups, and the broken lines represent those for the household groups. If the landholder offers his property to the highest bidder, the urban land is allocated as shown by the heavy line in Figure 11-4. The highest bidder for the most central location is industry group A. The low-income group locates next to the urban center. Industry groups B and C enclose the low-income group. Finally, the middle-income group resides at the outer fringes of the urban area, and the high-income group resides in the more distant suburbs.

Since Figure 11-4 represents the urban land-allocation pattern in every direction from the urban center, our theoretical model

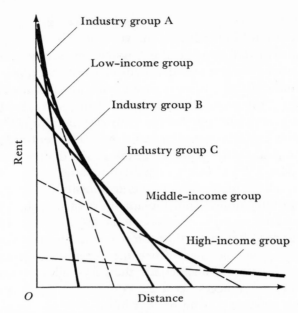

Rent

Industry group A

Low–income group

Industry group B

Industry group C

Middle–income group

High–income group

O

Distance

Figure 11-4   Urban land allocation for single urban core

supports what Burgess found from his empirical investigation of several large cities (Chapter 10). The urban area develops radially as a series of concentric zones.

In actuality, however, several conditions may affect the concentric-zone regularity in many urban areas. Natural barriers such as mountain ranges or rivers and lakes will influence the radial expansion of the urban area. Urban facilities such as railroads or highways create other barriers. Conceptually, this can be reflected in rent-bid lines for these sites; the rent for such sites will be lower than for sites of similar distance from the urban center which are not bounded by barriers. The construction of a major access route, on the other hand, will tend to improve the overall access of sites served by the route. As a result, the rent offered for these sites increases and a relocation of land use follows. Sites that were residential areas before the construction of the route become attractive commercial and industrial locations.

Land Use and Urban Growth

Thus far our discussion of access and urban land use has been centered around the notion of a single urban center, the urban core.

The theoretical development of a rent-bid line was used to explain how a land-use pattern develops around that core.

As residential development continues to expand outward and around the city, new markets for retail goods and services are created and profit-maximizing businesses seek location in these new market areas. This development can be described in a rent-bid analysis similar to that for the single urban core, Figure 11-4. An illustration which includes only one household group and one business group can indicate this.

In Figure 11-5, the business group's rent-bid line declines out to distance D_1 from the urban core. For some distance beyond point D_1, the business group's rent-bid line rises, and then it declines for the more distant sites in the new market area. For the new market area, the site where the rent-bid line reaches a peak represents the site of greatest overall access. Thus, the price the business group will bid for sites will decrease with distance from this new center at a rate just sufficient to offset any decrease in total revenue and increase in total operating costs.

Between D_2 and D_3 of Figure 11-5, businesses are shown to offer a price for land higher than the household group is willing to pay; thus, all land in this area will be ultimately allocated to businesses since landholders seek highest returns for land use.

An earlier discussion of the theory of central places (Chapter 6) indicated that the urban center will contain a greater number of functions than those found in the smaller commercial center between D_2 and D_3. Land values presumably will be lower between D_2 and D_3 than they are within the urban center since fewer businesses bid

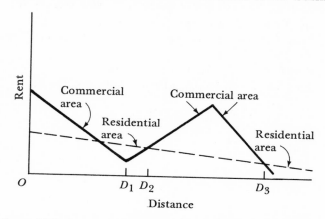

Figure 11-5 Urban land allocation for multiple commercial areas

for land in those areas. However, the growth of outlying business centers may ultimately lower the urban-core rent-bid lines of business by stimulating a decentralization of business activity from the urban core to outlying business centers.

SUMMARY

The primary concern of this chapter was to shed some light on the role of the free market in determining the allocation of urban land use. The value of the rent-bid argument is that the concept reveals the economic importance of alternative sites by depicting the willingness of firms and households to offer different prices for different sites and the desire of landholders to supply land on the basis of the highest price offered for their property.

In reality, the allocation of urban land is also guided by in-stitutional factors (i.e., zoning regulations). More will be said about the effects of institutional factors on urban land use in Chapters 13 and 14.

REFERENCES AND SUPPLEMENTAL READING

Matthew Edel and Jerome Rothenberg (eds.), *Readings in Urban Economics* (New York: The MacMillan Company, 1972), pp. 124–74.

William H. Leahy, *et al.* (eds.), *Urban Economics* (New York: The Free Press, 1970), pp. 55–63.

J. R. Meyer, *et al.*, *The Urban Transportation Problem* (Cambridge: Harvard University Press, 1965), Chapters 5, 6, and 7.

Edwin S. Mills, *Urban Economics* (Glenview, Illinois: Scott, Foresman and Company, 1972), Chapter 4.

Harvey S. Perloff and Lowdon Wingo, Jr. (eds.) *Issues in Urban Economics* (Baltimore: The Johns Hopkins Press, 1968), pp. 237–48.

12

The Public Economy
of Urban Regions

State and local governments are empowered to create and administer policies that affect the industries and individuals in their constituency. Unfortunately, taxing and spending policies, as well as regulatory policies, have economic consequences often only casually understood. Government policy can be used to consciously amplify desirable economic trends or to mitigate the effects of adverse developments.

In this chapter we will examine the rudiments of public-sector economics so that these principles may be applied in subsequent chapters dealing with urban-region problems and policies.

THE DIMENSIONS OF STATE AND
LOCAL GOVERNMENT

From their historic roles as the providers of protection and a few services for their constituency, state and local governments have moved into positions of greater influence in shaping the economic development of their region. In part this simply may be a result of increased awareness of the impact of state and local government actions on the quantity and quality of economic progress. But at least three major factors have contributed to the enlarged role of state and local government: urbanization, structural change, and the sheer size of state and local budgets.

Urbanization has brought a different mix of problems with which state and local governments must cope. The public-service requirements are greater and more varied for a large urban area than for a small village or rural population. Increasing density is generally associated with more externalities, benefits and costs spilling over to parties not involved in a particular transaction. Growth, decline, and stagnation resulting from differential regional growth rates give rise to a variety of problems. Government response to nongrowth or decline can be at least as perplexing as the problems of a growing area.

Structural change in nearly every regional economy has been dramatic. Increased productivity in agriculture has reduced the labor requirements, resulting in the well known out-migration from farming. Depletion of natural resources has resulted in numerous depressed areas. Federal government spending programs have stimulated the growth of various areas. Technological change transforms regional economies both dramatically and subtly. These and similar growth factors have been considered in previous chapters.

Taxation and expenditure policies have grown in importance simply because of their magnitude.

As indicated in Tables 12-1 and 12-2, revenue and expenditures of state and local government have increased rapidly. Although

TABLE 12-1. *State and Local Government Revenue, 1950, 1960, 1970*
(millions of dollars)

	1950	1960	1970
From federal government	2,486	6,944	23,257
Public welfare	1,107	2,070	7,574
Highways	438	2,905	4,608
Education	345	950	5,844
Social insurance	168	325	664
Other	428	724	4,567
From state and local sources	23,153	53,302	128,248
Property taxes	7,349	16,405	34,054
Sales and gross receipts taxes	5,154	11,849	30,322
Individual income	788	2,463	10,812
Corporation income	593	1,180	3,738
Utility and liquor store revenue	2,712	4,877	8,614
Other	6,557	2,285	40,708
TOTAL	25,639	60,277	151,505

SOURCE: Department of Commerce, Bureau of the Census, *Governmental Finances*, annual reports.

TABLE 12-2. *State and Local Government Expenditures, 1950, 1960, 1970*
(*millions of dollars*)

	1950	1960	1970
Education	7,177	18,719	52,718
Highways	3,803	9,428	16,427
Public welfare	2,940	4,404	14,680
Health and hospitals	1,748	3,794	9,668
Police and fire protection	1,264	2,852	6,518
Natural resources	670	1,189	2,732
Sanitation and sewerage	834	1,727	3,413
Housing and urban renewal	452	858	2,138
Local parks and recreation	304	770	1,888
Other	3,595	8,135	21,148
TOTAL	22,787	51,876	131,332

SOURCE: Department of Commerce, Bureau of the Census, *Governmental Finances*, annual reports.

the federal government has increased its assistance to state and local government, their predominant revenues are the local property tax and sales tax. Education receives the greatest share of the expenditures, followed by highways, public welfare, and health and hospitals.

Increasingly, governmental units are confronted with "trade-offs"—choosing among several alternatives of expenditures and taxes. For instance, should more be spent for welfare or for education? Should land be used for parks or industrial sites? Should more be spent for penal institutions or law enforcement?

Types of Government Units

About 81,000 subnational governmental units exist in the United States, divided approximately into the following categories:

    50 state governments
 3,000 county governments
18,000 municipalities
17,000 townships
22,000 school districts
21,000 special districts for purposes such as sewers

This political fragmentation can both alleviate and accentuate governmental problems. Political fragmentation will receive further attention in this and subsequent chapters.

SOME ECONOMIC RATIONALES FOR GOVERNMENT

State and local units of government have had an increasingly important role in shaping urban-regional growth. This governmental intervention has several economic rationales; we will consider the primary ones.

Market Imperfections

In order for the free-market mechanism to allocate resources in an optimal fashion, competition and increasing costs must exist in all markets, all buyers and sellers must have perfect knowledge, resources must be completely mobile, firms must behave as profit maximizers, and consumers must react so as to maximize their utility. In actual practice these conditions frequently are violated. Market failure results from the departure from any of the stringent conditions mentioned above.

A breakdown of the allocating mechanism of the market may provide the basis for governmental intervention to correct the misallocation. Monopoly power and insufficient consumer knowledge are common causes of collective action.

Further, although the market may be perfectly capable of optimum resource allocation, its slow response to change may be undesirable. Government action is often considered to be desirable to expedite the ordinarily slow market response.

Collective-Consumption Goods

Occasionally a city or other unit of government provides a service or capital which may benefit individuals even though they make no payment for the service. For instance, a flood levee protects everyone in the city, including those who do not wish to pay for such protection. Only government can force all persons to pay for a collective-consumption good such as the levee.

Externalities

When a meatpacking plant dumps animal remains into a river, downstream swimmers may encounter more than they bargained for. If your neighbor builds a swimming pool and frequently invites you to use it, you benefit from his expenditure without making one of your own. These are examples of externalities, or spillovers, which are common and in some situations lead to governmental action.

An externality exists where an economic action affects parties not directly involved in the transaction. Benefits or costs spill over on parties other than the primary participants in the transaction, thereby falling outside the reach of the price system. A negative externality exists where a person incurs identifiable costs for which he receives no compensation. A positive externality occurs where a person benefits from the action of another without being required to make compensation.

The concern over externalities stems from the breakdown in the market mechanism and a corresponding divergence of equity and efficiency solutions expected of the free market. From an equity viewpoint, some persons are "harmed" and others "helped" through no action of their own. Also, if externalities are present in the production of a good, a nonoptimal quantity of the good will be produced. Let's examine this latter statement in more detail.

Suppose that the market-equilibrium price and quantity for a product is represented by P_0 and Q_0 in Figure 12-1, where SS and DD are the corresponding supply and demand curves with all costs and all benefits embodied in each. At this equilibrium, marginal benefit equals marginal cost. But if there are externalities, some of the benefits and costs are not included in the demand and supply curves. For instance, if some of the costs are excluded from the market-supply curve, such as in SS', the market price will be lower and the quantity produced will be greater than the optimal price P_0 and quantity Q_0. Conversely, where benefits are excluded from the market-demand curve, the output and price will be lower than the socially optimum level. This situation is illustrated in Figure 12-2. In the case of either the cost or the benefit externality, a less than socially satisfactory market solution is achieved. In the case of the meatpacking plant, although the private costs of processing meat are included in the supply curve, the water pollution costs are not. These spill over on society.

The idea of externalities can be illustrated with a simple two-party externality depicted by Figure 12-3, where the marginal net benefits to producer X from undertaking a given activity are illustrated by the line AB and the value of the marginal costs to party Y are illustrated by line OC. As the level of output by X increases, the marginal net benefits to X decrease and the marginal net damages

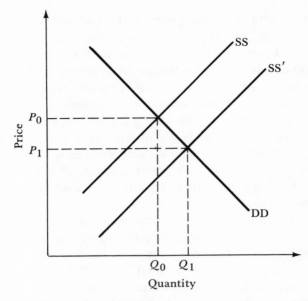

Figure 12-1 Socially optimum market conditions vs. cost externality

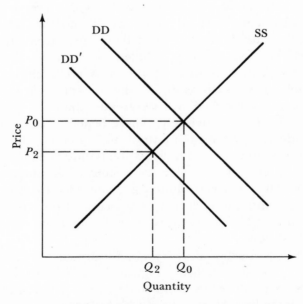

Figure 12-2 Socially optimum market conditions vs. benefit externality

to Y increase. If the production by X had no impact on Y, then X would produce at level B, because this would maximize net benefits to X. But given Y's marginal-damage function, the level of activity is unlikely to reach B. Y is willing to pay a price to have X's activity reduced, and the price increases with each increase in X's output, but is not relevant until level R is reached. Beyond this output level, Y is willing to pay X more than the marginal net benefits received by X from further output. The basis for a negotiated reduction of X's output to level R exists for any output level between R and B. A similar conclusion would result even if Y had the right to prevent X from undertaking any production. X would be willing to pay Y up to $ORDA$ to produce level R. The foregoing simple example is based on two important assumptions: legal rights exist to allow one of the two parties to take action to protect property rights and decision-making costs are zero.

What can be done to bring about a socially optimum solution in markets exhibiting significant externalities? Collective action in the form of government intervention usually is required to promote greater efficiency in instances of significant externalities. This intervention may take a variety of forms. At the extreme, the government may become the producer in order to achieve a more optimum output. In part this explains the government's role in education,

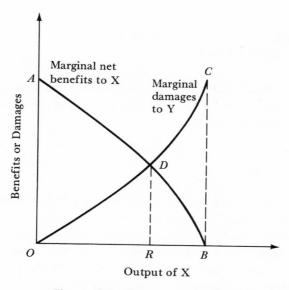

Figure 12-3 Two-party externality

protection, and health services. But within the private enterprise framework, the government may use taxes and subsidies to adjust for disparities that exist between private and social costs and private and social benefits. If the tax is equivalent to the difference between private and social costs, the effect will be to have firms make decisions on the basis of total social costs. This is sometimes referred to as "internalizing" externalities. Likewise, subsidies can elicit optimum output levels from private firms.

Interjurisdictional Spillovers

The political fragmentation described earlier in the chapter gives rise to a particular type of externality as a result of governmental structure. The provision of public services in one jurisdiction often spills over onto residents or industries in another area. These interjurisdictional spillovers result when benefits or costs resulting from the action of one government unit accrue to residents of another jurisdiction, even though the latter did not participate in the decision-making process. Such spillovers have become a serious problem in metropolitan areas which consist of a multiplicity of governments. This problem is discussed in greater detail in the next chapter.

FORMS OF GOVERNMENTAL INTERVENTION

A governmental unit may intervene in the free-market economy in four basic ways: rule making, producing goods and services, gifts and grants, and taxation.

Rule-Making

Rules may be imposed to require or prevent certain types of activities. In general, the rules are set forth to bring about a closer correspondence between social and private costs and benefits. Rules apply to business as well as individuals. Zoning laws are a set of rules designed to reduce negative externalities resulting from uncontrolled land development. Individuals are required to send their children to school partly because of the overall benefit to society.

Public Expenditures

About 30 percent of all expenditures in the United States each year are made by some form of government. Of the total government expenditures, about one-third was spent by state and local government for various activities as indicated in Table 12-2. How effective are these expenditure programs in providing benefits to people and industry?

Efficiency Criteria. In the private sector of the economy, economic efficiency is encouraged by responses of producers and consumers to price signals. But in the public sectors these signals are either weak or nonexistent. However, it is possible to set forth similar efficiency criteria to those applied to the private sector.

Ideally, the *benefit* derived from the last dollar spent on a public service should be greater than or at least equal to the *cost*. Such a criterion would assume that every expenditure for a public service would yield a benefit at least equal to the value of the goods foregone in the private sector. Also, it would assure that such an expenditure would not prevent a more valuable public expenditure in some other public service.

These benefit-cost criteria, if they can be implemented, will be vastly superior to the more frequently used budgeting guidelines such as the "requirements" approach and the "budget first" approach. The former specifies certain "needs" and proceeds to meet these needs regardless of cost or alternative competing programs. The "budget first" approach considers what can be afforded by the amount of funds available, thereby ignoring comparisons with private-sector alternatives. Even if the benefit-cost criteria are difficult to apply, the efficiency results are generally superior to alternative partial criteria.

Although the proper measure of a particular public-expenditure program is that marginal benefits equal marginal costs, the difficulty comes in identifying and measuring the benefits and costs. Let us examine some of the approaches of state and local government in making public-expenditure decisions.

The Demand for Public Services. The trend of spending by state and local government partly reflects increased demands for public services throughout the nation. Rising incomes and changing industrial structure have significantly altered the magnitude and composition of the demand for public services. The evidence indicates that consumers have preferred to spend a higher percentage of their additional incomes on services—both public and private. The demand for better education, health services, roads, welfare, recreation, and protection has risen more rapidly than income.

The changing composition of the demands for state and local government is also a reflection of a change in industry mix and employment patterns. Increased urbanization, declining farm population, and the emergence of new industries have altered the service requirements of regional governments.

A lack of responsiveness of government to changing demands for public services will result in substantial inefficiency. This may cause obsolete services to be continued and desired new services to be implemented slowly. In either case the benefit-cost criteria for efficiency is violated.

Supplying Public Services. Public services are generally not subjected to the rigors of market forces to encourage efficiency. But increasingly it has been argued that more public services should be priced in accord with costs associated with providing them. Traditionally, public services such as water, sewer, and refuse collection have tended to be priced on the basis of cost criteria. But many services such as education, recreation, and highway travel have not been priced to users. When services are underpriced, purchasers will tend to undervalue them and may use them wastefully. This is not to recommend that the public sector resort to a total-pricing system for its allocation of resources. In many cases public services are offered well below cost in order to maximize the use of the service. The view that access to an education is desirable for all has been a long-standing position of governments. But state and local governments have begun to experiment with more user pricing of recreation, transportation, and health services in order to accomplish a better allocation of resources.

As an alternative to price signals in promoting the proper responses of government, an encouraging development is the modification of the institutional arrangement of government agencies responsible for providing public services. The objective is to simulate conditions which will force the government decision makers to arrive at expenditure decisions which are efficient. The operations of the agency are structured so that conformity to the operating routine encourages efficiency. Best known of these schemes is the planning-programming-budgeting technique pioneered in the Defense Department. These newer management techniques have been implemented in varying degrees in state government, but have been only slowly adopted at the local-government level.

At the local-government level one of the chief obstacles to efficiency is size. Political fragmentation has resulted in units of government which are too small to gain the advantages of economies of scale. The result is an inadequate and expensive public-service system. The prime example is represented by county governments, most of which are not viable units of government from the standpoint of economic efficiency. They were designed to service an economy which no longer exists. Just as school consolidation greatly improved the efficiency of the educational system, so the consolidation of other functions will promote greater efficiency in other public services. Regional health programs have developed and so have, more recently, regional law-enforcement programs. In addition to consolidation, cooperation among overlapping units of government has been encouraging. County, city, and school board have cooperated in providing a recreation-athletic complex in one community. City and county have cooperated in utility networks. Consolidation and cooperation among units of government is crucial to reducing public-service costs.

Subsidies

Over the past 20 years the use of subsidies, primarily to attract industry, has grown at a rapid pace. States and communities hoping to gain a competitive edge have devised a variety of these subsidies to encourage new firms to locate in their region. The most popular of these subsidies is the industrial revenue bond. Since the pros and cons of other subsidies are much the same, we will restrict our discussion to the industrial revenue bond.

There are two general classifications of bonds which municipal governments may issue to raise capital for public undertakings: the revenue bond and the general-obligation bond.

Revenue bonds are bonds which are serviced and redeemed exclusively out of the net earnings of undertakings which they are issued to finance. They are secured by only a mortgage pledge on the properties of these undertakings with no responsibility on the part of the community to service the debt in case of default.

The revenue bond is, by definition, issued for investment

in a revenue-earning project. The general-obligation bond may or may not be issued to raise capital for a revenue-earning project. The crucial difference between the two is the obligation of the community to service the debt. The general-obligation bond is backed by "the full faith and credit" of the community. When general-obligation bonds are issued for investment in a revenue-earning project, the bonds will be backed not only by the earning power of the project being financed but also by the general credit of the community (and its taxing power).

As might be anticipated, when financing is supported by only a pledge of revenue it costs more (the interest rate is higher) than it would if based on a pledge of full faith and general credit, because the risk of loss through default is higher. The revenue bond has become a community financial tool because it lends itself to certain situations when the general-obligation bond could not be used.

Industrial revenue bonds have been utilized by communities in an attempt to attract industry to their locality, thereby providing jobs for their local unemployed or stimulating population growth. The bonds may be used to finance industrial buildings; and since these buildings are municipally owned—and therefore tax exempt— it is possible to effect a very favorable lease arrangement for any industry coming into the community.

Two types of subsidies normally are present in industrial revenue bonds. First, the industrial building funded by the sale of the bonds belongs to the government and is not subject to property tax (a local-government subsidy). Second, the interest paid on the bonds is exempt from the federal income tax (a federal-government subsidy). The subsidies involved in the use of industrial revenue bonds are major points of concern in the debate about the desirability of using industrial revenue bonds.

A community considering alternative approaches to solving its unemployment problem or attempting to stimulate population growth should consider two basic questions regarding any proposed solutions.

1. Will the proposed development policy accomplish the objective?
2. Is the proposed approach the most efficient way to reach the objective?

Effectiveness. Cost and demand factors are the major considerations influencing location. Local subsidies do not appear to eliminate or even reduce the importance of such factors. It appears, however, that under certain circumstances other economic and noneconomic factors may play a significant role. Although some locations are ruled out by cost and market considerations, there remain several alternative locations which are feasible. It is at this stage that local subsidies—in their present form and with present dollar values —may exert some influence on industrial location.

The subsidy provided by revenue-bond financing may be of some direct economic value. "With existing forms and levels of subsidization, this advantage is of limited significance in most cases, particularly when compared with the cost disadvantages that may result from choosing a poor location. Nevertheless, it may be advantageous for a firm to accept a subsidy if the community offering it is closely comparable to other possible locations in all major respects."[1] Subsidies now do not operate to negate traditional location considerations but rather extend the decision-making process another step.

Location theory indicates that the importance of the different factors influencing industrial location varies depending on the type of industry. As an example, for certain types of manufacturing a continuous source of power, in large amounts, may be the predominant factor in the location decision. Other industries —for example industries assembling prefabricated parts—may not need this "high-grade" form of power but may instead emphasize an abundance of labor as a prime location determinant. (Of course several factors must be weighed together.)

The potential incentive of a local subsidy appears to be related to the size of the firm. Small enterprises seem to find the type of subsidy provided by revenue-bond financing a relatively strong attraction. The reason would appear to be two-fold. First, construction of the plant by the community and financing under a long-term lease or lease-purchase agreement allows the company to conserve its limited capital for use as working capital. Second, while large firms may be able to internally finance expansion operations, the smaller firm may find that financing either is just not available or is available only at a very high interest rate. This is particularly true when the small firm is also a young one.

The financing shortage, or "credit gap," exists primarily in rural communities. The small and medium-sized industrial concern, considering starting manufacturing operations or expanding them into a rural community, seldom has cash for construction. This,

1. J. H. Thompson, "The Community Subsidy to Industry," *Business Horizons*, Spring, 1963, p. 48.

coupled with the fact that the conventional credit facilities in rural areas may be inadequate in terms of capability or willingness to provide financing for industrial buildings, leads to the conclusion that local government may be the *only* entity that has the motivation and power to command capital for this use.

An additional consideration, which may be useful in attempting to judge the potential of industrial-revenue-bond financing as a location incentive, involves distinguishing between new firms which are just entering the economic community and old firms which are involved in expansion operations. The location of a new firm probably constitutes a genuine decision in the sense that possible alternatives are carefully weighed and some attempt is made to arrive at the optimum location. This is important from the community standpoint because the local subsidy stands a better chance of working its way into the decision-making process when an attempt is being made to consider fully the advantages and disadvantages of each location.

In contrast to relocation, which may not be seriously considered unless persistent problems develop, the need for expansion probably will result in the detailed comparison of alternative locations. The advantages of having the new facilities nearby will be carefully weighed against the cost and marketing advantages of more distant locations. This careful consideration means that the local subsidy stands a chance of at least receiving consideration at some stage in the reasoning process.

Community subsidies usually represent a great deal less than windfall gains to the firms that receive them. The community that offers a subsidy often does so because it is deficient in other respects. To such a community, "buying" industry may seem a cheaper, easier alternative than attempting to remedy serious shortcomings in local services and institutions. Second, the advantage that a firm obtains from industrial-revenue-bond financing is temporary. For example, it is not unusual for a firm that has received a property-tax exemption to find itself paying higher-than-average property taxes at the end of the exemption period.

It is not possible to make a generalization regarding the effectiveness of local subsidies in attracting the desired industry. For certain firms the type of assistance provided by industrial revenue bonds may serve to compensate for minor shortcomings of the community as a location for industry. Other firms may assign this type of assistance a very low priority. The effectiveness of any community in attracting new industry depends, not on a single factor, but on how the community compares to other potential locations in terms of the overall advantages offered to that particular firm.

Efficiency. Subsidies also should be examined with reference to benefits and costs in addition to their ability to accomplish their objective. The benefits to the community may be calculated by computing the discounted value of the estimated increase in income resulting from the investment undertaken in the community because of the inducement program.

Two alternative measures of cost have been used. First, the cost element consists of the discounted value of the decrease in local income resulting from the investment *not* undertaken because of the inducement program. Second, the cost consists of the discounted value of the decrease in local income resulting because some of those financing the inducement program would, as a result, have lower incomes. For instance, taxpayers might have lower net incomes because of the higher taxes they had to pay in order to recover tax revenue lost because of the exemption program.

In the latter case considerable concern has been expressed that the additional employment and service requirements of the subsidized industry will generate an excessive burden on the local governmental units, particularly education. If the new industry were to draw in a large number of new employees, which is often the hope, this could increase the service load on local government, necessitating increased expenditures without a corresponding increase in tax revenue. Such a situation would result in a tax increase for the original residents of the community with no increase in services to them.

Often, however, firms that are attracted by industrial revenue bonds are also oriented to a labor-surplus area, so they do not draw many additional workers into the area. As a result, the additional costs to local government would be small. The actual benefit/cost ratio can be positive or negative depending on the individual circumstance.

Taxes

Taxes paid by business are frequently the subject of scrutiny for their effect on attracting industry and stimulating economic development in the state. In the course of attempting to raise revenue to finance government services, state and local governments are often accused of retarding the growth rate of the area with a comparatively unfavorable tax structure. As a result, most studies of the impact of the state-local public sector on economic growth have concentrated on the effects of the state-local tax system. More specifically, analysis of the influence of the tax system on industrial location in a particular state has been considered the way to measure the impact of the public sector on economic growth.

This method has generally led to inconclusive results or results showing that state tax differentials have little impact on industrial location decisions except for a few cases where all other locational factors are similar. For example, a firm that has decided to locate in the Kansas City area may decide to locate on the Kansas side if Kansas's local tax structures give that particular firm a tax advantage.

However, studies such as those by Campbell[2] and Sacks[3] have shown that little correlation exists between the level of taxation and the rate of economic growth. They set forth several reasons for lack of a significant relationship between level of taxes and economic growth. The main consideration is the conflicting influence, on economic growth, of taxes and levels of government services financed by taxes. High taxes may discourage firms from locating in a particular area while high levels of government services may attract industry. Alternatively stated, an area may lose an industry not because taxes are too high but because they are too low. Thus, it is difficult to isolate the influence of taxes on economic development.

The firm does not consider tax levels to be a major locational influence according to Due[4] and Greenhut.[5] They point out that taxes are a small percentage of total cost and thus can increase or decrease significantly without greatly affecting profits. On the other hand, even small shifts in large-cost items such as wages will have a large influence on profits. Furthermore, the shifting of business taxes forward to the final consumer or backward to factors of production certainly exists.

Also, state business taxes are deductible from federal taxes,

2. A. K. Campbell, "State and Local Taxes, Expenditures, and Economic Development" in *State and Local Taxes on Business*, Tax Institute of America, 1965, pp. 195–208.

3. S. Sacks, "State and Local Finances in Economic Development," in *State and Local Taxes on Business*, Tax Institute of America, 1965, pp. 209–224.

4. J. Due, "Studies of State-Local Influences on Location of Industry," *National Tax Journal*, June, 1961, pp. 163–173.

5. M. Greenhut, *Plant Location in Theory and Practice, the Economics of Space* (Chapel Hill: The University of North Carolina Press, 1956), pp. 137–139.

which effectively reduces the cost of state business taxes by approximately 50 percent.

There are dissenting views, notably those of Struyk,[6] who has shown that when considering a set of 50 similar-sized cities throughout the United States, there is a significant negative relationship between economic growth and the degree of taxation. His analysis shows that total state taxes and the local property tax both exhibit an inverse relationship with growth.

Thus, although taxes may vary from area to area, apparently they are not an overwhelming consideration in a location decision. Since high taxes are generally associated with greater quantity and quality of public services and facilities, firms requiring such services and facilities would be attracted to these areas.

An Analytical Framework. Business taxes affect not only the business on which they are imposed, but also the industries with which the taxed industry buys and sells. Depending on the supply and demand conditions in the market, a firm may be able to pass on the entire tax to its customers (forward-shifting) or to its suppliers (backward-shifting). Thus, in order to understand the eventual impact of business taxes, the interdependency among industries should be conisdered. This can be accomplished with input-output analysis.

The direct- and indirect-requirements matrix can be converted into a regional-tax matrix. Each entry of the regional-tax matrix shows the amount of regional business taxes embodied in the purchases of each sector as each sector makes a $1.00 delivery to final demand. Furthermore, each column sum of the tax matrix shows the total amount of regional business taxes embodied in each dollar of sales to final demand by each sector. Thus, the regional-tax matrix takes into account the tax pyramiding in each sector, as regional business taxes are assumed to be shifted forward to the purchaser. Such an analysis has been performed for West Virginia[7] and Kansas.[8] An example from the Kansas analysis is presented in Table 12-3. For instance, Table 12-3 indicates that the total direct and indirect taxes associated with producing $1.00 of corn for final demand equal nearly 0.7 cents.

6. R. J. Struyk, "An Analysis of Tax Structure, Public Service Levels and Regional Economic Growth," *Journal of Regional Science*, Winter, 1967, pp. 175–182.

7. R. W. Bahl and K. L. Shellhammer, "Evaluating the State Business Tax Structure: An Application of Input-Output Analysis," *National Tax Journal*, Vol. XXII, pp. 203–216.

8. M. J. Emerson and M. Henry, "The Impact of the Public Sectors on the Growth of the Kansas Economy," in *State and Local Finances in Kansas* (Kansas State University and the University of Kansas, 1972).

TABLE 12-3. *Total State Tax Per $1.00 of Final Demand, Kansas, 1965*

Industry	Dollar
1. Corn	.006905
2. Sorghum	.006757
3. Wheat	.011876
4. Other grains	.007871
5. Soybeans	.005676
6. Hay	.005875
7. Dairy products	.015015
8. Poultry and poultry products	.006903
9. Cattle	.004624
10. Hogs	.006991
11. Other agricultural products	.007885
12. Agricultural services	.009739
13. Crude oil and natural gas	.005851
14. Oil and gas field services	.006631
15. Nonmetallic mining	.003329
16. Other mining	.002427
17. Maintenance and repair	.006303
18. Building construction	.016238
19. Heavy construction	.020295
20. Special trade construction	.006303
21. Meat products	.006035
22. Dairy products	.014693
23. Grain mill products	.012321
24. Other food and kindred products	.006887
25. Apparel	.007585
26. Paper and allied products	.008364
27. Printing and publishing	.008442
28. Industrial chemicals	.006225
29. Agricultural chemicals	.007943
30. Other chemicals	.003157
31. Petroleum and coal products	.004628
32. Rubber and plastics	.002677
33. Cement and concrete	.010842
34. Other stone and clay	.004387
35. Primary metals	.005238
36. Fabricated metals	.008728
37. Other fabricated metal products	.009666
38. Farm machinery	.006232
39. Construction machinery	.006754
40. Food products machinery	.004533
41. Electrical machinery	.012946

TABLE 12-3. *(Continuued)*

Industry	Dollar
42. Other machinery	.021731
43. Motor vehicles	.013539
44. Aerospace	.003684
45. Trailer coaches	.006849
46. Other transportation equipment	.001508
47. Other manufacturing	.005733
48. Railroad transportation	.032534
49. Motor freight	.070545
50. Other transportation	.057555
51. Communications	.005167
52. Electric gas and sanitary services	.004303
53. Groceries	.004014
54. Farm products	.006368
55. Machinery and equipment	.006374
56. Other wholesale trade	.002912
57. Farm equipment dealers	.023627
58. Gasoline service stations	.004089
59. Eating and drinking	.003963
60. Other retail trade	.009517
61. Banking	.006744
62. Other finance	.015044
63. Insurance and real estate	.013890
64. Lodging services	.004936
65. Personal services	.014637
66. Business services	.004691
67. Medical and health services	.007418
68. Other services	.003068
69. Education	.047751

SOURCE: M. J. Emerson and Mark Henry, "The Impact of the Public Sectors on the Growth of the Kansas Economy," in *State and Local Finances in Kansas* (Manhattan, Kansas: Kansas State University, 1972).

These state-tax coefficients, which indicate the state business-tax burden for each sector, can be used to determine the effect of the state tax structure on the competitive position of state industries that compete in nonstate markets. For instance, if the export-base theory of regional growth is valid, a tax structure that enhances the competitive position of a region's export base would promote growth. For instance, a statistical analysis of the tax data in Table 12-3 indicated that state business taxes did not favor the export-base industries whereas local taxes did.

SUMMARY

The role of state and local governments in the growth of urban and regional areas has expanded at a rapid pace in the last two decades. Their roles have expanded because of urbanization, structural change, and budget size.

Government interference with the market mechanisms is often justified by market imperfections, collective-consumption goods, externalities, and interjurisdictional spillovers. Intervention takes the form of rule making, expenditures, subsidies, and taxes.

REFERENCES AND SUPPLEMENTAL READING

Robert L. Bish, *The Public Economy of Metropolitan Areas* (Chicago: Markham, 1971).

Werner Z. Hirsch, *The Economics of State and Local Government* (New York: McGraw-Hill, 1970).

Julius Margolis, "The Demand for Public Services," in *Issues in Urban Economics,* Harvey S. Perloff and Lowden Wingo, Jr. (eds.), (Baltimore: Johns Hopkins, 1968).

J. E. Moes, *Local Subsidies for Industry* (Chapel Hill, N.C.: The University of North Carolina Press, 1962).

R. J. Struyk, "An Analysis of Tax Structure, Public Service Levels, and Regional Economic Growth," *Journal of Regional Science,* Winter, 1967.

Charles M. Tiebout, "A Pure Theory of Local Expenditures," *Journal of Political Economy*, Vol. 64, October, 1956.

13

The Economics of Urban Poverty and Housing

At first impression, today's large cities are no longer workable —economically, politically, and socially. Economically, the inner cities are poverty-stricken with their high rates of unemployment, intolerable living conditions, and general congestion. Moreover, they are bankrupt at a time when their residents are dependent as never before upon public services for education, waste treatment, fire and police protection, and welfare. Politically, America's cities are faced with increasing political fragmentation, a problem which makes economic and social problems ever more difficult to control. Finally, there is the growing feeling that cities are places where man can no longer live in safety, with convenience, with a sense of security, or with a feeling of human dignity.

Such an impression of urban life is not new. We have read of it, we have heard of it, and many of us have experienced such conditions. But few people genuinely understand the perplexity of the urban socioeconomic structure. In this and the following two chapters, we will sketch the major economic problems of urban America. Matters of policy will also be considered in these chapters.

Specifically, this chapter is concerned with the economics of urban unemployment and urban housing. Matters of transportation and pollution will be discussed in Chapter 14. In both this chapter and Chapter 14, special emphasis is placed on the externalities of an urban economy. Chapter 15 will discuss political fragmentation and will examine the private real-estate market's influence on urban land-use practices. Chapter 15 should help us understand how today's local government structure and urban land-use practices aggravate the problems discussed in this chapter and Chapter 14.

The private-market system provides our basic rationale for allocating resources to the consumption and production of consumer goods and services. In order for the market to allocate these resources efficiently, a necessary condition, as indicated in Chapter 12, is that marginal private benefits must equal marginal social benefits and, similarly, marginal private cost must equal marginal social cost. In short, externalities (or spillover effects) must not exist in the production and consumption process.

When the nation's economy was basically that of a "cottage" industry, the externalities which existed were negligible and of little concern. A frontier family's efforts to produce food for home consumption or to spin wool into yarn for the weaving of clothing neither adversely affected nor benefited other families. Practically speaking, the economy was self-sufficient.

All of this changed as the young nation's people prospered and demanded more goods and services. Most noticeable in this change was the urbanization which reflected the growing complexity and interdependency of the economy. The externalities of today's urbanization are at a level where significant adverse effects do occur. (The deadly exhaust fumes from automobiles are a serious threat to life in many of the large cities.) But the private-market system does not consider such externalities. It is guided solely by private benefits and costs. Consequently, the private market fails to allocate resources efficiently whenever there are substantial indirect costs or benefits connected with the production and consumption of goods and services.

URBAN POVERTY AND EMPLOYMENT PROBLEMS

One result of technological change has been the urban concentration of people who live in poverty.

Simply defined, poverty is the inadequate consumption of

necessary goods and services. Implied in this definition is the notion of a minimal standard of living, a standard determined by the social values of the time, values which are influenced by the nation's capacity to produce goods and services. In defining poverty, the Social Security Administration determines standards for minimum food and other basic requirements necessary to good health and weights its standards by considering such factors as size of family and area of residence. On this basis, the federal government considered the poverty-cutoff family-income level for an urban family of four at $3,774 for 1970.

Some Characteristics of Low-Income Groups

The Department of Commerce and the Department of Labor issue regular reports on the social and economic conditions of families and unrelated individuals living in urban and rural regions of the country. An examination of these reports, though they are essentially data compilations, reveals the general characteristics of the nation's poverty groups and allows one to understand the trends which poverty is taking. Naturally, one must be cautious in any interpretation of these data, for they do not take into account future structural changes in social and economic conditions that may radically alter the nature and direction of any given trend. The trends discussed are for the 1960s.[1]

The Extent of Poverty. Overall, the number of poor persons in the United States declined at an average rate of about five percent a year. The 1970 poverty figure was 26 million, down from 39 million in 1959. The decline in poverty was much more rapid for whites than for blacks, and the number of poor persons declined more rapidly in nonmetropolitan areas than in metropolitan areas.

Geography of Poverty. For the United States in general, the major proportion of poverty shifted from nonmetropolitan to metropolitan areas. The proportion of poor persons living outside metropolitan areas declined as the result of a substantial reduction of poor persons among farm residents. For metropolitan areas, an increasing proportion of poverty was found in the central cities of the largest SMSA's

1. From reports published by the U.S. Department of Commerce, Bureau of the Census, and the U.S. Department of Labor.

(standard metropolitan statistical areas). The central cities of the smaller SMSA's showed no change in their proportion of poor.

Unlike the national trends, those for the South still showed a majority of both white and black poor persons residing outside metropolitan areas at the end of the decade.

Income of Poor. The median poverty gap[2] for urban families declined. Black families with incomes below the poverty line were more impoverished than were poor white families. In the central cities (where 80 percent of all metropolitan black families below the poverty level live), the average poor black family had an income which was about $1,000 below the poverty line at the end of the decade. The comparable figure for a poor white family was about $700.

Family Structure. The decade saw an increase in the number of poor people living in families without a male head. The number of families headed by women increased, especially black central-city families. These increases reflect the growth in the number of broken homes. Among blacks in central cities, only six out of every ten children were living with both parents at the end of the decade.

Education and Job Opportunities. Lack of education and training is the source of the largest disparity among individual earnings; low earnings are almost always associated with low educational and skill levels. For the decade of the 1960s, the proportion of young adults finishing high school in both central cities and suburbs increased substantially. For instance, the proportion of blacks in central cities who completed high school rose from 43 percent in 1960 to (about) 60 percent in 1970. What is not revealed in these aggregate percentage figures is the fact that gains in educational attainment among blacks as well as whites have been largely concentrated in families with incomes above the poverty level. The educational picture for individuals living in metropolitan poverty areas still remains dismal.

Changes in the nation's social and economic structure during the 1960s led to a moderate decline in the unemployment rates for both blacks and whites. Changes which probably helped most in increasing the employment opportunities among blacks as well as whites during the decade are: (1) The long-term rise in the educational level of blacks and whites, which has enabled more individuals

2. The poverty "gap" is the difference between the total income of families and unrelated individuals below the poverty level and their respective poverty thresholds.

to enter occupations where joblessness tends to be low; (2) the impact of government manpower programs, which have enrolled a relatively large proportion of blacks; and (3) greater emphasis by employers on the hiring and retention of black workers. Despite the moderate gain in employment opportunities, especially for the minority groups living in central cities, minority workers are employed in the low-level, low-paid jobs to a much greater extent than white workers. Such low-pay and "dead-end" job opportunities offer little hope of freeing oneself from poverty conditions.

Though educational levels and job opportunities have generally improved both for blacks and whites living in urban areas, female heads of poor families must be singled out as individuals who fall far behind in the gains made by the low-income group as a whole. As might be expected, an increasing proportion of all poor families living in central cities are female headed—especially black families— where the typical mother lacks the necessary education for the better-paying jobs. The economic situation of the female-headed poor family is dramatically underscored by public welfare statistics.[3] For example, 27 percent of Maryland's population is located in Baltimore, yet 72 percent of Maryland's Aid to Dependent Children (AFDC) expenditures is to be found in the city. And Boston, with 14 percent of Massachusetts' population, accounts for 40 percent of that state's AFDC expenditures.

Causes of Low Income (Unemployment)

Unemployment and its consequent poverty result from several conditions: automation, inadequate education, physical handicaps, age, sex and racial discrimination, broken homes, geographic job displacement, changes in industry demand, and inadequate aggregate demand. These economic and social factors are more obvious in urban areas with their population concentration, but they are not necessarily the result of urbanization. In fact, automation in agriculture and mining triggered much of the migration of rural workers to the cities.

Of the list of factors just cited, the economic factors of automation, inadequate skills, and geographic job displacement are

---

3. Advisory Commission on Intergovernmental Relations, *Urban and Rural America: Policies for Future Growth* (Washington: U.S. Government Printing Office, April 1968), p. 26.

perhaps more identified with urbanization than are the nationwide economic factors of changes in industry demand and inadequate aggregate demand. Though obviously interrelated, we will treat automation and inadequate skills as a topic separate from the matter of geographic job displacement.

Automation and Inadequate Skills. During the decade of the 50s when rural-to-urban migration was at its peak, the sheer size and rapid growth of urban areas seemingly promised jobs to even the migrant with modest skills. Such unskilled jobs as elevator operators, or building custodians, or pinsetters at the growing number of bowling alleys were often cited as possible employment for the less skilled migrant. For the better-educated migrant, the expansion of urban manufacturing and construction activities was regarded as a continuing source of employment.

During the 1940s and early 1950s, the rural-to-urban migrant did improve his occupational status and income as he entered the urban labor force. But this was short-lived. While the migrant's vision of a job in the city lingered on into the 60s, the actual likelihood of finding unskilled or semiskilled jobs in the inner city declined sharply by the end of the 1950s. As a result, unemployment rates for the inner cities began to climb.

One reason for the declining job market for the migrant was, of course, that automation was rapidly taking the place of the unskilled worker. The pinsetter was being replaced by the automatic pin-setting machine that could do the task in a fraction of the time required by the pinsetter. The elevator operator was replaced by a self-service, push-button system.

In manufacturing, the semiskilled worker faced a similar situation. One Bureau of Labor Statistics estimate shows that approximately 200,000 manufacturing jobs disappeared annually between 1953 and 1959 as a result of improved methods of production. Much of this technological unemployment occurred in the cities.

Geographic Displacement. A second determinant of inner-city low-income and high-unemployment rates is the decentralization of industry. In manufacturing, for example, the multistory plant has given way to the one-story plant layout and this has necessitated the general movement of industry to the suburbs where suitable space can be found to construct a one-story structure.

A recent study, *The Manpower Report of the President, 1971,*[4]

4. U.S. Department of Labor, *Manpower Report of the President, 1971*, pp. 89–90.

analyzing the employment effects of decentralization, found that 54 percent of the added employment in ten large metropolitan areas went to the suburban rings between 1959 and 1967. Five had 70 percent or more of the employment growth outside cities. A similar study of eight metropolitan areas[5] showed that between 1965 and 1967, central-city employment grew at an average annual rate of three percent, while it grew at six percent for the suburbs.

Inner-city employment growth in semiskilled trades did not develop as well as similar suburban employment. Indeed, in some cities factory employment declined. Those that showed gains had rates lower than did suburban areas. *The Manpower Report of the President, 1971* indicated that manufacturing employment for the ten metropolitan areas concentrated 80 percent of its 1959-1967 growth in the suburbs. Employment gains in retail and wholesale trade showed similar patterns: 78 percent of retail-trade and 68 percent of wholesale-trade employment increases took place in suburban areas.

Generally speaking, two conditions have prevented the inner-city resident from following jobs to the suburbs. First, because traditional commuting patterns have dictated urban transportation systems that emphasize suburban-to-central-city patterns, the commuter finds that public transportation to the suburbs is "usually expensive, often circuitous, or simply not available."[6] The central-city worker is economically "trapped" in the inner city. Second, low-income families have not been able to relocate in the suburbs because of the shortage of low-cost housing. This shortage reflects, in large part, a history of discrimination in the sale of suburban real estate to lower-income groups—particularly minority groups. Zoning practices have tended to bar low-cost housing by increasing residential minimum lot sizes to the point where only middle- and upper-income families can afford the houses built on them.

Alleviating Poverty

"I fight poverty—I work."

This bumper-sticker slogan reflects the blend of inevitable value judgments and economic theory involved in policies designed to alleviate poverty. Back in colonial times, poverty was considered

5. Charlotte Freman, "Central City and Suburban Employment Growth, 1965–67" (Washington: The Urban Institute, 1970, unpublished), A summary of the findings is reported in the *Manpower Report of the President, 1970*, p. 89.

6. Dorothy K. Newman, "The Decentralization of Jobs," *Monthly Labor Review*, May 1967 (Washington: U.S. Department of Labor), Reprint No. 2526.

a curse on disreputable people. The corresponding colonial anti-poverty solutions were corporal punishment, religious training, and banishment from the community. This attitude that poverty resulted from sin and laziness predominated until nearly this century. Views on the causes of poverty began to change and were rapidly altered with the Great Depression of the 1930s, when 15 million Americans were unemployed. The public began to view poverty as outside the control of the individual.

Current antipoverty programs reflect a diverse array of value judgments. We will not dwell on these, but rather we will concern ourselves with the characteristics of the policies. Antipoverty policies may be divided into two groups. Numerous policies have been designed to treat the *symptom* of poverty, which is a lack of income. Another group of policies attempt to attack the *causes* of poverty, which are generally a lack of human capital and discrimination.

Treating the Symptoms. A variety of policies to raise the immediate income of the impoverished have been tried or suggested. In this section we will consider employment programs and income-maintenance programs which are the two main types other than aggregate-demand stimulation.

Even when the economy is performing well by aggregate standards, unemployment rates for certain groups, particularly blacks, tend to remain high. In an economic expansion the new jobs are most frequently in the suburbs and require at least some degree of skill. But the vast majority of the urban poor live in the inner city and have poor access to these new jobs either because of inadequate transportation links to the outlying areas or because of skill or education deficiencies.

Two types of employment policies have attempted to bridge the spatial gap separating the ghetto unemployed from the suburban job-market expansion. One approach is to bring jobs to the ghetto, the other is to bring ghetto residents to the jobs.

Tax credits to business firms have been proposed to entice firms into the ghetto. The tax credit would be structured to offset other higher location costs, particularly land costs and risk. Potential new firms would include not only manufacturing plants but also retail and service establishments which are currently of meager quantity and quality.

Wage subsidies to reduce the cost of hiring ghetto labor in manufacturing and service jobs and the construction of new housing or the rehabilitation of old housing in the ghetto using ghetto labor have also been suggested.

But policies to attract firms to the inner city run counter to current strong decentralizing trends. A multiplicity of economic forces have been pushing and pulling economic activity to the suburbs and beyond. It may well be easier to develop policies that capitalize on such trends rather than run counter to them.

Another difficulty associated with the location of new firms in the inner city is the high density. New firms competing for land that is scarce would put additional pressure on an already over-crowded housing situation.

Even if firms were successfully attracted to the ghetto, they would tend to be low-wage, unstable industries. Their low-wage characteristics would mean little chance for upward mobility. The past record of low-wage industries has been one of locational in-stability. They tend to remain in a location only as long as wages remain low, and then move to another low-wage location.

Moving people to jobs is the reverse policy path. An improved transportation system from the inner city to the suburbs would provide better access to suburban jobs for ghetto residents. Such transportation would need to be low-cost public transportation since most persons below the poverty level cannot afford private transporta-tion or even some of the existing public transportation fares. It has been argued that low fares are feasible for inner-city residents because they would be traveling in the opposite direction of heavy usage at times when the trains and buses are virtually empty moving from the inner city to the suburbs.

A major difficulty in providing better public transportation from the inner-city ghetto to the jobs in the suburbs is the wide dispersal of suburban jobs. Public transportation depends on popu-lation concentrations which tend to decline as distance from the central city increases.

Consequently, proposals have been made to build housing in the suburbs nearer job opportunities for ghetto residents. But the high cost of housing and persistent discrimination have thwarted such policies.

In addition to the spatial mismatch of jobs and the unem-ployed or underemployed, there is also the mismatch of skills. Nu-merous training programs have been designed to upgrade the skill levels of the unemployed. Training and retraining programs are hardly new, but training programs aimed at elevating the skills of many ghetto residents must overcome several initial disadvantages of the trainee, including little prior, successful, formal schooling, little work experience, and little confidence in job opportunities. These factors result in high training costs, but when compared with the potential increase in earnings for the trainee, they have a high payoff.

Each of the policies to raise employment levels for poverty-stricken people bumps up against a longer-run problem of a lack of investment in human capital for those living in poverty and discriminatory practices which have denied minority groups an equal opportunity for jobs even when qualified. We will return to these longer-run problems later in this chapter.

Employment programs, even if successful, will not improve the plight of nearly one-half of the urban poor. About one-fourth of the urban poor are either elderly or members of households headed by a disabled male, and another one-fourth are members of households headed by a female under 65 with dependent children.

For this one-half of the urban poor a variety of income-maintenance programs have been devised which provide income payments to individuals below the poverty level. They are transfer payments in that no work is required of the recipient. A wide spectrum of programs have been developed, including those based entirely on need and others that are based on prior contributions. The need-based programs are more commonly referred to as welfare programs and have been the subject of considerable public controversy.

The welfare (public assistance) programs are listed in Table 13-1. Of these the Aid to Families with Dependent Children (AFDC)

TABLE 13-1. *Public Assistance Programs, 1971*

Program	Number of Recipients	Average Monthly Payment per Recipient or Case
Old-Age Assistance	2,024,000	$ 77
Aid to Families with Dependent Children	10,651,000	52
Aid to the Blind	80,000	106
Aid to Permanently, Totally Disabled	1,068,000	102
General Assistance	566,000	112

SOURCE: U.S. Social and Rehabilitation Service, *Public Assistance Statistics*, monthly.

is the largest and most controversial. It is intended to help poor families with young children, primarily where the male head of the household is not present.

The disparities in the AFDC program among various geographic areas can be observed for a few selected states in Table 13-2.

TABLE 13-2. *AFDC Payments per Family in Selected States, February 1973*

State	Payments Per Family
Alabama	$ 74.77
Connecticut	248.31
Florida	95.84
Hawaii	277.43
Louisiana	90.49
Massachusetts	268.61
Mississippi	52.81
New York	274.31
Wisconsin	270.84
National average	188.86

SOURCE: *Public Assistance Statistics,* Department of Health, Education, and Welfare, Washington, D.C., February, 1973.

Poor families of four, typically a mother and three children, received an average of $274.31 per month in New York compared with $52.81 per month in Mississippi.

To correct the deficiencies and inequalities of AFDC, several reforms have been proposed, including the Family Assistance Program (FAP). FAP and similar programs are designed to provide greater work incentive. A family receiving assistance could receive a basic income payment until its income from wages and assistance reached a certain level. As the total family income continued to rise, welfare payments would decline but at a slower rate than the rise in income.

Among the variety of welfare-reform proposals, the negative income tax (NIT) has attracted the most attention. NIT is mechanically similar to FAP but is more encompassing. Its coverage would include not only poor families with children but also other impoverished groups. The workings of NIT are illustrated in Figure 13-1. Suppose that an income base of $4,000 is established for a family of four. This is the amount the family would receive even if no one in

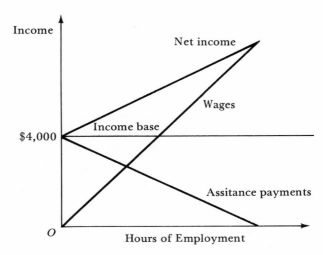

Figure 13-1   The negative income tax

the family worked.   Suppose that there is a negative-tax rate of 50 percent so that as the family's wages rise by $1.00, the amount of assistance declines by $.50.

This hypothetical situation would be universal and provide a work incentive, but it would also be expensive to provide some income support for all families with total income less than $8,000. Although this is only a hypothetical situation, it underscores a major drawback of NIT, an unacceptable cost.

Correcting the Causes of Poverty.   Explanations for poverty range from laziness to an inherent, uncorrectable character of the United States economy.   If there is a majority explanation, it centers around discrimination and a lack of human capital. Improved education and training and equal opportunity legislation have been the main policy thrusts to correct the causes of persistent poverty.

Human capital is a mixture of acquired and innate labor skills which may be marketed in exchange for income.   But there are wide disparities among individuals in the amount of embodied capital. Although a significant part of the difference reflects native ability, another important factor is unequal opportunity to acquire skills.

The acquisition of skills, of increasing the stock of human capital, depends importantly on training or education.   An expenditure for education may be considered an investment, since the increase in the individual's stock of human capital results in returns in the form of future higher earnings.

For a major segment of people in poverty there are barriers which impede the educational process. Numerous policies have been directed toward improving the situation. Since the early 1960s the federal government has rapidly expanded its role in providing job-training programs. By mid-1971 more than one million persons were enrolled in these programs, as indicated in Table 13-3.

TABLE 13-3. *Federal Manpower Programs, Fiscal Year 1970*

Program	Number Enrolled
Manpower Development and Training (MDTA)	221,000
Neighborhood Youth Corps (NYC)	482,100
Operation Mainstream	12,500
Public Service Careers	3,600
Concentrated Employment Programs (CEP)	110,100
Work Incentive Program (WIN)	92,700
JOBS	86,800
Job Corps	42,600
TOTAL	1,051,400

SOURCE: U.S. Department of Labor, *Manpower Report of the President*, 1971 (Washington, D.C.: Government Printing Office, 1971).

The Manpower Development and Training Act established in 1962 was the first full-scaled government training program. A concern for technological obsolescence of labor was the main thrust behind this effort. New skills were taught either in a formal class-room setting or in on-the-job training. The program had the potential to improve an individual's job opportunities, but matching training programs with manpower needs sometimes proved to be a difficult task.

Evaluating the impact of MDTA on unemployment and poverty is difficult because of the simultaneous influence of other factors. Some workers may have obtained training anyway. Also, employers presumably would provide the needed training for workers which were needed. If this is the case, the government may be providing training that private industry otherwise would have provided; therefore little, if any, net gain in job skills and employment is obtained. Furthermore, employers attempt to hire the best of the trainees. Usually these are not the poor, who have educational deficiencies. Of the MDTA trainees who had been receiving public assistance prior to completing the training course, 30 percent have remained unemployed. However, even with its shortcomings, MDTA has provided training for persons which allowed them to obtain jobs that raise them above the poverty level.

Another example of job training to alleviate poverty is the Work Incentive Program (WIN). This program is restricted to the public assistance program in that it is limited to adult recipients of AFDC assistance and is mandatory for them. The motive behind the program was probably more a belief that welfare recipients were trying to avoid work than it was a concern for human capital development.

Since a mismatch of people's skills and job requirements may persist even with better training programs, some have suggested that more jobs should be created by the federal government. In addition to the stimulation of aggregate demand, the government might also employ more people, particularly those in poverty. Such a program was pursued during the 1930s with the Works Progress Administration and more recently with the 1971 Emergency Employment Act.

Public service employment of this sort has the dual advantages of providing needed public services and also expanding employment opportunities. Its major criticism has been that it is make-work activity. In addition there is potential conflict between public and private markets.

Discrimination in both education and jobs is a major cause of poverty in the United States. Minority groups have a poorer educational opportunity and even with appropriate educational attainment, discriminatory barriers to employment exist.

Although a few antidiscriminatory labor-practice policies surfaced in the 1940s and 1950s, it was not until President Kennedy's executive order in March of 1961 that the federal government moved with any force to halt job discrimination. The 1961 executive order pledged the federal government to eliminate discrimination in its own agencies and, by threat of contract termination if the firms did not comply, to promote equal opportunity in all private firms that performed work for the federal government.

A second major step was taken in 1964 when Congress passed the Civil Rights Act, forbidding discrimination by corporations, unions, or other labor-market participants. The Equal Employment Opportunity Commission (EEOC) was created to enforce this act, but was given very limited enforcement power until 1972, when it received authorization to initiate court action against discriminatory practices.

Although weak enforcement of equal employment opportunities policies has blunted this effectiveness, the policies have had an impact. The greatest effect has been in improving the employment situation for minorities that have skills and education. In contrast, the unskilled minorities have experienced little improvement in their employment situation through antidiscriminatory policies.

Equal educational opportunity is at least as difficult to accomplish through policy measures as are job opportunities. Although the Supreme Court decision of Brown vs. the School Board of Topeka made intentional school segregation illegal, school integration has been difficult. Because minority groups tend to be concentrated in a few areas of a city, segregation often occurs as a result of school boundaries. Thus, *de facto* segregation continues even though *de jure* segregation is illegal. The quality of education in minority areas is poorer in no small measure because of lower financial resources to support education.

URBAN HOUSING

The amount of federal legislation dealing with housing over the past two decades leaves little doubt as to society's concern over this problem. To live in a decent home is the American's dream. This concern was outlined in the first housing act of 1949, when the National Housing Act called for "the realization as soon as feasible of the goal of a decent home and a suitable living environment for every American family." This has been the recurrent theme of all subsequent federal housing legislation. The passage of the 1968 Housing and Urban Redevelopment Act, for example, reaffirmed the place of housing as the major component in urban redevelopment and gave the highest priority to meeting the shelter needs of the underprivileged.

The Present Urban Housing Situation

One recent study[7] found that one in every eight American families cannot afford to pay the market price for standard housing.

7. "United States Housing Needs: 1968–1978" by TEMPO, General Electric's Center for Advanced Studies. Reprinted in *Urban Studies* by Louis K. Loewenstein (New York: The Free Press, 1971), pp. 346–64.

Assuming the present market price for standard housing and the arbitrary judgment that a family's housing costs should not exceed 20 percent of its income, it is not difficult to realize that an overwhelming majority of low-income families live in substandard housing units.

The Bureau of the Census has established four criteria to determine the substandard classification: (1) structural condition, (2) plumbing facilities, (3) occupation density, and (4) cost in relation to the income of the occupant. In the first instance, a housing unit is substandard if it has one or more critical structure defects (i.e., holes in the roof, substantially sagging floors, etc.). Second, the Census Bureau classifies a unit as substandard if it does not have a private toilet, a bath or shower, or if it lacks hot running water. Third, the usual measure of overcrowding is an occupancy ratio of more than one person per room. Finally, housing costs are unacceptable if they exceed 20 percent of an occupant's total income.

Judged on the basis of these indicators, recent urban-housing data indicate progress in attaining the goal of a decent home for every American family.[8] During the 1960s, the number of housing units in metropolitan areas rose from about 38.6 million to roughly 46.5 million, an increase of about 20 percent. As would be expected, the growth in the number of housing units was greater in the suburban areas than in the central cities. In the suburbs, housing units increased by 31 percent and in the central cities, 11 percent.

The growth in home building during the 1960s decreased the number of housing units lacking adequate plumbing. By 1970, only 3.5 percent of such metropolitan area homes existed (down from 9.1 percent in 1960)—significantly, the figure is the same for suburban areas. Though one would expect a difference between the figures for the two areas, three reasons account for the similarity. First, many recent urban-redevelopment programs include the construction of low-cost public housing. In fact, the 1968 Housing and Urban Redevelopment Act called for the construction of approximately 1.5 million public housing units during the period from 1969 to 1978. Though it is doubtful at this time whether Congress will appropriate sufficient funds during the 1969 to 1978 period to meet the goal of 1.5 million units by 1978, some federal funds have been used for the construction of public housing. Second, higher personal-

8. 1970 Census of Population and Housing, United States Summary, *General Demographic Trends for Metropolitan Areas, 1960 to 1970*, PHC (2)-1 (Washington: U.S. Department of Commerce, Bureau of the Census, October 1971), pp. 15–20.

income levels and recent increases in federally supported home mortgages have increased the turnover rate for housing units. As new housing construction exceeds urban population growth and the rate of increase in substandard houses, families of modest income are able to "upgrade" their living unit by moving into housing units vacated by higher-income families. Third, the percentage of substandard homes is similar in the two areas partly because the suburbs themselves also have a share of low-income families. The newer cities, Phoenix and Houston, for instance, have suburban, low-income families whose numbers tend to equalize the proportion of substandard housing units for both areas.

There was a decrease, also, in the number of overcrowded units during the 1960s. In 1960, ten percent of all occupied units in metropolitan areas had 1.01 or more persons per room. By 1970, housing units with more than one person per room decreased in the central cities (eleven to nine percent) as well as in the suburbs (ten to seven percent).

Although there was an improvement both in the quality of housing units and in the conditions of crowding during the 1960s, the cost of housing (in real terms) increased. This was true for the suburban areas as well as for the central cities, though the increase in costs was greater in the suburban areas.

In summary, urban housing has improved since the 1949 housing act. Although costs are higher, there is less crowding and there are fewer substandard units. Unfortunately, the improvements have not been great enough to put an end to the ghetto image of most inner-city neighborhoods or to ensure a feeling among the poor that things are improving.

Causes of Inadequate Urban Housing

Obviously the chief cause of inadequate urban housing is the low income level of inner-city families. If urban dwellers in areas of poor housing conditions had ample incomes, then home repairs and new dwelling starts could greatly change the housing picture. But while acknowledging the importance of family-income levels, we must also call attention to two other contributing conditions: the adverse effect of urban-housing externalities and the limiting effect of rising home-construction costs.

Externalities in Housing. A glance at urban conditions highlights obvious externalities in the urban-housing market. As long as private investors must be concerned with seeking adequate and comparative investment returns for their investments, the externalities of urban-housing investments must play a role in decisions affecting the financing of improved urban housing.

Certain indirect benefits, positive externalities, result from significant neighborhood improvements. The construction of one or more relatively expensive homes increases the value of adjacent sites. Large-lot development and neighborhood private-park developments result in similar advantages. But, by the same token, urban conditions give rise to indirect costs, negative externalities, as well. Investors must take note of the ultimate effect on their investments of such conditions as unsightly neighborhood properties, excessive noise levels created by inner-city population density, and the mixing together of sometimes incompatible social and economic groups. Doubtless such indirect costs are not intrinsic to urban America and doubtless, too, many are "social" in origin; but regardless of their nature, for many investors their existence is sufficient enough to lessen the marginal attractiveness of urban-housing investment.

A brief example highlights the effect which externalities have on the private real-estate market's influence over urban-housing conditions. Frequently private investors face the need to improve their urban properties, but frequently, also, these investors must ask if the cost of needed improvements (marginal private costs) will not exceed probable increases in value (marginal private benefit). Often such investors conclude that the potential increase in value will be offset by the negative externalities, that the outlay of $1,000 in property improvements will, because of the location of their property, add far less than that to the property's market value. Obviously, faced with such a probability, the investors are reluctant to improve their property. To be sure, if all investors in an urban area would carry out simultaneous, comparable improvements, much of the negative externalities would disappear, but the private market provides no mechanism to bring about such concerted action. Thus, the private market has a perverse effect on older neighborhoods, and it is the older neighborhoods that become the inner city's slums.

Negative externalities in housing are also operable in new-area developments. If a worker wishes to live in a new suburban-housing area near to his place of work, he will encounter difficulties if that area is one of expensive housing sites. Unless he can afford the area's prices, he will find a host of building and zoning codes that will prevent his building relatively low-cost housing in the area. Thus the homeowners in such areas, wishing to protect themselves against potential negative externalities, erect barriers that become, for potential homeowners, another source of indirect costs. The worker, deprived of such a residence site, must pay additional transportation costs to his place of work and must continue to experience other negative externalities at his inner-city residence.

Other social costs are apparent, also. The development restrictions in new areas contribute to inner-city congestion and its consequent social costs. It would be nearly impossible to compute the overall obvious and subtle costs incurred by overpopulation on city transportation systems, on increased fire and police protection, on overpopulated school systems, on public medical facilities, and on the necessarily proliferating social agencies. On the whole, the social costs resulting from discriminating land practices quite likely far exceed the private benefits for which the practices were instituted.

High-Cost Housing. The fact that about 12 percent of American families cannot afford standard housing has concerned critics of the housing industry and has led to accusations that the industry has failed to develop cost-savings techniques in home construction. This failure is blamed on the nature of the industry. Basically, the industry is characterized by many small firms which typically lack both the capital resources and the extended life expectancy requisite to a serious research and development effort, an effort that would lead to reduced costs in material and labor. The critics insist that as long as the industry is tied to labor-intensive techniques that do not reflect industrial efficiency, low-income families will be priced out of the private-housing market.

Questioning the critics' charge of inefficiency is a recent study[9] of housing which concludes that the housing industry operates with greater efficiency and response to innovation than is commonly thought. The study noted that one major reason for high costs is the nature of the external constraints which affect the construction industries. There are, for instance, approximately 23 major public and private direct participants in the production process (some involved in more than one phase) and approximately 17 major public

9. "United States Housing Needs: 1968–1978" by TEMPO, General Electrics Center for Advanced Studies. Reprinted in *Urban Studies* by Louis K. Loewenstein, ed. (New York: The Free Press, 1971), pp. 346–64.

and private sources of laws, rules, and practices that restrict and influence the process practically every step of the way.

A concluding comment comes from a recent report by the Advisory Commission on Intergovernmental Relations[10] in which the commission summarized the most frequent charges concerning building codes:

1. Local building codes extensively regulate construction by determining building material restrictions rather than by setting performance requirements, and thus tend to favor traditional products and methods over product innovations that might perform as well or better at less cost.
2. The extreme decentralization of building-code agencies makes it possible for small enclaves to restrict the use of new building materials and construction methods and to add, thereby, to the cost of urban housing.
3. The best-intentioned local governing body, if it lacks access to objective technical advice, cannot detect regulative proposals designed to favor particular construction projects or labor practices and groups.
4. Builders and developers incur considerable expense in tracing out and complying with the great diversity of local regulations.

The commission's investigation into home-construction costs concluded that the substantial diversity in building codes within the same urban area hampers large-scale home construction and standard marketing approaches. The commission further noted that the typical small-volume home builder is a critical factor in high-cost home construction.

Better Housing

The National Housing Act of 1949 established a national goal of "a decent home and a suitable living environment for every American family." But this proved to be an elusive goal. The approach was both inadequate and inappropriate to meet or even make reasonable progress toward the ambitious goal. Nearly 20 years later, the Housing and Urban Development Act recognized the nonattainment of the 1949 goal.

Improving the housing situation requires two types of policy

10. Advisory Commission on Intergovernmental Relations, *Urban America and the Federal System* (Washington: U.S. Govermnent Printing Office, October 1969), p. 54.

orientations: one to retard, if not reverse, the current degradation of existing housing and another to add new units to the housing stock. After a brief look at housing conservation, policies to increase the housing supply will be considered in four main groups:

1. Taxes—primarily property taxes which affect housing investment and its maintenance
2. Subsidies—financial assistance in the construction of housing and rent
3. Credit—cheaper and more readily available credit
4. Construction costs—elements which reduce construction costs, such as elimination of burdensome housing codes, and which encourage cost-reducing construction practices

Housing Conservation. The stock and growth of housing is often influenced by existing taxes, building codes, zoning, and related policies. Although these effects are generally unintentional and indirect, significant disincentives exist for property maintenance and improvements which, if corrected, would aid in the conservation of the existing housing stock.

Foremost among the barriers to conserving housing stock is the property tax. Estimates indicate that average property taxes represent the equivalent of a 25 percent sales tax on housing consumption and range as high as 35 percent in some of the heavily urbanized areas of the Northeast, Great Lakes, and West. This tax is particularly burdensome to the lower-income groups, who do not receive the federal tax advantages because they are primarily renters.

Considerable evidence suggests that property improvements increase the owner's property-tax bill more than in proportion to the value of the improvements. If this additional cost is not recovered in higher rents, thereby preserving the return on investment, disincentive to improve or repair property results. In many situations property taxes serve as a penalty for property improvement, and deterioration occurs. Removing such a disincentive would help conserve the existing stock of housing.

Taxes. As suggested above, the property tax is in part related to the income tax. Property taxes are deductible in calculating federal taxes. But income taxes tend to be progressive (rise as a percentage of income), resulting in a comparatively favorable treatment for high-income families and a comparatively unfavorable treatment of low-income families because of the allowable property-tax deduction.

In addition, low-income families tend to be renters and the net impact on renters is unfavorable compared with home owners.

Property taxes have the additional effect of discouraging housing construction in central cities and encouraging it in the suburbs. Suburban homeowners have their property taxes more directly tied to the services they receive, but central-city property taxes go to support a diverse group of services that are not perceived by the resident as a direct benefit to him.

The recognition that taxes have an impact on housing leads to tax policies designed to improve housing. The most obvious of such policies is to reduce property taxes. Since the help is needed at the lower end of the income scale, property taxes could be reduced or eliminated on lower-income and even middle-income housing. The federal government and some states have moved toward such policies. Many have argued that property-tax reductions should be on a broad scale rather than selective, in anticipation that private investors will respond by providing more housing.

Subsidies. Although European governments had been in the housing subsidy business for some time, the United States did not embark on such a program until the 1930s and then only on a small scale. But in the subsequent 40 years government subsidization of housing greatly expanded.

Three forms of subsidy are most common. First, the government may finance the construction of new housing and rent the property or provide it free after it is completed. Second, subsidization of private-sector construction can also serve to increase supply and lower the cost of housing. Third, rent subsidies may be provided to low-income families to enable them to secure better-quality housing.

The United States Housing Act of 1937 enabled the federal government to subsidize housing for low-income persons. By 1950, when the 1949 National Housing Act replaced it, 202,000 units had been built. The federal housing effort was greatly expanded with the 1949 act, which set a goal of 800,000 units in a six-year span. The program was carried out through a local housing authority which issued bonds for the housing, and the federal government subsidized the interest costs and repayment. Rental charges, scaled to the income of the residents, were to pay operating costs.

The program fell far below its goal with fewer than 600,000 units built in the 20 years following the passage of the act. Although the reluctance of Congress to appropriate funds was an obvious cause of the shortfall, several other factors were underlying.

Conflicts in the location of the subsidized housing were numerous. Land was most abundant in the suburbs and outlying areas, but opposition to low-income housing was encountered by the predominantly middle-income residents in these areas. Such conflicts were intensified with a racial overtone when blacks and other minority groups needed an increasing share of the low-income housing units. Alternately, the construction of housing in areas of dilapidated housing in the inner city would necessitate temporary, if not permanent, displacement of areas to be renewed. An additional objection to rebuilding ghettos and slums is spatial segregation of the poor.

The problems associated with finding satisfactory locations for housing projects created a program of high-rise housing units providing as many units as possible on one site. Since high-rise units generally have higher building costs, construction funds provided fewer units.

The 1949 act, in addition to providing subsidies for low-rent housing, subsidized land acquisition in blighted areas for urban renewal. Local governments would purchase and clear the land in blighted areas and transfer it to private developers or public agencies for redevelopment. The new developer would generally buy the land for one-fourth the cost of the land and site-clearing costs. The federal government would pay two-thirds of the difference or "write-down."

Although a part of the 1949 act, urban renewal was not primarily intended to increase the supply of housing but rather to improve deteriorating neighborhoods through a change in land-use patterns. In fact, urban renewal has brought a net loss in housing units. This occurred either because industrial or commercial uses replaced run-down housing or because the displaced housing was very high-density and was replaced by lower-density housing developments.

A relatively new form of housing subsidy is the rent supplement. Under a program enacted in 1965, families eligible for assistance pay 25 percent of their incomes as rent and the federal government makes up the difference to the landlord. This approach has several advantages over public housing projects. Economic segregation is less likely because of a greater choice in residence.

Families are not forced to move if their income rises above the minimum level as with public project housing. Also, the program is tied to family needs as reflected in their income.

Credit. Policies designed to reduce interest costs and improve the availability of credit have been the most popular of the various policies. The subsidization is indirect and less visible, thereby evoking less controversy than direct construction subsidies. Also, everyone may benefit from the credit policies, not just the poor.

The primary form of government credit policy has been the guaranteeing or insuring of mortgages. This policy created a national credit market which greatly increased the supply of funds and lowered the risk and interest rates. Mortgage funds could move with minimum risk across the nation. A financial institution in one location can invest funds in house construction at another location because of the government's underwriting of the risk.

The contrast of the mortgage-guarantee programs with the earlier situation is striking. Prior to the Federal Housing Administration (FHA) in 1934, down payments were usually one-half or more of the purchase price of the house. The mortgage was generally for five years. If the mortgage was not paid off in that time, refinancing was necessary and sometimes not available. The FHA and related programs have lowered down payments to ten percent or less and extended mortgages to 20 years or more. The influence of the FHA and Veterans Administration loan policies caused conventional mortgages to be comparable. Conventional mortgages are the dominant credit source today.

Although the mortgage-guarantee programs have been popular, they have had little direct impact on increasing the accessibility of housing for low-income families. Few families with incomes below the median family income (one-half the nation's families) can afford a single-family house with FHA, VA, or conventional financing.

To penetrate the lower-income-housing mortgage market, the federal government created the Federal National Mortgage Association (FNMA). FNMA borrows funds to be reloaned at interest rates lower than private-market rates. States and cities have followed similar practices of borrowing at lower interest rates which they are able to obtain. The funds were then reloaned to individual borrowers and builders. The interest saving is significant and results in lower mortgage payments for individuals and lower rent for renters. Government borrowing of this sort is not without its costs. The primary one is the effect that additional government borrowing has on interest rates generally. The additional government demand for investment funds tends to drive up interest rates, thereby increasing the costs of other types of construction.

A further step which has been taken by the government to assist housing construction and acquisition involves providing loans at rates below those paid by the government to borrow the funds. Such a policy tends to reach further into the lower-income groups, where the housing needs are most acute.

Construction and Land Costs. Since housing costs prevent a high portion of the population from acquiring adequate housing, can the government pursue policies which will reduce costs? Several approaches, aimed at different cost components of housing, have been tried or suggested.

In order to understand the necessity for a multifaceted-policy approach, a review of housing costs and influences is desirable. Construction costs are typically divided into 20 percent on-site labor costs, 35–40 percent materials, and 35–40 percent for land costs, overhead, profit, architects fees, and miscellaneous costs. Little advance has been made in productivity in construction in the last 20 years. Estimates indicate that construction productivity has increased less than 1 percent annually compared with 2.5 to 3.0 percent for the economy as a whole. But even if more dramatic productivity increases had been accomplished, mortgage repayments from land and construction costs represent only about one-half of the total monthly housing cost of a resident. Even large declines in construction costs will have a small impact on the total housing expenditure necessary by the house owner or renter. This is not to discourage policies which could lead to lower construction costs, but rather to indicate that substantial reductions in overall costs require reductions in other costs such as builder's markups, taxes, maintenance, and utilities.

Local-government policy has generally not been conducive to cost reduction. Zoning and building codes have discouraged innovations which might bring lower costs. Reliance on the property tax has encouraged such policies. Local governments try to encourage high-value housing development where the property-tax yield will be at least as high as the additional public-service costs of the residents of the new housing. Zoning and building codes, although not originally intended for this purpose, have been used to restrict lower-income housing development which tends to add more to the public-service load, particularly education, than is received in property-tax revenue. This rather natural response of local government discourages housing cost reduction via policies which promote high-value housing. Large lot sizes, for instance, are encouraged.

Efforts to shift the financial base of local governments away from the property tax will alleviate some of this difficulty. Revenue sharing has this capability. Another policy shift would be in the direction of regional land-use policies which would discourage such zoning practices.

Building codes also deter housing-cost reductions. In most cases local building codes were established with good intentions, but new techniques are difficult to introduce because of outmoded building codes. Attempts to change the codes often encounter resistance from vested-interest groups, mainly contractors and building-trade unions.

Changes in building codes are a necessity for adaption of new building technology. Current trends are favorable despite the above mentioned difficulties.

For summary and selected readings, see the end of the next chapter.

14

The Economics of Urban Transportation and Pollution

In this chapter, as we turn to the problems of urban transportation and pollution, the discussion once again focuses on the externality issue. A discussion of various policy measures concludes each section.

URBAN TRANSPORTATION

An urban transportation problem exists because we have developed an urban structure where we "move mostly at the same time and mostly to and from the same place. . . ."[1] Increasingly, we do this in the comfort and speed of our private automobiles. Wilbur Thompson describes our intracity travels as "an experience to be done with as quickly as possible. . . ."[2] Thus he notes that speed becomes the main objective, and traffic the main problem.

Demand for Urban Transportation

The growth of urban areas has had an obvious effect upon the demand for urban transportation. As mentioned in Chapter 11,

1. Wilbur Thompson, *A Preface to Urban Economics* (Baltimore: The Johns Hopkins Press, 1965), p. 333.
2. *Ibid.*

approximately 74 percent (or 236.4 million) of the estimated 320 million persons who will populate this country by 2000 will be living in major metropolitan areas (or urban regions). This means, generally speaking, that the urban population will at least double during the 40-year period from 1960 to 2000.

But the demand for urban transportation is expected to more than double during this same period.[3] In 1960, the total vehicle-miles driven in urban areas was about 331.6 million. By as early as 1980, however, that total will increase about 2⅓ times the 1960 figure, or to about 770.3 million vehicle-miles. As personal incomes increase and as the income inelasticity of services affecting urban transportation increases, a higher proportion of household income will be used for entertainment and recreation. This means additional trips and an increase in demand for urban transportation. The demand will increase as more and more urban workers will require transportation to and from their employment.

Mass Transportation. Because of the war, the total demand for inter- and intracity mass transportation by rail, trolley coach, and motor bus reached an all time high in 1945 with about 23.2 million passengers. By 1970, the figure had declined to less than 8 million.[4] Although these figures include inter- and intracity trips, they are suggestive of the substantial drop in the demand for urban mass transportation as urban travelers have shifted to private automotive transportation. This shift closely parallels the movement of households to the low-density, single-dwelling suburban areas and reflects the suburban householder's preference for the flexibility in transportation which the automobile provides.

Present mass-transportation technology is best suited for high-density areas that have a uniform pattern of demand. A low-density area poses a problem of collection and delivery. For instance, commuter trains or even buses cannot collect riders on a door-to-door basis in a residential area of single-family housing units and then deposit them at their individual destinations. Also, commuters seem unwilling to forego the extra time required to commute on a mass-transit system as compared to the travel time for private vehicles. This attitude is underscored in a study of the price elasticity of demand

3. Committee for Economic Development. *Developing Metropolitan Transportation Policies*, April 1965, p. 21.
4. American Transit Association, *Transit Fact Book*, annual report (Washington: U.S. Government Printing Office).

for urban transporation.[5] The study suggests that the cross-elasticity of demand between the private automobile and the public transportation system might be so low that actual cash payments would have to be made to automobile users to induce any considerable number to shift from private vehicles to mass transportation systems.

Even if train stations are strategically located in residential areas, commuter trains may have to reach speeds over 80 miles an hour between some stations in order to compete with the private automobile traveling at 30 miles an hour. Under present technology and with the low-density patterns of most cities, such speeds are impossible. Moreover, the use of train stations requires the need for some kind of transportation to them. The private automobile would likely be used here, and the incentive would be strong to continue the journey to the final destination by private automobile.

Similar problems are confronted at the commuters' destinations. Urban decentralization has greatly lengthened that portion of the trip between arrival at the transportation system's terminal and the commuter's arrival at his final destination. Consequently, the lengthening of the trip from the terminal to a destination has made the whole transit ride less attractive.

Finally, the greatest demand for urban transportation reflects commuters' work schedules and comes during a two-hour period in the morning and again during a two-hour period in the afternoon. Such a concentration of demand means that for many transit companies 80 percent or more of the volume of travel takes place in 20 hours of the week. The expansion of a mass-transit system's capacity to handle peak loads means that much of the capacity will be under-utilized most of the time, and this situation leads to high operating costs for the mass-transit system.

In summary, today's major mode of urban transportation is the private automobile. We should not, however, overlook the importance of mass transit, for it still moves 30 percent or more of the total number of commuters during the peak periods in large metropolitan areas. On balance, though, the demand for mass transit in urban areas has declined as the demand for private-vehicle transportation has increased.

Automobile Transportation. Estimated 1980 motor vehicle registration figures indicate the growing demand for private-automobile

5. Leon N. Moses and Harold F. Williamson, Jr. "Value of Time, Choice of Mode, and the Subsidy Issue in Urban Transportation," *Journal of Political Economy*, No. 71 (June 1963), pp. 247–264.

travel. By 1980, registrations will grow from the 1960 figure of 73.8 million to 120 million. Of the latter figure, 100.6 million will be the 1980 registration of private automobiles. Thus, by 1980, Americans will register automobiles at a rate of one for every two people. In 1960, the comparable figure was one for every 2.4 persons.[6]

As long as family incomes continue to rise and as long as urban residents prefer low-density residential living, an increase in the use of the private automobile relative to mass transportation is inevitable under present competitive conditions. In addition, urban-transportation specialists see little change in urban-transit technology during the next 20 or more years.[7] This is understandable in light of the continuation of the urban sprawl, which seems to impose an impregnable technological barrier to the development of mass transportation that is competitive with the privacy, convenience, flexibility, speed, and prestige of the private automobile.

The Cost of Urban Transportation

As mentioned in Chapter 12, there are two kinds of costs— private and social, and the difference between these is the negative externalities of the production and consumption of an item. Similarly, there are two kinds of benefits—social and private. The difference between these is considered positive externalities.

If substantial negative or positive externalities exist in providing urban transportation and the marginal social cost is not equal to the marginal social benefit at the present level of output, then the efficiency in the allocation of economic resources to urban transportation has not been achieved.

This section will examine urban transportation to see if it has become economically efficient in these terms. We shall begin with a discussion of the social cost of urban automobile transportation and resource allocation. This is followed by a discussion of urban mass transportation and pricing.

Cost of Urban Automotive Transportation. The vast resources that must be channeled into the construction of urban highways, streets, and parking areas in order to meet the needs of the private vehicle for

6. Committee for Economic Development, *Developing Metropolitan Transportation Policies*, April 1965, p. 21.
7. Louis K. Loewenstein (ed.), *Urban Studies* (New York: The Free Press, 1971), p. 419.

the next several decades raises serious doubts in the minds of public officials and concerned citizens as to the desirability of such investments. The cost of building urban freeways in the interstate system has averaged $3.7 million per mile.[8] Such excessive construction costs for urban highways are due to a number of factors. First, the high-density problem of urban areas necessitates the elevating or tunnelling of much of the roadbed. Second, the construction of continuous-travel entry and exit ramps in the central business districts requires vast amounts of expensive land. Finally, urban highways are even more expensive because they must be built to accommodate rush-hour traffic rather than the less expensive normal-time traffic flows.

The figure of $3.7 million per mile is a direct cost of urban automobile transportation. But there are also *indirect costs* (negative externalities). Such costs are seen, for example, in the construction of a limited-access freeway. With limited access, certain parts of the city are directly cut off from nearby areas. This leads to increased travel in affected areas and a possible reduction in market and sales areas for some businesses. More obvious is the indirect cost to an urban community when businesses and households must move to make way for the construction of the freeway, a move which results in increased unemployment for inner-city residents and the resulting problems of unemployment for the community. The removal of housing units also aggravates the problem of inadequate urban housing. Still another kind of indirect cost to the community is the loss of tax revenue through the removal of private real estate, revenue which is desperately needed to finance the cities' growing public needs. Finally, automobile emission pollution must be considered an indirect cost to the urban community. To say the least, automobiles are a prime contributor to the economic costs of air pollution in America's inner cities.

Additional economic costs of automotive transportation are the private owner's automotive costs. Although the private owner generally sees only the immediate cost of such out-of-pocket expenses as money for gas, oil, and possibly parking fees, a more responsible view would also consider the expenditures for depreciation, insurance, registration, and taxes. The overall cost of private ownership, then, comes to a quite considerable average of 16 cents per mile to drive and maintain a standard size late model car for ten years. However, as long as the motorist considers only the obvious costs, he will

8. *Ibid.*, p. 437.

believe that the cost of operating an automobile is quite competitive with the rates charged by public modes of transportation. When other factors, such as convenience, speed, privacy, and social prestige are added, it is understandable why the private vehicle is the most preferred form of urban transportation.

The gasoline taxes paid by the motorist are frequently used to finance the construction and maintenance of streets and highways, and other taxes include vehicle property taxes, registration fees, and tolls. Contrary to common belief, urban motorists as a group actually pay more in user taxes than all direct urban highway and street costs. Although it is true that some municipalities use general tax funds to pay for local streets, this is no indication that urban highway users are subsidized. Rather, it suggests the existence of problems in the intragovernmental handling of funds. Incidentally, an argument for shifting a portion of general tax funds to urban highway and street construction can be made, since the construction of urban highways and streets provides access to the abutting properties and increases the site value of these properties.

It is apparent, then, that a considerable cost is expended for private-automobile transportation. It remains to be seen if these urban, automobile, transportation costs represent an efficient allocation of resources, that is, if marginal social cost equals marginal social benefit. The graphic analysis of marginal costs and benefits discussed in Chapter 12 will be used here. The private costs have been identified as out-of-pocket costs plus the costs of depreciation, insurance, and taxes. As already mentioned, the taxes paid by automobile owners and users adequately finance all direct urban highway and street costs. Social costs include all private costs plus such indirect costs as business and household relocation costs, job displacement costs, and pollution costs.

Figure 14-1 shows the relationships between marginal private cost, marginal social cost, and marginal social benefit. Urban highway and street capacity is measured along the horizontal axis, where capacity is measured on the basis of (a) the number of vehicles accommodated per hour per lane, and (b) the average speed of the vehicles. Benefits and costs of automobile transportation are measured along the vertical axis.

The marginal-social-benefit curve for varying levels of highway and street capacity is shown as a downward-sloping curve and is assumed to be equal to marginal private benefit. Admittedly, there may be certain indirect social benefits associated with urban auto-

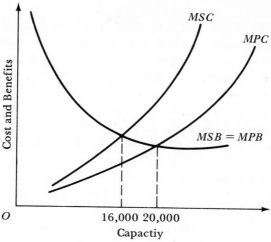

Figure 14-1 Negative externalities of urban automobile transportation

mobile transportation. Such indirect benefits would be indicated by showing the marginal-social-benefit curve to lie above the marginal-private-benefit curve. However, in order to simplify our analysis, we have simply assumed that marginal social benefit equals marginal private benefit.

The marginal-private-cost curve is shown to be an upward-sloping curve to indicate that each additional unit of capacity costs more than the previous unit. The marginal-social-cost curve is shown to "pull" away from the marginal-private-cost curve in an upward direction. Though indirect costs are difficult to measure, it seems reasonable to assume that the difference between marginal social cost and marginal private cost will increase with higher levels of capacity. The basic reason for this difference is due to the relationship between capacity and its negative impact upon the community. For instance, the construction of an eight-lane urban freeway will have a greater disruptive effect upon the community than the construction of a street.

In Figure 14-1, consider that the actual allocation of resources to urban highways and streets yields a combined capacity of 20,000 units. At this level, marginal private benefit is equal to marginal private cost (and marginal social benefit). In this situation, an overallocation of resources to urban highway and street construction has occurred since marginal social cost exceeds marginal social benefit. Marginal social cost equals marginal social benefit at 16,000 units of capacity, the efficient level of resource allocation.

Charging a user fee based on social costs (and not private costs) would increase the cost of automobile transportation to something more than 16 cents per mile and would encourage present users to reduce unnecessary vehicle trips or shift to less expensive modes of travel such as buses or rail systems.

Although it can be argued that substantial indirect costs do exist in urban automotive transportation and that they lead to an overallocation of resources to urban automotive transportation, it is quite another matter to measure these indirect costs. How does one, for example, accurately measure the undesirable effects of nearby freeway traffic? Or how can one measure the loss in receipts and jobs that result from the construction of a nearby six-lane limited-access freeway? It is extremely difficult, if not impossible, to measure accurately such indirect costs, because they are largely deceptive. The fact remains, nevertheless, that where indirect costs are substantial, there will be a considerable overallocation of resources.

Before turning to the cost and pricing of mass transportation, we need to discuss briefly the matter of discriminatory pricing in the use of urban highways. Presently, the user-fee system of financing urban highways and streets does not differentiate between the peak-period user and others. But clearly, when highways are built to handle the maximum loads of rush hours, their costs are greater than they would be if they were built to accommodate only "normal-hour" traffic loads. This additional cost, the proponents of discriminatory pricing systems argue, should be passed on to those who use the highways during the peak traffic periods. Thus, they argue, if a four-lane urban highway is adequate to handle the typical offpeak-period demand and an additional two lanes are built to handle peak-period traffic, the additional construction costs should be reflected in a higher user fee charged to peak-period travelers.

Such variable-fee systems, as they relate to the use of urban highways and streets, raise at least two interesting questions. First, how does one actually determine capacity requirements for peak-period demand and for offpeak-period demand? Capacity, we previously mentioned, is measured on the basis of (a) the number of vehicles per lane accommodated in an hour, and (b) the average speed of the vehicles. This means that different combinations of vehicles accommodated and average speeds will give the same level of capacity. For example, a figure of 1400 to 1500 vehicles per hour per lane at an average of 40 to 50 miles per hour may give the same capacity measure as 1700 to 1800 vehicles per hour per lane at an average speed of 30 to 35 miles per hour. In view of the relationship between the number of vehicles accommodated and their average speed, it is possible that offpeak-period users may demand the same (or about the same) level of capacity as peak-period users.

Second, would a variable-fee system create a different system of inequities? If the user fee were substantial enough, those who have control over their own work schedules, the higher-income workers, could avoid the fees by traveling at times other than the peak periods; consequently the higher-user fees would be borne by lower-income workers, those who cannot determine their own work schedules.

One final difficulty with discriminatory pricing is that it does not have the full blessing of government. In fact, there are laws against extreme versions of such practices. The general official feeling, as reflected in legislation, seems to be that price discrimination is justifiable only when there is some underlying cost justification. Since it is difficult to measure capacity as it relates to demand for periods of peak use and offpeak use, the argument of cost differences may be more theoretic than actual.

Pricing of Urban Mass Transportation. Some criticism has been voiced about the discriminatory nature of present fee-charging systems in mass transportation when rush-hour travelers oftentimes pay a lower average fee than that paid by the offpeak-period traveler. Some transportation companies, for instance, sell books of tickets at prices below the cost of those tickets purchased individually. Obviously the system works to the advantage of the frequent ticket user since others use the tickets too seldom to make book purchases feasible. The critics of the system consider the pricing to be excessively discriminatory.

The critics find it ironic, too, that the mass-transit companies give price advantages to the very customers who have been most responsible for the high operating costs of such transportation systems. Since these systems must be built to facilitate rush-hour commuter flows, they necessarily incur much greater costs than they would otherwise. Thus, say the critics, those who create the costs pay less than their share of them. Frequently, the total operating cost of a mass-transit company's operation exceeds the company's revenue. For example, during the 1962 to 1963 fiscal year the New York City Transit Authority incurred a deficit of $146.1 million, which was largely attributable to the substantial fixed costs which resulted from

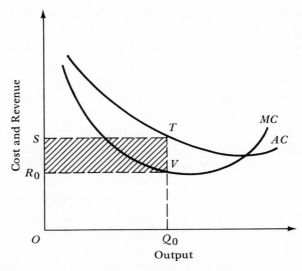

Figure 14-2   Marginal cost pricing for public transportation

building capacity to meet the peak-period demand.[9] Such evidence, the critics argue, shows that the peak-period user of mass transportation is not paying the incremental cost of the service which he demands during peak periods—a problem similar to that encountered when urban highways are built to meet peak-period demands. What is needed, say the critics, is a system of incremental cost-pricing.

The principle of incremental cost-pricing in mass transportation can best be understood with the use of a simple diagram. Such a diagram will also make apparent that whenever scale economies are realized in mass transportation, the practice of incremental cost-pricing will actually result in a deficit. Figure 14-2 shows a user fee of R_0 set by a transit company. When incremental cost-pricing principles are applied, the transit company will provide Q_0 in mass-transit service, the point at which marginal cost (incremental cost) equals price (rate). But the total operating cost at a level of Q_0 is S and, since the revenue from Q_0 amount of service is only R_0, a deficit of R_0STV is realized.

One possible solution to the problem is to subsidize the transit company by the amount of R_0STV. From a purely economic standpoint, the subsidization is justified since it is only through this that the consuming public can reap the full benefits of scale economies.

9. Committee for Economic Development, *Developing Metropolitan Transportation Policies*, April 1965, p. 75.

Benefit-Cost Analysis of Urban Transportation

The purpose of urban transportation is to transport individuals and goods between geographic points. The ultimate impact of the overall urban transportation system of streets, highways, and rail lines is its influence upon the locational development of the basic components of an urban region, i.e., its retail and service centers, industrial parks, and residential areas.

A city's transportation system represents, in large part, the long-term development of its users' preferences for the different modes of transportation. Since new preferences are constantly arrived at, transportation systems undergo continuous change, a change that ultimately results in specific modifications in urban land-use. Some of these changes have adverse effects upon certain groups. The construction of a freeway may improve access to the downtown area for residents living in a distant suburb, but its construction means that some households and businesses must move from their present location. Thus, an indirect consequence of the construction of the freeway is a social cost to those who are required to leave their established places of residence and business and look for new location sites.

What is implied here is that urban transportation is a public good primarily because of the various spillover effects connected with its development and use. In order to approach an optimum urban transportation system, all the indirect costs and benefits connected with urban transportation need to be considered along with its direct costs and benefits. Obviously, many of the indirect costs and benefits are difficult to measure, but an awareness of their existence is a step in the right direction. Hopefully, better estimating procedures can be developed.

Once all indirect and direct costs and benefits can be measured, the general rule for allocating resources to alternative proposed transportation systems is simple. Investments should be made in those transportation alternatives which provide the greatest relative benefits at the least relative costs, that is, the transportation system should maximize net social benefits.

Finally, the benefit-cost analysis approach to urban transportation requires the full cooperation of all political units of urban government. At present, it is doubtful if this kind of cooperation is possible—a topic of discussion in the next chapter.

Improving Urban Transportation

"You can't get there from here" is both a title of an Ogden Nash book of poems and an exaggerated description of the urban transportation system. Nash is humorous, a clogged urban highway is not. Access in a city is a paramount urban problem which has several ramifications depending on the vantage point of the viewer. A city's resident is concerned with access to and from work, shopping, services, recreation, and friends. A businessman sees transportation as an influence on business potential and land values. To a planner, transportation is the network which is interrelated with housing, poverty, industrial land use, and similar interrelated factors forming the structure of the city.

The economist, as indicated at the beginning of this chapter, views the urban transportation problem from a combined perspective. How can the service be provided efficiently and equitably? Sizeable externalities have developed in transportation services which are the distortion of these criteria. In an effort to alleviate this situation, numerous policies have been designed, generally in two categories: pricing policies and subsidies.

Pricing Policies. As indicated in an earlier section of this chapter, the pricing of transportation in urban areas contributes to the congestion and other inadequacies. The existing transportation facilities are the product of past decisions, so that in the short run an improvement in transportation is concerned with more efficient utilization of existing facilities.

The problem of traffic congestion is essentially a problem of externalities, where the social costs of additional users of the transportation structure exceed the private costs incurred by those users. Several pricing strategies to alleviate this situation have been suggested. Each recognizes the necessity to ration existing capacity, particularly at certain times of the day.

From Figure 14-1 it is apparent that increasing congestion is associated with a divergence of marginal social costs from marginal social benefits. This divergence continues to exist until marginal private costs and marginal private benefits are equal.

In order to reduce the use level during the times of day when such an externality exists, price can be used as a rationing device. If marginal social benefits are known or can be estimated, a price could be charged reflecting the difference between marginal social cost and marginal private cost. The price would be higher during the heavy-use time of day and would drop to zero during the times of day when use is low, so that there are no externalities.

The charges to users during peak periods would have several potential consequences. Motorists may shift from the toll roads to other streets, increasing the congestion on them. There would also be an incentive to switch to public transportation because of the new relative prices. Car pooling would also be encouraged. All of these potential shifts have the effect of reducing the flow on major congested expressways during peak periods.

The imposition of prices to more efficiently allocate existing transportation facilities is not without its drawbacks. One such criticism involves the administrative costs. Toll collection is not only expensive but reduces the flow of traffic. New developments in automatic toll collection may reduce this problem, but the problem of measuring the indirect costs and corresponding appropriate charges is particularly difficult. Experimentation with different charges seems to be the best alternative.

An equity argument has also been raised against increased road-user charges. It is argued that low-income persons will be less able to pay the higher charges. But the majority of the poor reside in the central city, and those that travel to jobs not in the central city are traveling in the opposite direction of the heavy flow at peak times.

Other forms of rationing, in addition to price, are also possible. Physical controls, staggered work hours, and downtown parking rates are a few of the major ones. The latter has been used with some success as an indirect form of price-rationing device. Higher parking rates, although providing less than an optimal solution, have tended to discourage some of the flow into the downtown area.

Short-run price policies of the sort suggested above can have some significant long-run effects. Employees may seek to avoid the higher costs associated with peak-hour traffic by seeking jobs in the suburbs, by preferring offhour job schedules, or by seeking higher wages to compensate for these higher transportation costs. Such decisions may exert a decentralizing effect on downtown businesses, which may alleviate some of the congestion but also may shift it elsewhere.

Subsidies. An alternative to price policy in encouraging short-run efficiency is subsidization. Subsidies of public transportation have been justified as a means of shifting automobile users to public trains and buses.

Since negative externalities are present on automobile expressways during peak-hour congestion, it has been suggested that government can justifiably subsidize other transportation modes to reduce these negative externalities. Since private-automobile users are not paying full cost, public transit systems should be subsidized as well.

The current extent of subsidization of transport systems is difficult to assess. There is a bias toward highway development, but even with such bias, highway-users taxes and related revenue are roughly equal to the amount spent for highways. But peak-hour highway users are in effect subsidized by offpeak users and users of other parts of the urban highway network.

The case for subsidization of public transportation systems rests heavily on the negative externalities of highway development, including air pollution, land use, and urban expansion.

POLLUTION

We sometimes fail to realize that the earth's biological system has polluted the environment since the beginning of time. In the cycle of life—birth, reproduction, and death—materials are consumed and then returned to the environment as waste materials. We also fail to realize that the earth's capacity to absorb waste materials is not infinite, a point made with increasing frequency by alarmed environmentalists. Their basic concern is the relation between man's increasing capacity to produce waste materials and the limited capacity of the earth to assimilate them.

Law of Conservation of Matter

As applied to production and consumption, the law of conservation of matter means that the mass of material used in the economy's production processes will ultimately result in a roughly equivalent mass of material wastes. The waste materials which stem from production plus the waste materials from consumption equal the weight of the basic inputs (minerals, fuels, water) used in the production of the goods and services.

The Pollution Problem

A pollution problem exists when total waste materials (effluent) exceed the environment's capacity to absorb or assimilate these materials. The problem arises when three conditions occur in combination: (1) a sufficient amount of goods and services are produced and consumed; (2) these goods and services are of particular kinds; and (3) the production and consumption of these goods and services are geographically concentrated.

Quantity of Goods and Services. Because the mass of materials used in the economy's production processes will ultimately result in a roughly equivalent mass of material wastes, pollution can occur only when goods are produced in sufficient quantities. The more affluent we become, the more we have to throw away as waste materials; thus, an affluent society is also an effluent society. It has been estimated that each American has about 50 times the negative impact on the earth's life support system as does the average citizen of India.

Kinds of Goods and Services Produced. Effluence is also related to the kinds of goods and services produced. A growing number of new items produced each year are not biodegradable, i.e., are not readily broken down into easily digestible or disposable by-products. Consider, for example, the increasing number of items that are either shipped in or contain some amount of synthetic material.

Geographic Concentration. Finally, the geographic concentration of producers and consumers is a major factor of pollution. The nation's technological progress and general economic prosperity have transformed our once rural landscape into a highly urbanized one. Chapter 10 indicated, for instance, that over 70 percent of the nation's population lives in urban areas. Such a concentration creates conditions where the emission of pollutants exceeds the capacity of the environment to dispose of these waste materials. In recent years, the urban pollution problem has been illustrated in various ways. We have estimated our volume of pollution or we have estimated our social costs from pollution; we have even satirically summed it up as in New York Magazine:[10]

"Beyond its natural loveliness, pollution serves the city of New York in so many ways. It helps keep the city from becoming overpopu-

10. Dick Schaap, *New York Magazine* (April 15, 1968).

lated, it insures that only the fittest survive and the rest move to the suburbs. It helps keep the city from becoming overgrown with foliage; it kills roses and tulips and other harmful weeds. It provides employment for window washers and car washers and eager little shoeshine boys. And it saves money; it provides all the joys of cigarette smoking without the expenses."

Obviously, a less concentrated population would alleviate urban pollution problems and their consequent social costs. Unfortunately, however, the case is one of mixed blessings. If we sought to disperse our population, we would lose the economic advantages which are characteristic of urbanized agglomerative economies. Cities such as New York provide businesses with very specialized services not found in smaller areas, and industries that are highly dependent on those specialized services gain from locating in an area rich in agglomerative economies. Thus, a movement away from the concentrated areas may help stem pollution, but it would do so at the expense of some agglomeration economies. The basic question, then, must pose the alternatives: Do the benefits of agglomeration economies exceed the social costs of urban pollution? Unfortunately, little comparative data are available.

Limitations of the Market

It has repeatedly been mentioned that geographic concentration tends to increase the extent of externalities. We saw this to be the case with urban transportation and with urban housing. Clearly, too, pollution in our urban areas creates greater negative externalities than does pollution in nonurban areas. The pollution from a few automobiles and the waste materials from one or two small factories in a small community create fewer negative externalities because the rural environment is capable of handling that degree of pollution. But, if the same number of cars and factories is added to an already concentrated area, the negative effects of the additional pollution would be substantial. As Figure 14-3 illustrates, net social benefits are maximized at an output level of Q', which represents a substantial reduction in pollution, but it also represents a substantial reduction in the firm's profits. Ways which government can intervene in the market in order to reduce pollution to a level where net social benefits are maximized will be discussed next.

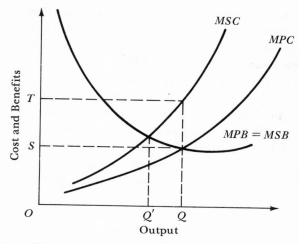

Figure 14-3   Negative externalities of pollution

Improving the Urban Environment

Environmental degradation has captured the attention of the public and policy makers. Although pollution and other forms of environmental decay are not new, the amount of damage experienced from it has risen to an unsatisfactory level. Specifically, a substantial divergence between total social costs and total private costs has apparently taken place.

If the present pollution-emission levels are such that these substantial negative externalities exist, is it possible to intervene in the private-market system in such a way that pollution can be reduced to a level where net social benefits are maximized? Apparently this can be done through one of any three ways: taxation, subsidization, or direct control.

Pollution Tax. If the firm is charged a tax or fine equal to the difference between marginal social cost and marginal private cost, the new maximum-profit level of production is Q' (Figure 14-4). The rationale is clear. When the pollution tax is imposed on the firm, the firm's marginal-cost curve becomes the marginal-social-cost curve. In effect, the pollution tax "internalized" the indirect social cost of pollution and, consequently, Q' becomes the new maximum-profit level of production (that is, marginal revenue equals marginal cost at Q').

Subsidy. Instead of imposing a pollution tax on production, pollution can be controlled through subsidy. As Figure 14-4 indicates, Q units of output represent the maximum-profit level of production and Q' represents the level of output at which net social benefits are at a maximum. If the producer cuts back his production to Q', he will obviously forgo some profit. The subsidy is used to compensate the producer for this loss. The producer is, in this case, paid a subsidy equal to his profit loss. The profits at Q' units of output plus the subsidy equal the amount of profit the producer would earn at the maximum-profit level of output Q. The rationale for this method is that the community is taxed in order to maximize desired net social benefits.

Direct Control. The simplest method of controlling pollution is to intervene directly in the private market. A government agency would simply reduce the output of the firm from Q units of output to Q' units.

A Trade-Off Problem. Regardless of the method used to control pollution to the extent of maximizing net social benefits, the amount of pollution that remains may still be above the level that can be absorbed by the earth's environment. We may still face the matter of alternatives.

We have seen that the dynamics of the private market have produced a highly urbanized economy (Chapter 6). The economic advantages accruing to firms which agglomerate have been the principal reason for urbanization, but the concentration of businesses and households has created a serious pollution problem.

It might be argued that we need to begin a program aimed at dispersing economic activity into less concentrated areas so as to make better use of nature's capacity to recycle waste materials. Such a dispersion, however, may lead to a substantial loss of certain economic advantages of concentration (i.e., agglomeration economies). Hence, we are faced with a potential dilemma. If the loss of agglomeration economies as a result of a dispersion program is greater than the gain from reducing the concentration of pollution, then the program may not be consistent with the goal of maximizing net social benefits.

In addition, a closer examination of ways to remove pollution from our streams, lakes, rivers, and atmosphere may indicate that there are cost savings associated with the treatment of waste materials in concentrated amounts. Simply put, it is quite possible that economies of scale can be realized in the treatment of waste materials, and the extent of scale economies would depend, in large part, on the existence of concentrated amounts of waste materials.

SUMMARY

Chapters 13 and 14 have emphasized the externalities connected with urban economies in order to examine the private-market failure to allocate resources efficiently to the production and use of the basic needs of urban regions—housing, job-training programs, transportation, and pollution. These chapters also reemphasized the notion that when external effects are substantial in the production and consumption of an item, a considerable difference will exist between the market's resource allocation for such production and consumption and the amount of resources that should be allocated to maximize net social benefits.

As we have seen in this and the previous chapter, the existence of substantial spillover effects is a basic cause of some of today's major urban economic problems. But before we can make much progress in eliminating this cause, we need to find some satisfactory way to "internalize" the more significant spillover effects. In effect, the major indirect benefits stemming from the production and consumption of a good or service need to be identified in order that all those who benefit from such production and consumption share in their costs. Conversely, the indirect social costs connected with production and consumption need to be identified in order to make these costs a part of the total cost of production.

The major problems of poverty, housing, transportation, and pollution have been attacked with a variety of policies, including subsidy, taxation, and regulation. Most of these measures deal in some way with the matter of spillover effects (or externalities). These measures can be categorically described as symptom-oriented or cause-oriented. The attractive feature of symptom-oriented measures is immediate effects. On the other hand, the effects of cause-oriented measures are not immediately apparent and, therefore, are characterized as long-term measures. This unattractive characteristic of cause-oriented measures can mean that symptom-oriented measures are preferred over cause-oriented measures. Unfortunately, symptom-oriented measures can be counterproductive.

REFERENCES AND SUPPLEMENTAL READING

Daniel R. Fusfeld, *The Basic Economics of the Urban Racial Crisis* (New York: Holt, Rinehart and Winston, Inc., 1973).

Matthew Edel and Jerome Rothenberg (eds.), *Readings in Urban Economics* (New York: The Macmillan Company, 1972), Parts 3, 4, 5, and 6.

Ronald E. Grieson (ed.), *Urban Economics: Readings and Analysis* (Boston: Little, Brown and Company, 1973).

Robert Gutman and David Popenoe (eds.), *Neighborhood, City, and Metropolis* (New York: Random House, 1970).

Joseph E. Haring, *Urban and Regional Economics* (Boston: Houghton Mifflin Company, 1972), Part Two.

Lawrence G. Hines, *Environment Issues: Population, Pollution, and Economics* (New York: W. W. Norton & Company, Inc., 1973).

R. J. Johnston, *Urban Residential Patterns* (New York: Praeger Publishers, 1972).

Heinz Kohler, *Economics and Urban Problems* (Lexington, Massachusetts: D. C. Heath and Company, 1973).

Louis K. Loewenstein, (ed.), *Urban Studies* (New York: The Free Press, 1971).

Edwin S. Mills, *Urban Economics* (Glenview, Illinois: Scott, Foresman and Company, 1972), Chapters 9, 10, 11, and 13.

William B. Neenan, *Political Economy of Urban Areas* (Chicago: Markham Publishing Company, 1972).

Dick Netzer, *Economics and Urban Problems*, 2nd ed. (New York: Basic Books, Inc., 1974).

Charles Sackrey, *The Political Economy of Urban Poverty* (New York: W. W. Norton & Company, Inc., 1973).

Arthur F. Schreiber, *et al.*, *Economics of Urban Problems: An Introduction* (Boston: Houghton Mifflin Company, 1971).

Wilbur R. Thompson, *A Preface to Urban Economics* (Baltimore: The Johns Hopkins Press, 1965), Chapters 6, 7, 8, 9, and 10.

15

Problems of Urban Government and Land-Use Practices

This chapter continues our discussion of urban problems with an examination of the deficiencies and merits of the current spatial organization of metropolitan governments. A popular view has it that the present organization of government in metropolitan areas is incapable of dealing effectively with major urban problems. As diagnosed, the symptomatic problem is the duplication of functions and overlapping jurisdictions of urban government, and the consequent result is a piecemeal handling of major problems. Still, some urban scholars believe that most metropolitan areas already possess "a very rich and intricate framework for negotiating, adjudicating, and deciding questions" that affect the diverse interests of urban residents.[1]

This chapter has three objectives. The first objective is to present a critical view of the present organizational structure of urban government. To this end the chapter begins with a discussion of the evolving organization of metropolitan government. The purpose of this discussion is to show how it might rightly be argued that the present organization of urban government is, indeed, a jungle of uncoordinated, overlapping, and competing jurisdictions. A liberal

1. Vincent Ostrom, Charles M. Tiebout, and Robert Warren, "The Organization of Government in Metropolitan Areas: A Theoretical Inquiry," *American Political Science Review*, Vol. 55 (Dec. 1961), pp. 831–842.

use of illustrations and observations of problems assertedly connected with political fragmentation will be given here. The second objective is to present the view that urban government presently offers features which fashion effective government. Therefore, to say that we have "too many governments and too little government" may be an illusion. Both views are presented in the following section. The final objective of this chapter is to turn to the matter of urban land-use practices. Closely related to a discussion of the effectiveness of urban government is the matter of land-use practices. Much can be learned about correcting questionable land-use practices from a study of the structure and behavior of government in metropolitan areas. The treatment of this topic follows the discussion of urban government.

HAVE URBAN AREAS OUTGROWN LOCAL GOVERNMENT?

Today it is easy to ask if urban areas have, in fact, outgrown local government (i.e., local government by districts, townships, boroughs, etc.). If this is the case, a suggested prescription might be a sweeping reorganization of urban government into a general metropolitan-government framework that possesses the capability to deal effectively and equitably with problems on an urbanwide basis. This prescription is rooted in the view that the evolutionary process of urban government has made the mishandling of local public responsibilities the rule rather than the exception.

The Evolving Topography of Urban Government

Features of Urban Government. Today a common feature of all metro-politan areas is the existence of many different local governments, ranging from city government down to special districts responsible for such diverse functions as fire protection, utility service, and port development. The 1967 Census of Governments shows that the average number of independent governments for a SMSA (standard metropolitan statistical area) in 1967 was 91 and that there were a total of 20,745 local units of government for all statistical areas. Viewed another way, in 1967 there were approximately 17.6 local units of government per 100,000 population living in the defined SMSAs. Chicago led the nation in the greatest number of local units of government—1,113.

With few exceptions, these local governments are relatively small geographically. For example, about half of the nearly 5,000 municipalities in the SMSAs have less than a single square mile of land area, and only one in five is as large as four square miles. As would be expected, the populations of these local governments are quite small. Two-thirds of them have fewer than 5,000 people.

A most striking feature of local governments is the extent of district overlap. The average central city has more than four over-lying local governments, and in parts of some metropolitan areas the number is much greater.

Finally, the government of some urban regions is divided into intercounty, interstate, and international metropolitan areas. In fact, approximately one-half of our SMSAs contain from two to eight county governments, and none of these intercounty metropolitan areas is located within the boundaries of a single general-purpose local government. There are 30 interstate metropolitan areas designated as SMSAs. Of greater significance, there are five metropolitan areas in the United States that are socially and economically tied to urban settlements of neighboring nations. One such international metropolitan area is the Detroit, Michigan–Windsor, Canada urban region.

The multiplicity of urban government can best be viewed as a map that pictures a "crazy-quilt" pattern of local governments. The St. Louis urbanized area shown in Figure 15-1 is typical of a governmentally crowded modern metropolis. The St. Louis SMSA is served by 474 local governments—232 in Missouri and 242 in Illinois.

Reasons for the Proliferation of Local Government. At least two historical occasions can be cited as primary reasons for modern political frag-mentation. The first is the *doctrine of home rule* as it has played a historical role in the formation of state and local government. Basic to the principle of home rule are maximum citizen participation and local control.

The widespread acceptance of home rule dates back to the earliest days of the republic, when two major types of local government developed. One type was that which was spelled out in state con-stitutions as a statewide system of county government. Within this

275

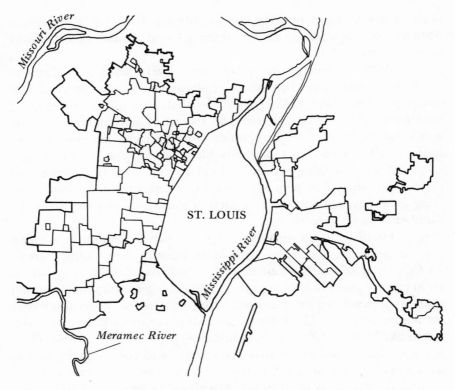

Figure 15-1   The St. Louis urbanized area. (Reprinted from a commission report on *Urban America and The Federal System,* p. 85, by permission of the Advisory Commission on Intergovernmental Relations.)

system, county government was administered by local control and was responsible for the various public services that were needed throughout a state.[2]

The second general class of local government was that of municipalities, which came into existence either by direct state legislation or by local action taken in accordance with an authorizing general state law. The creation of municipalities was authorized by the states to provide services and facilities peculiar to villages, towns, and cities. They were also given the power to tax their residents.

With the increased demand for such special services as education and fire protection, a third class of local government emerged,

2. In some parts of the nation, a statewide system of townships was created in order to bring local government closer to the people.

276

called special districts. Unlike counties, townships, and municipalities, special districts were responsible for only one function
(e.g., public education). Special districts had the power to tax the
local residents to provide the special services.

The second historical occasion for the fragmentation and
the proliferation of local government is the limited role of local
government. Historically, county and city governments have been
given only limited roles. In most parts of the United States, county
government is regarded as a state agent which performs those general
services which are demanded by urban and nonurban areas. Since
much of the financial support for these statewide services comes from
county taxes, most counties lack the authority and the capacity to
supply the special services demanded by residents of the urban parts
of their territory.

Cities are also restricted by state law in their power to expand
their boundaries to provide the needed services to the sprawling
urban areas. In many states, laws require that annexation proceed-
ings be instituted by the owners of the property to be taken into the
city, and in some instances a two-thirds majority of these property
owners must indicate their favor through referendum.

As would be expected, property owners residing in suburban
areas usually oppose annexation because it generally leads to higher
taxes—taxes to pay the burgeoning costs of, for instance, city welfare
and crime protection.

Too Many Governments and Too Little Government

The Paradox of Home Rule. It can be reasoned that the historical
sacredness given to maximum citizen participation (i.e., the principle
of home rule) largely led to the development of a system of competing,
overlapping, uncoordinated, independent political units of government in most urban areas. Consequently, fragmented local government is likely to limit the ability and authority of local government to
meet today's needs. The Advisory Commission of Intergovernmental
Relations takes note of the paradoxical situation in this way:[3]

3. Advisory Commission on Intergovernmental Relations, Message from the President
   of the United States Transmitting the Final Report of the Commission on Intergovernmental Relations, Pursuant to Public Law 109, 83rd Congress (Washington,
   D.C.: U.S. Government Printing Office, 1955), pp. 54–55.

Self-determination in one isolated local unit of a large community often restricts the opportunity for genuine home rule in the whole community.

Unfettered local control can be injurious to local as well as to broader interests. For example, it is generally agreed that houses cost more than they need to because local building codes, sanitary regulations and inspections, licensing requirements for artisans, and zoning and subdivision controls are often inadequate, outmoded, or conflicting. Complete home rule with respect to these matters by ill-equipped local units has been frustrating for the building industry and the public, and has produced complications for national and state housing programs.

The Problem of Fiscal Disparity. The political fragmentation of metropolitan areas has led to a separation of resources from needs. The Advisory Commission on Intergovernmental Relations so describes the predicament that besets our metropolitan areas:[4]

> The metropolitan areas of the United States account for 80 percent of the nation's bank accounts, three-quarters of federal personal income tax collections, and 77 percent of the value added by manufacture. Yet, it is in these same metropolitan areas that civil government faces its fiercest challenge with rising crime and delinquency; city schools that are becoming jungles of terror; neighborhoods that are blighted; poverty and disease that are rampant; and gravest of all, with millions of citizens feeling completely alienated from government and the whole concept of liberty with order.
>
> In brief, most of America's wealth and most of America's domestic problems reside in metropolitan areas. Why, then, cannot this vast wealth be applied through vigorous social measures to meet the growing problems? Because the resources exist in one set of jurisdictions within the metropolitan areas and the problems in another. Through a large part of the country this disparity between needs and resources is the disparity between the central city and its suburbs.

The property tax, the levy upon land and improvements, lies at the root of the urban financial problem. Traditionally, the property tax has been the main source of revenue for local governments, including the cities. In the United States, it comprises 87.7 percent of total tax revenues for local governments. For municipalities, this tax contributes more than 70 cents of every incoming tax dollar.

4. Advisory Commission on Intergovernmental Relations, *Urban America and the Federal System* (Washington, D.C.: U.S. Government Printing Office, October 1969), p. 1.

Not only is the property tax at the root of the urban financial problem, but urban areas have not been able to free themselves from this dependence. Historically, local units of government have possessed only residual taxing powers, and since the broadened income-tax and sales-tax base has been used largely to finance public services provided by state and federal governments, local governments have usually been left with the property tax as the principal means of financing local services.

As high-tax-yielding activities have moved away from inner-city sites to the metropolitan suburbs, city officials have been faced with an eroding tax base. To compound the problem, city officials face simultaneously increasing costs for better education, for higher welfare costs, for improved police and fire protection, and for better treatment of the mounting environmental pollution of the inner cities.

Faced with the dual problems of a decreasing tax base on the one hand, and rising social costs on the other, cities, not surprisingly, are looking for ways to cut back on total public expenditures. In the winter of 1969, Newark, New Jersey, for example, was forced to consider closing its libraries to meet its city-hall payroll. A rash of cities have considered cutting weeks off the school year because of the shortage of funds.

Compared to that of the central cities, the financial situation of the suburbs is bright. One reason for this is the suburbs' "local tax-and-zoning game." The Advisory Commission on Intergovernmental Relations describes this practice:[5]

The fiscal contest among municipalities in the same metropolitan area might be described as the local Tax and Zoning Game. In order to hold down education costs, suburban legislators are under strong temptation to use a low-density approach to residential zoning. Although the one-acre suburban lots can be denounced as an example of "snob" or restrictive zoning, they are also hailed as an act of local financial prudence—the only sure way of placing a lid on school costs and property-tax rates. The zoning of great stretches of suburban land for commercial and/or light industrial purposes is another example of fiscal zoning. There is always the hope that a large share of the local tax burden can be exported to neighboring communities by snagging the giant shopping center, the industrial research park, or the massive public-utility installation. In brief, the name of the game is cutthroat intergovernmental competition, and the object of the game is to "zone in" urban resources and to "zone out" urban

5. Advisory Commission on Intergovernmental Relations, *Urban America and the Federal System* (Washington, D.C.: U.S. Government Printing Office, October 1969), p. 12.

problems. Operating under a logic that goes back to the Domesday Book of William the Conquerer, each autonomous principality has the unchallenged and exclusive right to protect and to exploit all taxable resources within its domain. While this "winner take all" philosophy makes good sense in terms of the old "balanced" community, it takes on a harsh and inequitable color in a sprawling metropolitan area inhabited by aggressive and lopsided governmental units. One jurisdiction can reap all the tax benefits of an industrial location while the neighboring communities are often required to pay the costs of educating the children of the new employees.

So far, we have noted the fiscal disparity between the central city and the suburbs. We would be remiss if we did not point out that in some metropolitan areas (particularly the newer metropolitan areas—Phoenix and Houston, as examples) the gap between the most affluent and the most impoverished jurisdiction is greater than that between central city and suburbia in general. This situation may become more widespread in metropolitan areas as an increasing number of lower-middle-class households move to the suburbs. This trend may increase the demand for special services in suburbs (e.g., public education) at a faster rate than the rate of increase in the local tax base.

Fragmented Public Utilities

One obvious result of political fragmentation is the piecewise development of public utilities. Metropolitan water services are handled largely by a series of small, separate governmental units and private companies. For example, a recent survey of the Sacramento metropolitan area showed that the water supply and distribution services were handled by 44 public and 55 private agencies and that these agencies were all operating independently.[6] A similar survey of the Minneapolis–St. Paul metropolitan area showed that 45 individual water utilities were operating without an organizational or operational tie except for minimal state-agency controls.[7] As might be expected, most of these independent agencies were found in the suburbs.

6. Advisory Commission on Intergovernmental Relations, *Metropolitan America: Challenge to Federalism* (Washington, D.C.: U.S. Government Printing Office, 1966), pp. 38–39.
7. Ibid.

The fragmentation of sewage-disposal services is similar to that of water-supply services. For example, in suburban Nassau County in the New York metropolitan area there were 41 districts for waste disposal and removal in 1966.[8] Similar examples can be cited for the suburban areas of other major metropolitan areas.

The consequences of such fragmentation are obvious. It leads to one or more of the following conditions: inadequate services, excessive duplication of services, or excessive high prices for the services.

The inadequate treatment of a metropolitan area's waste materials is frequent. At times, small municipalities and sewer districts do not process wastes at all. The usual reason for this failure is that many small governmental units simply lack the resources to finance a "full-treatment" processing plant; consequently, they dump raw sewage or inadequately processed sewage in streams and rivers.

A striking example of excessive duplication of facilities is found in the Seattle area. There, a suburban water district recently spent $1 million for a filtration plant to treat the polluted waters of Lake Washington.[9] Independent of this decision, the City of Seattle followed by spending $1,950,000 to construct a pipeline to transport virgin water from the Cedar River in the Cascades to some suburbs adjacent to the water district. The irony surrounding the two independent decisions is that the pipeline laid to transport water from the Cascades was large enough to meet the needs of both the Seattle water district and the suburban water district which had just invested in an expensive facility to treat inferior water.

Clearly, excessive duplication (and underutilization of facilities) leads to excessive prices for public services. The Seattle case quite likely resulted in excessively high prices for the services.

Urban Development Programs and Political Fragmentation

Massive city programs such as highway construction, urban renewal, park development, and public housing are increasing. Since much of this construction activity takes place in heavily populated urban areas (i.e., the inner city), thousands of persons and businesses are forced to relocate every year. The Commission on Intergovern-

8. Ibid.
9. Ibid.

mental Relations notes that it has been estimated "that between 1964 and 1972 the federally aided urban renewal and highway programs alone will uproot 825,000 families and individuals and 136,000 business and nonprofit organizations."[10]   Clearly, the sheer magnitude of such a shift requires the entire metropolitan area's coordinated effort to handle the many relocation problems well.

Responsive Government from Large Numbers

We would be remiss if we did not discuss two basic character-istics of public services, since an understanding of these characteristics have a bearing on the question of whether the statement of "too many governments and too little government" has any validity. These basic characteristics are spillover effects and scale economies.

A basic function of government is to provide public services (or goods).   A service (or good) becomes a public service in the event that it cannot be easily "packaged" and sold to an individual in the private market place (recall the discussion of public goods in Chapter 12).   Thus, a public service is characterized as a service that yields substantial spillover effects.   Fire protection, as an example, is a nonpackageable item.   The private purchase of enough fire protection to cover the value of the purchaser's property would most certainly benefit the owners of nearby property.   The provision of fire protec-tion, then, becomes a matter of local government because of its apparent nonpackageable feature.

The notion of "packageability" has an interesting and im-portant implication in the case of public services.   If the above basic definition of a public service (that is, an item that cannot be packaged and sold to an individual without incurring notable spillover effects upon other individuals) is expanded to include a collection of in-dividuals, it can be seen that public services are packageable on an areawide basis.   The exact size and shape of the area would largely depend upon the nature of the spillover effects.   If a service area has been defined on the basis of the spillover effects, it can be said that the spillover effects have been "internalized."

In at least one respect, the internalization of spillover effects makes public services similar to private items.   That is, as the late Charles Tiebout pointed out,[11] urban residents can "shop around"

10.   Ibid., p. 63.
11.   Charles M. Tiebout, "A Pure Theory of Local Expenditures," *Journal of Political Economy*, Vol. 64 (October, 1956), pp. 416–24.

and locate in the area that provides the kinds and quality of public services that best fulfill their satisfaction relative to the tax-dollar outlay. And the fact that we now have a plurality in urban government makes shopping around possible. One of the effects of shopping around is to encourage competition among the various jurisdictions, as each jurisdiction strives to offer services corresponding to a certain preference set. It can further be argued that this would cause local jurisdictions to be more sensitive to the diverse preferences for public goods and services.

There are at least three drawbacks to the "shopping around" notion. One has to do with the "freedom" to shop around. The shopping-around notion assumes that urban residents have the economic and social opportunities to locate freely in the area of their choice. As most of us know, this freedom is severely limited for many minority groups. A second drawback relates to the sheer number of jurisdictions that might have to be formed to accommodate the many different residence-preference patterns. There would be a need for as many jurisdictional units as there are notable differences in preference patterns. This is further complicated by the good chance that each public good and service provided by the urban area will have its own areal net of jurisdictions (or districts), where the quantity and quality of that service would vary among the jurisdictions in accordance to consumer preferences. (A network of jurisdictions for each public service is similar to, but not identical with, the central-place notion of market areas discussed in Chapter 6.) It is extremely doubtful that it would be politically and administratively possible to create enough jurisdictions to correspond exactly to all the particular sets of residence preferences. A final drawback of the shopping-around notion has to do with the question of preference satisfaction. Whose preference is being satisfied in the case of an individual who lives in suburbia and works in the inner city? The daily mobility of this individual means that he will be consuming public services from several jurisdictions. Consequently, his preference pattern for public services is not confined to a single jurisdiction, but, in fact, may extend over the entire urban area.

The second characteristic of public services is the matter of economies of scale in the provision of public services. The mention of this characteristic here is not to suggest that the case of scale economies is unique to public services. In fact, the actual provision of a public good or service does not differ significantly from that of a private item. Both require labor as a basic input. Certian technological knowhow is put to use in both cases. And both generally require material inputs. Therefore, both are subject to internal economies (and diseconomies) of scale.

The existence of scale economies is mentioned here because of its importance in determining the size of service areas. If efficiency is a concern with urban government, then it should be seen that jurisdictional areas correspond to the most favorable level of operation for providing the service. For some services, the most efficient level of operation may be at an output level that can only serve a small area. In contrast, the efficient operation in the provision of other services may require an area equal to the entire urban area. Since the efficiency levels quite likely vary with the various services provided in an urban area, it seems desirable that service units (or districts) of some kind be formed to take advantage of internal economies of scale. It might be argued, therefore, that a governmental organization which is best able to deal with economies of scale is one that has the authority to develop districts of any size where such matters as spillover effects and economies of scale are considered.

One feature of the present organization of urban government is that an elaborate web of governmental districts already exists, ranging from the small district to the state and federal government agency. This network of governmental units may somewhat approximate a network of districts based on such factors as scale economies and spillover problems. Still, it is doubtful that the present network of governmental units would so nearly correspond to a satisfactory network of districts that there would not be a need for some kind of cooperative arrangement among existing jurisdictions or a reorganization of some jurisdictions. It would be a mistake to think that cooperative arrangements are easily secured, for it is likely that most cooperative arrangements would result in a reallocation of public services among the participating political units. A conflict of interest would no doubt be the rule, and a failure to cooperate would suggest that the disputing political units seek a higher level of government in the quest for an agreeable solution to the interests of all involved.

Considering Reform in Urban Government

This chapter's concern with the consequent functional and administrative problems stemming from our system of uncoordinated local government, plus the emphasis in Chapters 13 and 14 on basic urban-region economic problems, points to a need for considering reform in urban government. Whatever kind of reform is necessary, it would be a mistake to ignore totally the possible merits of the multiplicity of political units that now exists in urban areas. Helpful in assessing the merits of the present political framework of urban government is a list of criteria, suggested by the Commission on Intergovernmental Relations, for evaluating the performance of governmental functions in metropolitan areas:[12]

1. The governmental jurisdiction responsible for providing any service should be large enough for the benefits from that service to be received primarily by its own population. Neither the benefits from the service nor the social costs of failing to provide it should "spill over" into other jurisdictions.
2. The unit of government should be large enough to permit realization of the economies of scale in the provision of a service.
3. The unit of government carrying on a function should have a geographic area of jurisdiction adequate for effective performance.
4. The unit of government should have the legal and administrative ability to perform services assigned to it.
5. Every unit of government should be responsible for a sufficient number of functions so that its governing processes involve a resolution of conflicting interests and balancing of governmental needs and resources. An overemphasis on assigning individual functions to different governments can create so many separate entities that it results in an undemocratic, inequitable, and inadequate assignment of priorities.
6. The performance of public functions should remain subject to public control. This is an essential condition of responsible government that is often violated by creating special districts whose decision-making power and purse strings are not subject to direct control by the voters.
7. Functions should be assigned to a level of government that provides opportunities for active citizen participation and still permits adequate performance.

URBAN LAND-USE PRACTICES

Some scholars believe that one of the most challenging problems facing urban regions in the next several decades will be that of

12. Advisory Commission on Intergovernmental Relations, *Metropolitan America: Challenge to Federalism* (Washington, D.C.: U.S. Government Printing Office, 1966), pp. 29–32.

proper land apportionment. Already some agree that we must accept either complete public control of private land or public ownership of land.

Such an attitude implies that the private real-estate market fails to apportion urban land in the best interest of the urban community. The private real-estate market faces three conditions that determine its actions: speculation often results in private land retention; private gain often stimulates land developments that are adverse to communitywide advantages; and the private real-estate market is most responsive to the existence of positive externalities of public investments.

An appropriate way to begin a discussion of these conditions is with a review of the economics of land use (see Chapter 11). Practically speaking, the supply of land is largely fixed in an urban area. Admittedly, an urban area can intensify its land use by, say, building taller buildings, but the truth of the matter is that this kind of growth indicates the almost perfectly inelastic supply of urban land.

The opposing market forces of demand and supply will logically apportion land on the principle of "best" use—best in the economic sense of allocation in accordance with effective demand. But the presence of the three conditions just cited has a definite influence on the efficiency of the private market to apportion land on the principle of best use.

Land Retention

Speculators enter the real-estate market to make a generous return on their investments. To some extent, they are encouraged to do so because local property-tax assessment practices encourage land speculation.

As already mentioned, the principal local tax is the property tax, one which taxes the assessed market value of real estate. Generally speaking, the property tax is levied against the value of the particular structure that occupies the site rather than upon the economic value of the site alone. The effect is oftentimes to encourage landholding which may not be in the best community interest, for frequently the city must build around those sites that are withheld from the market. A vacant building in a downtown area exemplifies this. The economic value of the site may be quite high, reflecting the effective demand for central location. But if the site is taxed on the basis of an empty building that is in need of much repair, the property owner is encouraged to hold the land for speculation. Consequently, he pays a relatively small tax as he holds the land for the "right" price, and that "right" price, ironically, is based upon what the owner believes to be the effective demand price for the site rather than upon the value of the structure that presently occupies the site.

Another problem is seen in a private owner's speculation with urban open tracts. Scattered almost at random within any urban region are various tracts without structures. Again, because open acreage for various reasons is taxed at a lower value than comparable occupied sites, many private owners withhold this land from the market in order to speculate with it. For instance, the landholder of raw acreage in a residential area pays only 62 cents in real-estate taxes for every dollar paid by the home owner next door.

To be sure, a landowner is encouraged by the local property-tax-assessment practices to withhold land from the market until the right price is offered. The advantage of holding property at a relatively low cost (the property tax) has been a major reason that organizations (e.g., corporations and estates) speculate with large investments in urban land. Such investments have led to monopoly tendencies in the urban-land market and to a slowdown in the turn-over rate of urban land use, particularly in the inner cities. Logically, the turnover rate of urban land use should reflect the dynamic nature of a competitive free-market economy and hence not be limited by monopoly power.

Discontinuous Land Development

We shall continue our example of open-tract speculation as an illustration of how this kind of real-estate speculation can lead to discontinuous land development. The case, though not documented, is a typical one. Involved is a land speculator seeking maximum profits by selling at the "right" price and a land developer who must purchase land economically. The two positions are not reconcilable, for the land speculator realizes that the value of his holdings will increase beyond the price that the land developer is willing to pay.

13. Roy J. Burrough, "Should Urban Land Be Publicly Owned?," *Land Economics*, XLII, No. 1 (February 1966), pp. 11–20.

Generally, the developer is forced to build in another location. Strapped for time and the demands of economy, he builds further out from the urban center where land costs are lower. In doing so, he increases the land speculator's holdings, for these have now increased in value as land development grows around it. The land becomes more valuable than it was earlier because it is now a choice site for commercial organizations that will seek to service the land developer's newly constructed residential areas.

The inevitable pattern, once the land developer begins to build in his second-choice site, is to create "discontinuous" land-development patterns—"leapfrogging" as it is frequently called. The land speculator is, then, in a position to seek a zoning change for his land, from residential to commercial, and when he is successful in doing so, he has realized a handsome increase in the value of his land.

Our typical case makes two practices of private land speculation clear, two practices made possible by local zoning and taxing practices and by federal tax laws. In each instance we have examples of how such practices result in inefficient urban land speculation.

There is little doubt that the land owner was encouraged to hold his land originally. Because that tax on unimproved acreage is considerably less than on improved sites, the speculator could retain his property by incurring a relatively slight tax cost, a cost more than compensated for by the expected increase in value his land realized. Also, the speculator was well aware that once his land became an attractive commercial site as a result of the use of the land around him, he could have the land rezoned as a commercial site and, consequently, realize a yet larger profit from it.

Finally, the profits earned from the sale of the land after the zoning change is taxed as capital gains. And the tax on gains for property held longer than six months is much less than the tax on earnings. Thus, in addition to the advantages to the speculator which local property taxes and local zoning codes offer, federal taxes add a further incentive to the property owner to speculate as the opportunity presents itself. In each case, we find something less than the soundest of means for urban land use.

Externalities of Public Investments

The third condition determining private real-estate actions is the existence of positive externalities of public investments. Public investments, such as parks and arterials, generally increase the value of abutting properties because of spillover advantages. The construction of an arterial, for example, improves the accessibility of adjacent areas to other parts of the metropolitan community. Recall that access is a basic determinant of economic land rent (see Chapter 11). With the construction of the arterial, the land-use pattern of abutting properties will eventually change from residential land use to commercial use; thus, a substantial increase in land value occurs. A similar situation occurs with the development of public parks. Several studies of land values and public investments clearly show that land adjacent to a park has a higher value than comparable sites located several blocks away.[14]

The existence of profitable spillover effects from public investments encourages land developers and land speculators to work closely with public officials to build desirable facilities near their land holdings. Such constructions may be in direct violation of comprehensive growth and development plans that were approved by the same public officials.

One way of avoiding this undesirable relationship, as suggested by some urban-land specialists, is for urban communities to levy a tax to capture the increment of rising land prices due to public investments so that rising valuations benefit the public rather than the individual landowner.

It was mentioned at the beginning of this section that urban communities may need to turn to either complete public control of private land or public ownership of land as the only way to manage land apportionment in the community's interest. Admittedly there is a need to bring the actions of landowners into harmony with the community's interests. But it may be possible to accomplish this harmonization through better use of existing public instruments. For instance, uniform zoning policies and building codes can be established for the entire urban region. Also, zoning practices and building-code practices could be made consistent with the comprehensive land-use plan of the urban region. Finally, the power to tax can be an effective tool for land-use control. For instance, taxation can be used to accelerate or delay the urbanization of tracts of land. In addition, taxation can be used to capture the "unearned" increment

---

14. It is interesting to note here that in metropolitan areas where crime rates are high, a growing number of suburban residents resist the development of parks in their neighborhoods. Parks are perceived as places where muggers can hide, thus endangering the safety of nearby residents. Economically, this perception lowers the value of nearby property as concerned residents move to "safer" areas.

of rising land prices due to the spillover advantages of public investments.

SUMMARY

A rather convincing argument can be made that the historical occasions of home rule and the limited role given to local government have been largely responsible for today's multiplicity of local government. There is little disagreement among urban scholars on this point. Differences of opinion begin to appear on the question of whether the multiplicity of local government means "too many governments and too little government." There is seemingly no lack of evidence to support this critical viewpoint of urban government (e.g., duplication of public facilities and urban land-use practices).

Many urbanologists have argued that a correction of the present political fragmentation of urban areas is a necessary prerequisite to solving problems. Even with adequate financial resources, the fragmented political units do not have effective jurisdiction over many of the urban problems which are areawide in nature.

Efforts to bring political consolidation or at least cooperation have been made for more than 20 years. Among the experiments have been annexation, city-county consolidation, intergovernmental contracting for specific services, sharing common facilities, regional planning commissions, special purpose districts, and councils of government. The problems which transcend traditional political boundaries are still in need of broader governmental jurisdiction for their solution.

Federal grant-in-aid programs have fostered the development of broader-scale regional agencies or intergovernmental agreements as conditions of the grants. The monetary inducement of sharing in federal dollars brought all levels of government into alignments. In the decade of the 1960s, 345 councils of government and 464 state planning and development districts were created. Unfortunately, proficiency in processing grant applications has been the greatest contribution for all too many of these regional agencies.

The search for viable forms of regional entities continues. Among the more promising is the Twin Cities Metropolitan Council in Minneapolis–St. Paul, Minnesota. Created by the state government, this umbrella agency has a governor-appointed policy-making body representing the entire metropolitan area. In addition to the usual planning and coordinating functions, it also supervises and directs the performance of operational responsibilities ranging from airport to water-sewer development.

REFERENCES AND SUPPLEMENTAL READING

Advisory Commission on Intergovernmental Relations, *Metropolitan America: Challenge to Federalism* (Washington: U.S. Government Printing Office, 1966).

Advisory Commission on Intergovernmental Relations, *Urban America and the Federal System* (Washington: U.S. Government Printing Office, 1969).

John C. Bollens and Henry J. Schmandt, *The Metropolis: Its People, Politics, and Economic Life*, 2d ed. (New York: Harper & Row Publishers, 1970), Chapters 5, 6, 10, 11, 12, 13, and 14.

Ray J. Burroughs, "Should Urban Land be Publicly Owned?" *Land Economics* XLII, No. 1 (February 1966), pp. 11–20.

Committee for Economic Development, *Reshaping Government in Metropolitan Areas* (New York: Committee for Economic Development, February 1970).

Mason Gaffney, "Land Rent, Taxation, and Public Policy," *The Regional Science Association Papers* XXIII (1969), pp. 141–153.

James W. Kitchen and William S. Hendon, "Land Values Adjacent to an Urban Neighborhood Park," *Land Economics* XLII, No. 3 (August 1967), pp. 357–60.

Louis K. Loewenstein (ed.), *Urban Studies* (New York: The Free Press, 1971), pp. 268–302.

Edwin S. Mills, *Urban Economics* (Glenview, Illinois: Scott, Foresman and Company, 1972), Chapter 12.

Dick Netzer, *Economics and Urban Problems* (New York: Basic Books, Inc., 1970), pp. 268–302.

John H. Niedercorn and Edward F. R. Hearle, "Recent Land-Use Trends in Forty-eight Large American Cities," *Land Economics* XL, No. 1 (February 1964), pp. 105–110.

William M. Shenkel, "The Economic Consequences of Industrial Zoning," *Land Economics* XL, No. 3 (August 1964), pp. 255–265.

16

Nonmetropolitan Problems

If word association were played with the word "rural," the list might include lush greenery, clean air, open space, and tranquility. But it might also include abject poverty, isolation, scarred land, and raped resources. The sharp contrast of such descriptive phrases points to the enigma of rural America, or in more contemporary terms, nonmetropolitan America. At the time of the first census in 1790, rural America was America. But today only about 30 percent of the United States population lives in nonmetropolitan regions. Recent surveys indicate that more would like to live in the open country than currently do,[1] and yet the concentration of population in the metropolitan areas continues.

A nonmetropolitan economy may be a resort area with an all-year population of 2,500 and a summer population of 15,000, a mining town in Appalachia with a declining economic base and severe poverty, an affluent farming area in Iowa, a retirement village in Florida, a new town in California. The economies of nonmetropolitan regions are both more numerous and more diverse than their metropolitan counterparts.

This chapter looks at the regional economies of nonmetropolitan America, economies which in total represent about 98 percent of the land area of the United States but only about 30 percent of the people. The nonmetropolitan population consists of those persons living in towns of less than 50,000, in the open country, and on farms. The largest share of the nonmetropolitan population,

1. See Chapter 9, page 174.

about 86 percent, is rural. The census definition of rural includes persons living in towns of less than 2,500, in the open country, and on farms. In practice, the definition of rural has been expanded to become nearly synonymous with nonmetropolitan. For instance, the Rural Development Act of 1972 had at least some applicability to cities up to 50,000 population.

SOME DIMENSIONS OF NONMETROPOLITAN REGIONS

Nonmetropolitan America is not easily captured with a few summary statistics. But a few broad, aggregate measures are useful to establish some important current trends.

Population

Historically, the United States has been a rural country. The first census in 1790 indicated that 95 percent of the population was rural. Even at the turn of the century 60 percent of the people were living on farms or in villages. As Figure 16-1 indicates, not until nearly 1920 did more than half the population live in urban places.

The fraction of the population living in nonmetropolitan

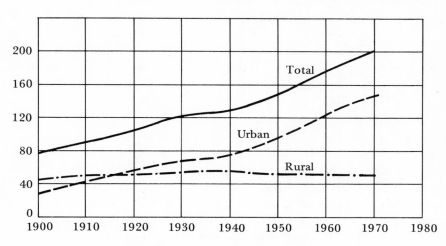

Figure 16-1 Population of the United States by urban and rural residence, 1900–1970 (in millions)

America has steadily declined. The distribution of the population by residence is summarized in Table 16-1 for 1950, 1960, and 1970.

TABLE 16-1. *Population of the United States by Residence, 1950–1970*

	Population in 1,000's			Percent of U.S. Population		
	1950	1960	1970	1950	1960	1970
Urban	96,847	125,269	149,281	64	70	73
Total rural	54,479	54,045	53,885	36	30	27
Rural farm	23,048	15,635	9,712	15	9	5
Rural nonfarm	31,431	38,410	44,173	21	21	22
Metropolitan	94,711	119,828	139,707	63	67	69
Total nonmetropolitan	56,615	59,494	63,458	37	33	31
Nonmetropolitan farm	N.A.	13,029	8,284	—	7	4
Nonmetropolitan nonfarm	N.A.	46,465	55,174	—	26	27

N.A.—Not Available

Although nonmetropolitan population has increased, its share of total national population declined from 37 percent in 1950 to 33 percent in 1960 and to 31 percent in 1970.

On the average, nonmetropolitan areas have grown less rapidly than metropolitan areas. Between 1960 and 1970 nonmetropolitan areas grew at a 6.7 percent rate compared with a 16.6 percent rate for metropolitan areas. But compared with the previous decade, the nonmetropolitan areas fared somewhat better. The growth rate of metropolitan areas declined from 26.5 percent during the 1950s to 16.6 percent during the 1960s, while the nonmetropolitan growth rate increased from 5.1 to 6.7 percent for the same periods. This was also reflected in the slowdown of migration from nonmetropolitan to metropolitan areas during the two periods. During the 1950s 6 million people migrated from nonmetropolitan to metropolitan areas, but during the 1960s this declined to 2.4 million.

The decline in rural-urban migration rates between 1960 and 1970 was not the result of a lower rate of movement off farms. As Table 16-2 indicates, the rate of decline in farm population was even greater during the 1960s than it had been during the 1950s. But, nonfarm nonmetropolitan population grew at a rate of 19 percent, greater than both the total national population growth rate and the metropolitan growth rate, as shown in Figure 16-2.

TABLE 16-2. *Change in the United States Population by Residence, 1950–1970*

Year	Total Population Pop. in 1000's	Percent Change In Previous Decade	Urban Pop. in 1000's	Percent Change In Previous Decade	Total Rural Pop. in 1000's	Percent Change In Previous Decade	Rural Farm Pop. in 1000's	Percent Change In Previous Decade	Rural Nonfarm Pop. in 1000's	Percent Change In Previous Decade
1950	151,326	14.5	96,847	29.6	54,479	−5.2	23,048	−24.5	31,431	16.8
1960	179,323	18.5	125,269	29.3	54,045	−.8	15,635	−32.2	38,410	22.2
1970	203,166	13.3	149,281	19.2	53,885	−.3	9,712	−37.9	44,173	15.0

Year	Metropolitan Pop. in 1000's	Percent Change In Previous Decade	Total Nonmetro Pop. in 1000's	Percent Change In Previous Decade	Nonmetro Farm Pop. in 1000's	Percent Change In Previous Decade	Nonmetro Nonfarm Pop. in 1000's	Percent Change In Previous Decade
1950	94,711	N.A.	56,615	N.A.	N.A.	N.A.	N.A.	N.A.
1960	119,828	26.5	59,494	5.1	13,029	N.A.	46,465	N.A.
1970	139,707	16.6	63,458	6.7	8,284	−36.4	55,174	18.7

The large and continuous decline in the farm population has tended to obscure the rapid growth of the nonfarm population living in the open country and small towns. The growth of nonmetropolitan regions is concentrated, however, in areas close to larger urban centers. Counties located within 50 miles of a metropolitan area were more likely to grow than those located further away. Counties located more than 100 miles from a central city were more likely to experience severe decline.

Thus, despite an overall increase in nonmetropolitan population, about 70 percent of all nonmetropolitan counties lost population between 1960 and 1970. These were generally counties which were located a considerable distance away from a metropolitan area or which did not contain a large town.

Employment

Productivity increases in agriculture in the past few years have been the most dramatic in history. But greater productivity with a fixed amount of land in agricultural production diminishes job needs in agriculture. This trend is likely to continue, but its impact on rural America will probably be different. A detailed examination of the 1970 census indicates the possible beginnings of

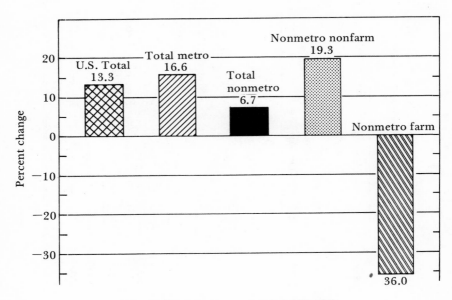

Figure 16-2   Population change, 1960–1970

this in several counties. These counties had registered population declines for several decades as a result of a lack of employment opportunities in agriculture. The decrease in agricultural employment was of such a magnitude as to overwhelm other developments in the county. Recently, although the rate of decline may not have changed, the absolute size of employment decline in farming has slowed. Employment increases in other sectors, which may be only modest, combined to show small employment gains and population growth in historically declining counties.

The rate of increase of nonfarm employment between 1960 and 1970 was slightly greater in nonmetropolitan counties than in metropolitan ones, as indicated in Figure 16-3. The rate of gain in

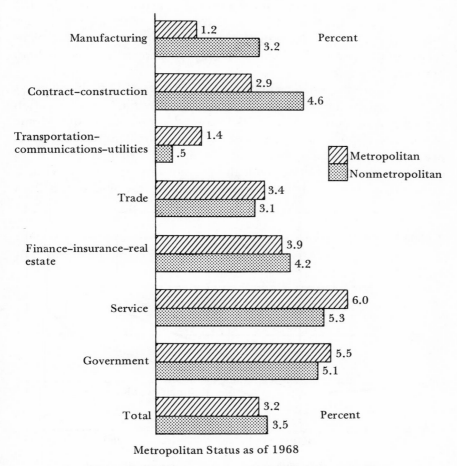

Metropolitan Status as of 1968

Figure 16-3 Employment gains for industry groups by metropolitan-nonmetropolitan location, 1960–1970

manufacturing employment in nonmetropolitan areas was nearly three times that in the metropolitan areas. Nonmetropolitan growth rates were also greater for construction, finance, insurance, and real-estate employment. However, the nonmetropolitan employment growth rates were moderately below metropolitan rates in service industries and government.

Income

Incomes in nonmetropolitan areas have been well below metropolitan areas as indicated by Figure 16-4. In 1929 metropolitan per-capita income was more than double that of nonmetropolitan areas. But over the next four decades the growth of nonmetropolitan per-capita income was 7.4 percent, compared with 5.9 percent for metropolitan areas. Nonetheless a sizeable gap still exists. Non-metropolitan per capita income is only 70 percent of metropolitan per capita income.

An important development in nonmetropolitan income has been the rise in the portion of income earned by the farm population from nonfarm sources. Table 16-3 shows that one-half of the income of the farm population comes from nonfarm sources. Farm operators near larger cities have found jobs in the city while continuing to operate their farms, which typically are not large enough to yield a sufficient income by themselves. In addition, the nonmetropolitan

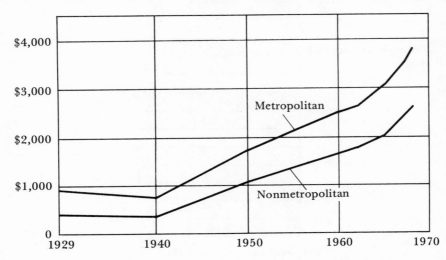

Figure 16-4 Per-capita personal income by metropolitan residence

TABLE 16-3. *Per-Capita Personal Income of Farm Population, 1960–70*

Year	From Farm Sources	From Nonfarm Sources	From All Sources	Percent Nonfarm is of Total Income
1960	$ 737	$ 458	$1,195	38
1962	856	573	1,429	40
1964	875	718	1,593	45
1966	1,243	903	2,146	42
1968	1,295	1,131	2,426	47
1969	1,430	1,240	2,670	46
1970	1,503	1,369	2,872	48

SOURCE: *Farm Income Situation*, FIS 216, Economic Research Service, July 1970, Table 7H, p. 56.

landscape is becoming dotted with manufacturing plants, particularly in the South. Thus, manufacturing has become the largest source of total income in both metropolitan and nonmetropolitan areas, as indicated by Table 16-4. Surprisingly, farming accounts for only about 13 percent of total nonmetropolitan earnings.

TABLE 16-4. *Earnings by Industrial Sources Where Earned, Metro and Nonmetro, 1968 (dollars in millions)*

Industry Sector	Sources of Earnings			
	Metro		Nonmetro	
	Dollars	Percent of Total	Dollars	Percent of Total
Manufacturing	126,804	30.2	34,380	26.7
Wholesale and retail trade	71,696	17.1	18,502	14.4
Government	67,137	16.0	26,162	20.3
Services	65,021	15.5	14,993	11.7
Construction	25,711	6.1	7,101	5.5
Transportation, communications, and public utilities	31,036	7.4	6,827	5.3
Finance, insurance, and real estate	25,233	6.0	3,501	2.7
Farming, mining, forestry, and fisheries	6,501	1.7	16,488	13.4
TOTAL	419,982	100.0	128,661	100.0

SOURCE: Survey of Current Business, May 1970.

In the often quoted report *The People Left Behind* prepared by the President's National Advisory Commission on Rural Poverty, the following statement bluntly states the rural poverty condition:

It may surprise most Americans to know that there is more poverty in rural America, proportionately, than in our cities. In metropolitan areas, one person in eight is poor, and in the suburbs the ratio is one in 15. But in rural areas one of every four persons is poor.

Some 30 percent of our total population live in rural areas, but 40 percent of the nation's poor live there.[2]

Poverty in rural areas is not of the same character as urban poverty. The rural poor have even fewer opportunities for work, and less access to adequate health care, education, and housing than do the urban poor. The broad geographic disposal of rural poverty hinders the effectiveness of programs designed to alleviate the poverty. However, much of the rural poverty is concentrated in "depressed areas" which are considered later in this chapter.

DECENTRALIZATION

The current economic landscape is the result of long-term agglomerating forces which have compressed economic activity into the largest urban areas. While most prognosticators expect this trend to continue, some decentralization, particularly of manufacturing activity, has been occurring.

Although about three-fourths of the nation's manufacturing employment is located in the 193 largest labor markets, the rate of increase in manufacturing jobs has been greatest in the smaller labor markets. Between 1962 and 1969 in all parts of the country but the West, the growth rate in manufacturing employment in the small labor markets exceeded that of the large labor markets. The large labor markets still had the largest absolute employment increase, however.

The movement of industry to nonmetropolitan areas is encouraged by several developments. The archaic central industrial district, traffic congestion, and rising land values have pushed industry further and further from the central city. The interstate highway

2. National Advisory Commission on Rural Poverty, *The People Left Behind*, (Washington, D.C.: U.S. Government Printing Office), 1967.

system and other improvements in transportation have increased the access to and from smaller communities. Relative costs of shipping goods to urban centers have been reduced for many smaller towns on or near improved transportation systems, particularly the interstate highways.

Our earlier discussion of location dynamics helps explain the tendency for some industries to decentralize. Increasing population in the major metropolitan areas may promote economies of scale for some public or private production but raise unit costs for others. As a result, certain types of industries experience rising costs in large metropolitan areas which worsen their competitive position, encouraging a movement at least to the edge of the metropolitan area.

In addition to changes in spatial cost patterns, markets also shift. The movement of the population to the West and South has changed the optimal production location for numerous firms, thereby encouraging relocations and new locations, some of which are in smaller-size places.

A variety of manufacturing industries have been appearing in nonmetropolitan areas, including food processing, mobile homes, apparel, pharmaceuticals, control equipment, industrial chemicals, appliances and electrical apparatus, recreational boats, and metalworking. In addition, several other types of industries have experienced significant growth in nonmetropolitan areas. The four which stand out are recreation, wholesaling and distribution, regional facilities such as medical and educational, and federal government activities.

On a national scale, manufacturing activity has been a shrinking component of total employment. During the past two decades manufacturing employment has dropped from 34 percent of nonagricultural employment to 25 percent. Service activities have been growing more rapidly. For the same recent 20-year period, while goods-related employment dropped from 50 percent to 38 percent of the nonagricultural employment, service-related employment increased from 50 to 62 percent.

Manufacturing activity is no longer the major growth component of the economy. Even though decentralization trends may be stronger, manufacturing no longer has the employment thrust it once had. Service-related employment tends to be even more metropolitan-oriented than manufacturing, with even less promise of subsequent dispersal.

Wilbur Thompson places manufacturing decentralization in

301

a slightly different perspective with his "filtering down" theory of location.

> In national perspective, industries filter down through the system of cities, from places of greater to lesser industrial sophistication. Most often, the highest skills are needed in the difficult, early stage of mastering a new process, and skill requirements decline steadily as the production process is rationalized and routinized with experience. As the industry slides down the learning curve, the high wage rates of the more industrially sophisticated innovating areas become superfluous. The aging industry seeks out industrial backwaters where the cheaper labor is now up to the lesser demands of the simplified process.[3]

DEVELOPMENT PROBLEMS

The small, isolated town has continually come up second best in its competition with larger urban places for economic growth. The economic disadvantages of the small town in a highly industrialized economy are numerous. And yet, as the recent statistical evidence suggests, many of these towns have been faring better, particularly in attracting manufacturing activity.

The Economic Base

Many small cities depend on a single industry or even a single firm as its economic specialty, while others have only a handful of basic activities. Such a lack of industrial diversification is the core of the economic problems facing small communities. Adverse changes in demand or costs can dislodge the entire economic base of a small town, plunging it into an economic depression. The viability of the small town is severely hampered by its lack of diversification. Its labor and capital are not readily adaptable to new industries, particularly if they have been highly specialized.

Historically, small towns have been service centers for the agricultural hinterland and raw-material processors (farm products,

3. Wilbur R. Thompson, "The Economic Base of Urban Problems," in Neil W. Chamberlain, ed., *Contemporary Economic Issues* (Homewood, Illinois: Richard D. Irwin, 1969), p. 8.

mining, or lumber). A few have specialized in a particular service function, such as a railroad town. As the base waned in importance, many of these communities experienced economic decline or collapse.

Nonmetropolitan regions have generally been considered to be labor-surplus areas as a result of unemployment or substantial underemployment by people who had been employed in agricultural pursuits. Many of the enterprises locating in nonmetropolitan areas have been labor-intensive in nature and are attracted to these areas in part because of lower labor costs. Prime examples of industries of this sort are apparel industries, electronic-assembly operations, and mobile-home manufacturing. These industries have a very low capital/labor ratio and require relatively unskilled labor for most of the jobs.

The recent significant industrialization of the rural South has been facilitated by the relatively high density of rural population. A labor force can be drawn rather readily from people living in small communities or farms who are within commuting distance to a new enterprise.

Another attraction for industrial growth in rural areas has been the low labor-force participation rate reflecting a low percentage of women in the workforce. Numerous firms have moved into nonmetropolitan areas in an attempt to tap the potential female labor force in the area.

The mix of skills in nonmetropolitan regions is understandably limited; however, in the past decade regional vocational-technical schools have made a major contribution to the grading of skilled levels of area populations, which in turn have led to the attraction of industries to nonmetropolitan areas. Arrangements are made for a vocational-technical school to provide the necessary training for workers to be employed in a new plant. Training is accomplished while the plant is being constructed so that a trained labor force is available once the plant is ready to start operations.

Wage rates tend to be lower in nonmetropolitan areas than metropolitan areas as indicated earlier in the chapter. Low wage rates, however, mean that it is difficult for areas to provide adequate public services because of the low incomes of the residents. A low quality environment is not particularly attractive to new economic activity.

But the basic issue with regard to wage rates is the relationship between wage rates and productivity. If wage rates increase more rapidly than productivity, this tends to discourage entry of new firms and weakens the competitive position of local firms.

Capital

A scarcity of both private and public capital impairs the growth of most thinly settled regions. Neither operating nor risk capital is as easily obtainable in nonmetropolitan towns as in larger cities. Likewise, infrastructure capital is generally less prevalent or of lower quality.

Private Capital. In Chapter 7 we noted that capital moved less readily to remote areas because of a greater degree of risk and uncertainty. In part this is attributable to imperfect information flows or at least to a belief that this is the situation. In addition the salvage value of fixed capital may be less in smaller communities because of its unadaptability to other uses. In a larger city, a building might be used for a variety of activities and thus have a greater resale value should the enterprise require liquidation.

The problems of obtaining risk capital in smaller communities has been partially remedied by a variety of federal, state, and local programs. These include guaranteed loans, industrial-credit corporations, industrial revenue bonds, subsidies, and tax concessions. Many communities have erected buildings to be offered to new industry. But since small-town banks lack sufficient size to handle many capital requirements, the financial centers of large cities still dominate the capital markets.

Even operating-capital requirements may be troublesome in small communities. Again, the lending capacity of a small-town bank is a limiting factor.

Public Capital. Roads, sewers, water, and other ingredients of infrastructure are important to industry but are often lacking or obsolete in small communities. Public capital consists of economic-overhead capital, which supports industry, and social-overhead capital, which supports the population. Evidence suggests that the provision of economic-overhead capital precedes growth and the provision of social-overhead capital follows growth. But while this may be generally true, there is no guarantee that investment in economic-overhead capital will guarantee industrial growth in a community.

It can be a strong contributing factor, and is probably a necessary precondition, but could backfire in the form of higher taxes should the strategy not attract new industry.

Housing in Nonmetropolitan Areas

Substandard housing is much more serious in nonmetropolitan areas than in urban areas. City slums and ghettos naturally receive more attention because they are compressed into a few areas of the city. Poor housing is more subtle in rural areas. The run-down or dilapidated housing is dispersed over the landscape in such a way that it does not attract the same attention.

Surveys indicate that in 1968 one in every six rural homes was substandard. About one million rural homes were dilapidated —literally falling down—and another two million were classified substandard. About five million of the 63 million housing units in the United States in 1970 were substandard, of which three million were located in rural areas or small towns of less than 5,500. In 1970 rural America had about 27 percent of the population, but it also had about 60 percent of the substandard housing.

Bad housing is a regional phenomenon. About 60 percent of substandard rural housing is located in the South. North Carolina and Kentucky contain more substandard housing than all of the 13 western states.

The ownership of the housing influences the rate of improvement. Studies indicate that owned rural housing has shown significant improvement more rapidly than rented housing. This is due in part to the fact that half the rented substandard housing is occupied by tenants who pay no cash rent. This is a throwback to the plantation and sharecropper days. Most of the residents of such dwellings are former laborers for the landowner, who no longer needs as much labor because of mechanization. The former workers continue to live in these dwellings and earn a meager living with part-time jobs.

Related to this problem is the persistently bad condition of rural housing occupied by blacks. About 75 percent of the housing they occupy is substandard. They also comprise about four-fifths of the no-cash-rent occupants. Almost all of these units are substandard and unlikely to improve. More than two-thirds of the homes owned by black families are substandard, compared with less than ten percent of those owned by white families.

Another serious problem is the rural housing of the elderly. In 1960 about 25 percent of substandard rural housing was occupied by elderly families, nearly 50 percent higher than their representation in the total population.

Housing for migrant workers has long been grossly inadequate. Migrant workers follow the harvests, never needed in one location more than four to six months, and often for much shorter periods. The houses in which they live at a harvest location are vacant the remainder of the year. The housing is generally provided by the grower at no charge to the worker, but is substandard and unattractive for rental during the remainder of the year. The migrant worker has little choice in housing because the grower-provided housing is usually all that is available for short-term rental to such a large influx of workers. The low wages of the laborers are, of course, a major obstacle to better housing.

The size of the problem is declining because the number of migrant laborers is fewer. Some growers are banding together to provide off-season employment for the workers, thereby eliminating them from migrant status. Legislative changes have also reduced the number of migrant workers. Federal housing support in the form of loans and grants has had a significant impact in the past few years. For instance, between 1970 and 1971 the Farmer's Home Administration upped their budget for loans and grants from $4 million to $13.8 million. Individual states have moved to alleviate the migrant-housing problem as well with varying degrees of effort and success.

A major obstacle to improved nonmetropolitan housing is cost. Although cost generally is a problem in providing adequate housing, it may be a more severe problem in sparsely settled areas where even the existing meager economies of scale are difficult to attain. In some areas it is difficult to obtain home builders because of the irregular market pattern for new housing.

Some form of industrialized housing may be the answer to this problem. Mobile homes are the most popular form of such industrialized housing in nonmetropolitan areas. In fact, most mobile homes are located in rural areas and on the outskirts of small- and medium-size cities. Zoning laws have tended to keep mobile homes out of most cities. Even so, in 1971 one of every three new single-family dwellings was a mobile home.

A basic appeal of mobile homes is price. In 1971 the average price of a mobile home complete with furnishings was $6,300, compared with a $23,000 average price of a new conventional house which did not include furnishings except appliances.

SPATIAL STRUCTURE

A major theme of this book has been the importance of spatial structure of economic activity. "Where it's at" makes a difference. The growth potential of a nonmetropolitan region is encouraged or inhibited by its spatial juxtaposition.

Access

The notion of input-output access, which we discussed in Chapter 7, is particularly relevant to the growth potentials of non-metropolitan regions. Regions with a good access to markets and a good access to raw materials are more likely to grow than regions with poor access to markets and a poor access to raw materials. Most nonmetropolitan areas lie somewhere in between these two extremes.

Access to markets and raw materials changes over time. The decline of many small communities occurred initially because of better access to larger communities through improved roads and the automobile.

Transportation technology has undergone a phenomenal change in the past 50 years and even in the past 10 years. Fifty years ago, an hour's travel by road covered about five miles. Today an hour's travel means 50 to 60 miles or more. The negative impact on the small town which was formed partially because of a greater friction of distance is well known. People bypass the small town to travel to the larger town where the variety of goods and services is greater.

In the past ten years the greatest change in surface trans-portation resulted from the completion of major segments of the interstate highway system. More small towns were bypassed as a result, but the improvements in the highway system are not all to the disadvantage of rural America. Relative costs of shipping goods to urban centers have been reduced for those towns on or near the interstate system. The remoteness of many small towns has been reduced and with it a greater interest on the part of firms that consider locating in these communities.

Conurbations

The spatial juxtaposition of smaller towns may make it possible for them to simulate some of the conditions of a larger urban area. If these communities are located close together and connected by good transportation, they may for many purposes take on the form of one larger place. With good access from one community to another, the labor market may be considered to be the entire group of interconnected communities. Certain public services and facilities could be located in one community to service the entire area, thereby achieving a better facility for all the area residents. An example of such a conurbation is the Chapel Hill–Durham–Raleigh triangle in North Carolina, which is a research and development area. A federation of communities improves both the competitive position of its industries as well as the quality of life of its residents.

Functional Economic Areas

A somewhat related notion of spatial economic structure of nonmetropolitan areas is that of functional economic areas. Pioneered by Karl Fox, this idea of spatial organization recognizes the potential commuting distances of the hinterland population around a city of some minimum size.

Central-place theory, discussed in an earlier chapter, is part of the central foundation of the notion of functional economic areas. You will recall that central-place theory emphasized the hierarchy of central places and equated the order of place with the functions which it performed. Functional economic areas stem from a consideration of the economies of size necessary to support various economic units such as food supermarkets, public schools, transportation facilities, health services, and entertainment, as well as a consideration of the range of choice of goods which contribute to a quality of life. A dispersed population living in small communities or the open country must depend on a larger central place to supply a large quantity of the goods and services unavailable to rural residents in the immediate vicinity. Thus the well-being of the people living in the hinterlands of a functional economic area depends importantly on the economy of the largest central place in the functional economic area.

The functional economic area becomes defined by the economic interactions of persons within the area. Improved services within the area, usually in the central city, benefit residents in the entire area. Similarly, the increased job opportunities anywhere in the area may benefit people living elsewhere in the area because of their proximity to the job opportunities. A natural economic cohesiveness binds the region together. Commuting patterns become a key indicator of the degree of economic integration in the area. Thus a functional economic area usually takes the shape of a rectangle or diamond-shaped region with a maximum commuting distance of 50 miles from the central city. The shape is rectangular because road systems are laid out on a grid. In order for the trade center to provide adequate services, it should have a population of at least 50,000 people.

NONMETROPOLITAN POLICY

One of the tendencies which people have is to classify things. Thus, a long-standing division of settlements in the United States has been urban and rural. A major intent of this book has been to avoid the urban-rural dichotomy with a regional framework. The latter makes more sense for a number of reasons explained earlier.

Nonetheless, there are some problems and associated policies which are unique to sparsely settled regions. In this section we will take a brief look at some of these policies that have been oriented to nonmetropolitan regions.

The Rural Development Act of 1972

Indicative of the policies to aid nonmetropolitan areas is the Rural Development Act of 1972, which ran into initial funding problems but contained numerous elements of previous legislation as well as new policies aimed at rural problems.

Rural Industrialization. Unemployment and underemployment with associated poverty are the target of several provisions of the act.

Almost all of the provisions of the act are designed to provide credit, investment, and equity capital to encourage rural economic development through private enterprise. Infrastructure receives special attention to provide the public-capital base necessary to attract private capital. Subsequent policies are directed at a major problem of rural areas—a lack of capital. As discussed earlier, a host of factors, some economically justified, have restricted the flow of both public and private capital into nonmetropolitan regions. To the extent that these restrictions are institutional, the bill is well-intended. Even if private capital does not follow public capital in these areas, better public services such as sewer and water will improve the well-being of the residents of the area.

Rural Housing. As indicated earlier in the chapter, the housing situation in rural America is in many ways worse than in urban areas. Improved credit conditions are provided in the bill, which extends to higher-income persons as well as middle- and low-income persons. The rationale for this extension is that it may serve as an inducement for industrial managers, physicians, and other professionals who consider locating in nonmetropolitan areas where there is a shortage of such personnel.

Rural Development Planning. Jurisdictional problems plague nonmetropolitan regions as well as metropolitan regions. Towns, counties, and special-purpose districts result in political fragmentation thwarting development efforts. For instance, at the time of their origin, county boundaries may have been appropriate to horse-powered travel on unimproved roads, but with today's transportation technology, most county boundaries are obsolete.

Regional development districts are encouraged under the bill in an effort to broaden the policy base to achieve scale effects and greater efficiency.

Environmental Policy

A variety of policies to encourage conservation have been pursued in rural areas for decades. Soil and water conservation practices have received a government stimulus along with reforestation and mine-land reclamation.

More recently, new problems have surfaced which have

brought new policy parameters into play. The rapid development of vacation homes has necessitated more stringent water pollution control measures. Fertilizers and pesticides have also created water quality problems necessitating policy action.

But environmental policy is not readily structured on an urban-rural basis. Urban effluents may impact rural areas and vice versa. Environmental problems are best handled on a broad regional or even national scale.

Human-Resource Development

A major portion of the nonmetropolitan problem has been the technological displacement of people from agriculture. Those that are displaced lack skills to move readily to other occupations. The federal government has done little to upgrade human capital in these areas. If displaced farm workers have received federally funded training assistance, it has been only after they have migrated to an urban center. In the past few years some vocational-technical training schools have been developed in nonmetropolitan areas, but this has happened long after the major impact of farm technology.

The upgrading of skill and education levels in nonmetropolitan areas has been left largely to state and local government. For the most part, the educational programs at this level have done a good job. For instance, the plains states, which have had massive outmigration from agriculture, have long ranked near the top in percapita spending for education. A sizeable portion of those receiving this education leave the state for better jobs elsewhere. Their mobility is increased by the investment made in their education and training.

Recreation

Changing attitudes, increasing leisure time, higher incomes, and greater ease of movement, as well as increasing population, are creating a 10 to 15 percent annual increase in recreational activities. Many nonmetropolitan areas are being strained by this boom in recreation. Lakes have become ringed with cabins and homes. Scenic mountain areas experience weekend traffic jams. Beaches are jammed to capacity.

311

This development has generally occurred without adequate planning to control the ensuing growth. The control of recreation development is just now being inaugurated in most areas not already under the control of some government body, such as national parks.

Land Use

Suburban sprawl, second-home developments, power-plant siting, and recreational developments have demonstrated the inadequacies of most rural land-use controls. In many areas land-use controls were virtually nonexistent until recently. In reaction to the adverse impacts associated with haphazard developments, the majority of states now have established some type of land-use control. These include such features as impact statements prior to development, land set-asides for special purposes, and restrictions or prohibitions of coastline development. A few states such as Hawaii, and more recently Florida, have adopted stringent land-use controls.

SUMMARY

Nonmetropolitan America has experienced no less a transition than metropolitan America. The ties between the two, if anything, have grown stronger. Improved transportation and communication technology have improved the access of metropolitan areas to non-metropolitan areas and vice versa. As a result, "urban" and "rural" are labels which are inappropriate classification schemes.

Rising incomes and increased leisure time have expanded recreational pursuits. The amenities of nonmetropolitan America for recreational activities have brought a significant new development to nonmetropolitan areas. Recreation, manufacturing decentralization, and improved communication are the dominant factors influencing the growth prospects of small towns. While many will thrive and serve a useful purpose, hundreds of others will continue to decline.

REFERENCES AND SUPPLEMENTAL READING

M. D. I. Chisholm, *Rural Settlement and Land Use: An Essay in Location* (London: Hutchinson University Press, 1962).

E. S. Dunn, Jr., *The Location of Agricultural Production* (Gainesville, Fla.: The University of Florida Press, 1954).

Economic and Social Conditions of Rural America in the 1970s, Economic Development Division, Economic Research Service, U.S. Department of Agriculture, Part 1, May 1971.

Niles M. Hansen, *Rural Poverty and the Urban Crisis* (Bloomington: Indiana University Press, 1970).

National Advisory Commission on Rural Poverty, *The People Left Behind* (Washington, D.C.: U.S. Government Printing Office, 1967).

17

New Towns and
New Communities

Though it can hardly be denied that urbanization has been a decisive factor in bringing expanded opportunities for millions of Americans in the form of better jobs, improving educational and cultural facilities, and greater social mobility, it can be argued that something has been lost in the process. What has been lost, say the alarmists, is the ability of our cities to serve human life.

A FRESH START

It is understandable why some question the possibility of achieving a "good life" in urban areas that are characterized by a deteriorating urban core and an awesome pattern of urban sprawl. But there is also the increasing belief that it is possible to develop a healthier environment for city living with the construction of planned new communities and new towns in America.

The basic purpose of this chapter is to discuss some recent efforts in the United States that deal with the development of new communities and new towns.[1] To accomplish this objective, we shall first define the difference between new-community development and new-town development. Second, we shall summarize the move-

1. Much of the discussion in this chapter is based upon Advisory Commission on Intergovernmental Relations, *Urban and Rural America: Policies for Future Growth*, A-32 (Washington, D.C.: U.S. Government Printing Office, April 1968), pp. 62–106.

ment of new-town and new-community development in Europe (particularly Great Britain), to which much of the development practices in the United States can be traced. Third, we shall discuss the variety of ways new communities and new towns have been and are being financed in the United States as we discuss a few of the more successful, planned new communities and new towns in America. Finally, we shall discuss some of the problems facing new communities and new towns.

New Towns and New Communities Defined

Common to new-town development and new-community development is that they both represent planned, concentrated areas of development, where the geographic size and population of the area have been predetermined.

The one basic difference between new towns and new communities is the degree of "self-containment." Generally speaking, new communities are largely dependent upon an existing urban area(s) as a major source of employment. The new community will offer some employment in the new services and trade establishments that are constructed in the community. In addition, the community may offer some employment opportunities in the limited industrial development planned for the community. The important point is that the economic base is not planned to employ all the community's residents. The economic base is primarily a service- and trade-oriented economy. In short, a planned new community is a residential area with all the desired amenities and within commuting distance of existing employment centers.

In contrast, new towns are planned as self-contained urban areas—that is, a planned community of a size large enough to provide economic opportunities within its borders for the employment of its residents. In addition, it is large enough to support a wide range of public facilities and social and cultural opportunities.

THE EUROPEAN EXPERIENCE

Several European countries have had considerable experience with planned new communities and new towns designed to accomplish social and economic objectives as part of a national policy. A variety of governmental and private institutional and financial arrangements have been used in the development of these communities. The British new-towns program, for example, was undertaken to accomplish the dispersion of population away from London and is presently administered by nationally chartered new-town corporations. Similar programs are found in Sweden and the Netherlands.

To pick a period when new-community and new-town development gained some recognition in Great Britain, one would have to begin with the efforts of Ebenezer Howard and a few close supporters in the development of the first "garden city"—Letchworth. Letchworth was and remains a representation of what Howard believed was possible in urban development—that is, a garden city where the residents enjoy favorable access to open spaces as well as reasonable proximity to work. A close observer of Howard's work notes that "Howard attacked the whole problem of the city's development, not merely its physical growth but the interrelationship of urban functions within the community and the integration of urban and rural patterns, for the vitalizing of urban life on the one hand and the intellectual and social improvement of rural life on the other."[2]

The concept of garden cities is well treated in Howard's book, which was first published in 1898 as *To-Morrow: A Peaceful Path to Real Reform*, and reissued with slight revisions in 1902 under the title *Garden Cities of Tomorrow*. In his concept of a garden city (and his notion of "total environmental development"), Howard placed upmost importance on three factors: (1) population size and area, (2) economic and social opportunities, and (3) land-use control. He firmly believed that in order to attain a desired balance between economic and social opportunities, the population and geographic size of the "new garden city" would have to be held to some specified limit. Basic to this belief was the notion that nothing is gained by unrestrained growth. In addition, Howard believed that there would have to be centralized control of land use in order to cultivate and preserve a desired balance between economic and social opportunities.

The development of Letchworth on undeveloped land was an amazing fact in itself. But the most significant achievement was that it turned a dream into a reality; that is, it demonstrated that a town based on modern industry can be economically and socially viable,

2. Ebenezer Howard, *Garden Cities of Tomorrow*, edited with additional comment by F. J. Osborn and Lewis Mumford (Cambridge: The M.I.T. Press, 1965), p. 35.

even if located beyond the economic influence of an existing urban area.

The development of a second garden city—Welwyn—followed the development of Letchworth. By the late 1930s, Letchworth and Welwyn were comparatively prosperous towns. The establishment of Letchworth and Welwyn, however, did not lead to a widespread new-town development program based on Howard's principles. The truth of the matter is that Howard and his few supporters were unable to generate continued interest and financial support to transform Britain's urban areas into the "garden cities" of tomorrow.

Renewed interest in new-town development returned in 1946 when Parliament enacted the New Towns Act. This act made available government aid in the development of new towns. Since 1946, Great Britain has established an unprecedented record in the designation of 21 new towns. By 1964, approximately 650,000 persons out of a projected population of 1,354,000 resided in these new towns.[3]

NEW TOWNS IN AMERICA

Emphasis on new-town development in America did not take place in any noticeable way until after World War I. In the words of C. S. Stein, this is how new-town planning started in America after the First World War:[4]

After the First World War there was a strong surge of enthusiasm for a better world. A group of us, including Lewis Mumford, Stuart Chase, Benton MacKaye, Charles Whitaker, and Henry Wright, formed the Regional Planning Association of America, to discuss regional development, geotechnics and New Communities. New York's great democratic governor, Al Smith, planned to replace the slums in which he had grown up. As a result, there was created the Commission of Housing and Regional Planning. He made me chairman. Up to that time in America our attack on housing had been regulatory—legal don'ts. In England "New Towns" and "New Towns after the War" were attempting to chart a way; the second Garden City, Welwyn, was being built. I returned to America a disciple of Ebenezer Howard and Raymond Unwin.

3. *The New Towns of Britain* (London: British Information Service, 1964), p. 5.
4. C. S. Stein, *Toward New Towns for America* (Cambridge: M.I.T. Press, 1969), p. 19.

We would be remiss if we did not mention the private development of planned communities and company towns in America before
World War I. Between 1830 and 1900 the private construction of
company towns and planned communities was quite common in the
rapidly expanding industrialized areas of this country. Unlike the
new towns in Britain, the company towns constructed during this
period were planned around one basic objective—to provide a place
of residence for the company's employees with the provision of some
services for the workers. Most housing and service establishments
constructed in the company towns were financed by the companies
and leased to residents and businessmen. Generally speaking, the
basic motive behind the development of company towns was profit
rather than long-range public benefit.

Some of the more familiar company towns developed during
this period were Gary, Indiana, built by U.S. Steel; Lowell, Massachusetts, built by Francis Cabot Lowell's textile-manufacturing company; and Pullman, Illinois, developed by the Pullman Company.
The economic base of these company towns was a single, dominant
firm—short of a balanced economic and social community as outlined
by Howard in his garden-city concept. Incidentally, these towns are
no longer company towns. As these towns grew in size, the companys'
exercise of authority gave way to democratic participation and private
ownership by citizens.

A period of largely new-community development followed the
era of the company town. As an example, real-estate development
groups attempted to develop attractive residential areas cut off from
the large industrial areas. The Intergovernmental Advisory Commission notes that the unique planning features of these communities
were the stability of land use, separation of residential and business
areas, and a continuous-planning function. These features made
possible the development of a "sense of neighborhood" so obviously
lacking in the company towns. Because of the high cost of construction and maintenance, only the high-income families could afford to
live in these communities. Consequently, they became showplaces
for those who could insulate themselves from the undesirable features
of urban living. The result? They ignored rather than relieved
urban problems of congestion, transportation, and adequate housing.

In general, it was demonstrated that large-scale private pro-
moters could plan and develop new communities and new towns in
America. Unfortunately, these early developments did not provide a
practical general alternative to unrestricted urban growth.

America's Garden Cities

From the imaginative minds and efforts of such urban planners as Clarence Stein and Lewis Mumford, Ebenezer Howard's theories concerning the development of garden cities were tried in this country in the 1920s as garden communities.[5] A distinction is made here between garden cities and garden communities, since the early efforts of these individuals were in the development of new communities. The first planned garden community in America was planned for a population of 25,000 on a square-mile tract at the undeveloped edge of New York City. Although the garden community was never developed, largely because the purchase of property within the tract could not be financed quickly enough to prevent the land being subdivided and thrown into the speculative market, many of the features proposed for the garden community were later developed in the new communities of Sunnyside and Radburn. Both communities were a part of the New York City urban region.

Sunnyside, a planned neighborhood in New York City, was constructed between 1924 and 1928. In contrast to Sunnyside, the Radburn, New Jersey project represented an attempt to build America's first garden city. The Radburn project called for the use of superblocks, roads for specialized uses separating pedestrian and motorized travel, and central parks. The garden city of Radburn differed from Howard's concept of a greenbelt city since Radburn did not include Howard's protecting greenbelt. There was not adequate available land surrounding the proposed town to establish a greenbelt area. The actual development of Radburn was halted by the depression of the 1930s. Consequently, the town was never completed, and the development of the planned economic base (industry development) did not take place.

Although Radburn fell short of the new-town concept, a major contribution to new-town development was made in the design of superblocks. Superblocks were large rectangular blocks that provided ample open space away from traffic. The basic purpose of the superblocks was to develop a town in which people could peacefully coexist with the automobile.

Finally, the Radburn project made it clear that new-town development required the cooperation of government. The task of developing new towns was simply too great for private or quasi-government corporations. It was apparent that the financial support

5. *Ibid.*, pp. 19–74.

of government is needed to acquire land at low interest rates and aid in the construction of the necessary utilities, highways and streets, and public buildings such as schools.

It is important to note that the Sunnyside and Radburn projects were undertaken at a time when there was little or no public support for such projects. The Sunnyside and Radburn projects were financed by the formation of a City Housing Corporation, a limited dividend company which was organized in 1924 for the ultimate purpose of building an American garden city.

Federal Government Projects

The federal government has been actively involved in the direct sponsorship of comprehensively designed residential developments since 1917. In contrast to the communities and new towns developed by Stein, the federal government's involvement in the development of new communities was tied largely to some role of its own. For example, in response to severe war-industry housing shortages, U.S. Shipping Board Communities were developed to provide housing and services to workers in shipyards during World War I. In March of 1918, Congress enacted the necessary housing legislation and appropriated an eventual total of $175 million—$75 million to the Emergency Fleet Corporation (EFC) of the U.S. Shipping Board and $100 million to the U.S. Housing Corporation (USHC) through the Labor Administration for the creation of permanent homes and communities. Absolute control in these projects was maintained by the government, with the USHC building and administering its communities directly, and the EFC maintaining complete control over rental, design, and management policy.

A second example of direct federal government involvement in new-community development was the development of so-called greenbelt communities. This came about as a result of the 1935 executive order which created the Resettlement Administration. Three sites were eventually selected for the development of greenbelt communities: Greenbelt (on the outskirts of Washington, D.C.), Greenhills (Cincinnati, Ohio); and Greendale (Milwaukee, Wisconsin). The total development stage of these projects covered a period from about 1936 to 1953. The development process of these greenbelt communities can be described as a movement from federal government involvement in land use to a stage where local government assumed all powers and services formerly reserved to the federal government. This last step was accomplished when the federal government liquidated all government holdings and the Public Housing Administration sold undeveloped land to private, nonprofit veterans' associations.

The lack of public interest, adequate financing, and proper land-use control were factors that severely limited the success of these communities as planned greenbelt communities. It would nevertheless be incorrect to conclude that the work of the Resettlement Administration was a failure, since their efforts made clear the importance of long-range planning embraced by a commitment to finance and govern the total development of planned communities.

To cite a final example, the federal government has been directly involved in the development of communities near large-scale power and reclamation projects. Two examples of such communities are Boulder City, Nevada (the Hoover Dam Project) and Norris, Tennessee (the Tennessee Valley Authority). The planning of Norris, Tennessee followed closely the garden-community concept of Radburn. The town of Norris was surrounded with a protective greenbelt. Within the town of Norris, there were parks, pedestrian underpasses, and community centers. Both communities now are under local authority as the federal government divested its land holdings in the communities.

CURRENT NEW COMMUNITY DEVELOPMENT

In recent years there has been a significant upsurge in the building of planned new communities in America, representing a pace of activity never before approached. Other countries are ahead in the construction of new towns, in the strict sense of self-contained, self-sufficient, independent cities; but in terms of those large-scaled planned developments which may be identified more broadly as new communities, none can challenge the United States.

There are several reasons for this revival of interest. First, the entry of a number of large corporations into the home-building and construction field either as land developers, home builders, diversified contractors, or investors has provided the corporate structure and a considerable portion of the financing necessary for such undertakings.

321

Examples of large corporations now engaged in the development of new communities are the Rassmoor Corporation (one of the nation's largest homebuilding corporations); Westinghouse (which has investments in Coral Ridge Properties, Inc., the developers of Coral Springs, Florida); General Electric (which plans the building of a community of 30,000 units and eventually to house 100,000 persons); the Pennsylvania Railroad (the owner and developer of the Porter Ranch new community in Los Angeles County and holder of over 100,000 acres of land in southern California); and International Telephone and Telegraph Corporation (which owns Levitt and Sons, one of the nation's largest and the most successful homebuilders). International Telephone and Telegraph Corporation provides the financial backing for Levitt and Sons to expand its operations and pursue a goal of creating independent self-sufficient "primary-employment towns," which would have enough business and industry to support as many as 250,000 residents.

These examples represent a small fraction of the number of corporations that have entered or plan to enter the new-community and new-town development field. One of the principle reasons why large corporations have entered this new investment venture is because of the nation's antitrust legislation which makes the merger of similar activities extremely difficult. Thus, corporations have turned to vertical integration as a way to expand operations and thereby avoid antitrust problems. For example, Kaiser Aluminum formed a land-development subsidiary known as Westwood Properties as a way to expand its market for aluminum products and thereby help combat the problem of overcapacity in the aluminum industry.

A second reason for the recent upsurge in new-community development is the sustained growth in population and prosperity since World War II. This has had a most significant effect on the demand for housing, particularly among the middle- and upper-income groups. Consequently, the profits from homebuilding and new-community development have attracted large corporations to the field.

A third reason, related to the second, is the unprecedented growth in suburban areas. As indicated in earlier chapters (Chapter 10 and 13), the rapid expansion of suburban areas represents, among other things, the desire of middle- and high-income groups to escape the crowded conditions of the inner cities. The desire to move out of the inner city coupled with the recent trend to move out of settled suburban areas to satellite communities has created a profitable enterprise of homebuilding and new-community development.

Finally, certain federal programs have encouraged suburban development and new-community development (satellite communities) near urban areas. The Federal Housing Administration (FHA) and the Veterans' Administration (VA) offer mortgage funds that have been most helpful to middle- and high-income groups in moving to the suburbs. The construction of interstate highway systems through urban areas, where the federal government pays a substantial portion of the total construction costs, has encouraged the development of satellite communities. These high-speed expressways provide easy access for commuters whose place of employment may be in the inner city.

The number of new planned communities is not fully known since the developers surround their development plans with utmost secrecy in order to forestall speculation of nearby land and premature development of these tracts. Preliminary estimates indicate that there may be a total of 50 projects in the United States with planned residential, commercial, and industrial features. These 50 projects would roughly fit the description of new towns. As regards to new communities, information as to the number of planned new communities is even more sketchy. It has been estimated that the actual number is in the vicinity of 200 to 250. There is little or no information as to the location of many of these new communities. It can be speculated, however, that most or all of these planned new communities will border those urban areas with the highest projected growth rates.

The most recent emphasis on new-community development and new-town development comes from legislation passed in 1970.[6] The legislation established the administrative machinery for dealing with new community development and authorized broad credit, loan guarantee, and grant assistance to qualified developers of new communities. A New Community Development Corporation in the Department of Housing and Urban Development (HUD) is responsible for the new-communities policy, and an Office of New Communities Development has been established to provide staff support for it. Some funding in the form of loan guarantees has already been approved by Congress. Additional funding is expected to be ap-

6. "New Towns U.S.A.," *Resources*, No. 39, January 1972 (Washington, D.C.: Resources for the Future), pp. 19–21.

proved by Congress as greater public interest develops in new-community development.

The recent federal policy is aimed at ensuring that public interests are realized in the course of development. The development of these federally supported new communities will be handled by private developers in the business for a profit.

Four kinds of new communities are to be considered eligible for aid: (1) economically balanced new communities within metropolitan areas; (2) additions to smaller nonmetropolitan towns and cities; (3) major new town–intown developments; and (4) new communities away from existing urban centers. This list allows for new-town assistance to just about everyone. Developer interest will be mostly in the first category—new towns in metropolitan areas where demand is strong. Reston and Columbia (near Washington, D.C.) fall in this group. Categories (2) and (4) are designed to appeal to nonmetropolitan areas, including depressed areas. The new town–intown concept qualified central cities for support under the act, thereby forestalling their opposition to outlying development.

SUMMARY

One characteristic of America's future can be predicted with some accuracy. As we have already indicated in an earlier chapter, it has been projected that as many as 300 million persons will be living in this country by the year 2000. Rural population will perhaps continue to decline and level off at about nine percent (give or take a percent) by year 2000. This means that 90 percent of the nation's total population will be working and living in urban regions. Roughly speaking, this means that approximately 90 million more persons will be living in America's urban regions by year 2000 as compared to the (approximately) 180 million persons now living in cities.

Taking the figure of 90 million, a striking estimate as to the demand for new towns can be made. Suppose, for instance, that one-half of the the 90 million persons settles in existing urban areas. This means that these urban areas will expand geographically, but this phenomenon is not new to us. Where might the remaining 45 million persons locate? A probable answer is new towns.

Given today's level of technology and market structure, the

city-size population figure of 250,000 is frequently cited as the threshold level for stable economic growth of an urban area. Let us assume that this figure does not change significantly by the year 2000. This means, generally speaking, that this nation could add 180 new towns with a population of 250,000 each by the year 2000.

The next question is this: Is it likely that we will see such a growth in the number of new towns by the year 2000? Mounting evidence seems to indicate that we will. In Chapters 13 and 14 and, again, in the opening pages of this chapter, we commented on the growing disenchantment with today's urban areas. Those who can afford to escape the ills of our cities do so by moving to suburbia or better yet to some satellite community beyond the fringes of the city. In short, decentralization of a kind is already occurring. Add to this the trend toward more market-oriented activities as opposed to resource-oriented activities (i.e., the importance of agglomerative economies) and we have before us the necessary factors for new-town development.

Of course new-town development requires massive investments in the required infrastructure (utilities, streets, schools, etc.), in housing, and in industrial development. But several of the nation's largest corporations have already shown an interest in providing the technical and management know-how and a considerable portion of the capital outlays necessary for residential and industrial development. With federal appropriations for the development of the infrastructure, new-town development is close at hand in this country.

New-town development could well be the "new frontier" in America's development, but there are at least three critical problem areas that cannot be overlooked. First, will a major program of new-town development solve the critical problems of our existing urban areas? The answer is no because it is unthinkable to believe that today's problems in our cities will somehow go away with the development of new towns. Furthermore, ways must be found to work out such problems as urban transportation, housing, pollution, etc. in order to avoid these same problems in the development of new cities.

A second problem area has to do with the extent of government involvement in the development of new towns. What role should the federal government play in the development of new towns? At one extreme is the situation where the federal government is given complete authority, through legislation, to control the use of land in order to protect the public's and the developers' interests. Once the new town is at a take-off stage of continued growth, an appropriate local governmental structure could be established to guide, direct, and serve the community in all future development decisions. This would also involve authority over virgin land surrounding the new town in order to avoid the balkanization of urban government that now plagues urban areas. The described role of the federal government certainly tests the sanctity of the doctrine of home rule and is sure to raise questions in the minds of many Americans as to the extent of government involvement. Certainly, the European experience in new-town development and this country's limited experience in new-community development indicate that centralized authority via federal government control is essential in the early stages of development in order to protect the long-range interest of residents and businesses.

A final (and more abstract question) has to do with the size and location of these new towns. What should be the optimal size of these new towns? Should they all be of the same size? Recall that the growth of cities seems to follow some hierarchical pattern of city-size development. Closely associated with the question of city size is the matter of location (see Chapter 6). Should these new towns be formed in areas that are already highly urbanized? Or should we follow a policy that would bring about a more uniform geographic distribution of people and activity? Admittedly, these questions are more difficult to answer than the previous one, but they do require an answer if we are to make new-town and new-community development a national policy.

REFERENCES AND SUPPLEMENTAL READING

Advisory Commission on Intergovernmental Relations, *Urban and Rural America: Policies for Future Growth*, A-32 (Washington, D.C.: U.S. Government Printing Office, April 1968), Chapters 4 and 5.

National Committee on Urban Growth Policy, *The New City* (New York: Frederick A. Praeger, Publishers, 1969).

F. J. Osborn (ed.), *Garden Cities of Tomorrow* (Cambridge: The M.I.T. Press, 1969).

C. S. Stein, *Toward New Towns for America* (Cambridge: The M.I.T. Press, 1969), Chapters 1 and 2.

The report of the Commission on Population Growth and the American Future, *Population and the American Future* (Bergenfield, New Jersey: The New American Library, Inc., 1972), Chapters 3, 6, and 14.

18

Alternative Futures

"We should all be concerned about the future because we will have to spend the rest of our lives there," stated inventor C. F. Kettering.

What does the future hold for urban and nonurban settlement patterns? Will current economic forces continue to shape the structure of regions? Can policies be implemented to alleviate our worst problems? Through better planning, can we control the future of our urban and nonurban regions?

In 1970 there were about 200 million people living in the United States. Projections indicate that the total may swell by another 100 million by the year 2000. Where will these additional people and the associated economic activity be located? Can existing metropolitan areas absorb a 50 percent increase in population in 30 years? Will most people live in "Bos-wash, Chi-pitts, and San-san"? Will new towns be developed to accommodate the increase?

This chapter looks at factors likely to shape the future economic landscape of the nation. Some of the constraints on development are considered. Alternative development paths are examined, including such issues as urban-rural balance and renewal versus new development. Urban and regional planning, which is essentially the consideration of alternative futures, is evaluated for its potential role in shaping the future. Finally, we sketch a few scenarios of alternative futures.

LIMITS TO GROWTH

A basic characteristic of most growth processes is the eventual encounter with an asymptote. An economic activity may grow rapidly for a time, but eventually its growth rate reaches a limit and often declines.

Economic-development potentials are constrained by resource and technology limits. Over a period of time, these limits change and accommodate different levels of activity. The current economic landscape still reflects the earlier constraints on economic development. For instance, waterways were the primary mode of transportation in early periods and the settlement system was oriented to them. The growth of the economy was temporarily constrained to this type of technology.

However, binding constraints change over time. Communication technology long has played a role in defining the limits to feasible development of many industries. Recently, the development of high-speed computers and the ability to transmit data rapidly from one location to another have freed many firms from traditional locations. Several potential limits to growth confront future development in the United States. Of these, the environment and energy deserve brief mention.

The Environment

Most past development has occurred on the premise of positive externalities while nearly ignoring possible negative spillovers. As air and water pollution reached critical levels in some areas and suburban sprawl and second-home development tore at open country, a major shift in development policy began to occur. Countless conflicts over the encroachment of development on environmentally critical areas brought pressure for change in development policies. The result has been major changes in land-use planning approaches and mechanisms. One of the effects has been to shift land-use planning and control from local units of government to regional and state governments. The federal government also is entering land-use planning in a more visible manner.

By 1973 approximately 34 states had some type of land-use legislation to reduce environmental degradation. Although the provisions varied, some of the more significant provisions of the state legislation were:

1. Require an impact statement for both private and public projects which are environmentally significant.

2. Provide tax incentives to preserve open space.
3. Establish state or regional review over major developments.
4. Control coastal development through state and regional commissions.
5. Establish statewide zoning and environment standards to be followed by local units of government.
6. Purchase of open space and critical areas.

Both state and federal governments have moved toward anti-pollution measures. Tax incentives, penalties, and regulations to reduce pollution have changed the firm's cost structure and brought dislocations of numerous firms. Society appears unwilling and unable to permit firms to externalize some of their costs. These new constraints imply locational shifts for some firms and possibly entire industries.

Energy

The settlement of the country was strongly conditioned by energy constraints which resulted in locations, such as ocean ports and rivers, that minimized transport. Water power was an important source of power and wood a major source of fuel. As the energy mode changed so did the spatial structure of the economy which had been tied to those energy modes.

More recently the spatial structure of the economy has evolved under conditions of generally cheap and abundant energy. This situation contributed to the footloose location nature of many industries during the past several decades. As these energy sources are reduced via depletion and higher prices, change will come.

The anticipated shift to new energy sources is likely to have a significant transformation effect on the spatial structure of the economy. Shifts from a petroleum-based energy supply to nuclear, coal, solar, or other energy sources is almost certain to precipitate major shifts in the location of economic activity and in life-styles.

GROWTH-POLICY OPTIONS

Should existing trends be allowed to shape the future economic landscape, or should the public sector pursue decisive policies to alter the spatial distribution of economic activity?

Proponents of a national growth policy argue that federal, state, and local government have a significant impact on the spatial distribution of economic activity, but their policies are often improperly and inconsistently oriented. The policy fragmentation which exists is reinforcing undesirable conditions. Not only are current difficulties being improperly treated but also desirable future-growth patterns are being ignored. A national growth policy is required to marshal more effectively government programs to correct current problems and allocate future resources to encourage economic efficiency and equity.

A contrary view holds that existing policy failures indicate that basic economic forces are difficult to change, that inadequate monitoring of individual and business response to economic incentives provides little basis for policy formulation, and that goods for development are often in conflict with one another. Basic market forces create fewer difficulties than managed growth by the public sector.

Controversies regarding urban-rural balance, optimum city size, new development versus renewal, and depressed regions versus rapid-growth regions usually emerge from policy discussions concerning the appropriate role of the federal government in influencing the spatial development of the economy. Since the role that government policy plays is overwhelming, even if inadvertent, such policy issues are important.

City Size

A theory of positive externalities underlies a broad policy framework for regional development. Agglomeration effects and external economies in industries with increasing returns to scale are assumed to transmit benefits from a policy such as a subsidy to a much broader group than those immediately gaining from a preferential government program.

In this regard considerable investigation and controversy has emerged concerning an optimal city size. Figure 18-1 reflects the nature of the question. The diagram indicates that the minimum aggregate average cost (AC) of providing public services declines as city size (population) increases until an optimum size is reached and then the minimum-cost point rises. Thus, a small city with an average-cost curve for public services represented by AC_1 is unable to provide public services at a unit cost as low as a larger city with an

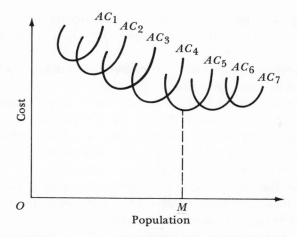

Figure 18-1   Hypothetical long-run city-cost curves

average cost curve AC_2 unless of course, the larger city is not at the minimum point on the average-cost curve. The minimum average-cost point continues to decline as city size increases until some optimum size of city is reached, as illustrated by AC_5 in Figure 18-1, after which it rises.   Do aggregate public service cost curves actually behave in this manner?

Ample evidence demonstrates that there are economies of scale associated with city size.   But is there some limit to these economies of scale?   Is there some optimum city size beyond which the unit-cost curves begin to increase as indicated in Figure 18-1?

Some evidence suggests that at least certain public-sector costs do rise as the city's population increases.   For example, New York City spends for other-than-school costs half again as much per capita as the other cities over 1,000,000, nearly twice as much per capita as cities between 500,000 and 1,000,000, nearly three times as much as cities under 500,000.

Explicit or implicit policies toward urbanization are concerned with the size of cities.   How big is too big?   How small is too small?

One approach to providing answers to these questions is to examine per capita costs associated with city size.   Numerous studies of this sort have found public costs to be a minimum somewhere between 10,000 and 250,000 population.   These studies, although illuminating, treat expenditures as costs without recognizing that by paying more, more may be received.   The basic assumption is

that per-capita output is constant.   In addition, institutional convention often dictates what are public costs and what are private
costs.

Βut even without data, a persuasive argument can be made
for an optimum size.   In a situation of rising costs, a firm will decide
to locate in a city on the basis of the average costs it encounters.   But
when costs are rising, marginal costs are greater than average costs.
Thus, negative externalities result with the urban area.   In this
situation the firm does not pay the total cost associated with its movement into the urban area; private costs are lower than social costs.

Some European countries have formulated a tax policy on
the basis of this argument.   Taxes are levied on firms (and people)
that attempt to locate in areas considered to be already overcrowded.
These taxes are a crude approximation of the difference between
private and social cost.

An alternative approach to the question of urban size has
been developed by Alonso.[1]   If it is true that per-capita output is a
function of urban size, then a look at the optimal size of city must
consider both inputs and outputs.   By viewing the city as an aggregate
productive unit, Alonso argues that cost and product curves for urban
areas can be constructed as in Figure 18-2.   Urban product is the
gross urban product and urban costs include infrastructure, public
service, and private costs.   Although P_a is the point of minimum per
capita cost, P_c is the point of greatest contribution to national income,
and therefore the optimal city size for maximizing total national
income is considerably larger than the point of minimum cost.

At the reverse end of the population scale are small towns,
many of which apparently are not large enough to be viable, efficient settlements.   Modern technology and higher income levels
have brought precipitous declines in the population and economic
well-being of the majority of small towns.   The small economic and
population bases are below threshold levels necessary to support all
but a few functions.   The range of choice of consumer goods and
services is limited, thereby restricting consumer welfare.   The limited
economic base restricts the vitality of the small community because,
as discussed in Chapter 15, the service base is not as amenable to
change as in a large city, consequently the possibility of self-sustaining
growth is low.

Studies of the minimum size necessary for self-sustaining
growth range from a few thousand to more than one million, with

1.   William Alonso, "The Economics of Urban Size," *Regional Science Association Papers*,
Volume XXVI, 1971, pp. 67–83.

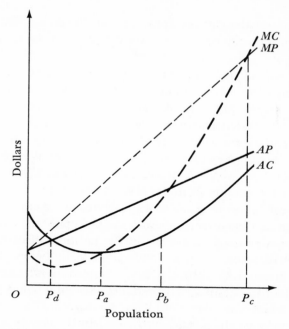

Figure 18-2   **Urban cost and product curves with city size.** (Source: William Alonso, "The Economics of Urban Size," *Papers of the Regional Science Association,* Vol. 26, 1971, p. 71.)

average estimates somewhere around one-quarter million. For smaller cities and towns a wide variation in growth rates is the usual pattern. An explanation of viability requires more than measuring population.

In retrospect, the flood of migrants into large urban areas often did little more than transfer a poverty problem from a rural to an urban setting. Individuals moved into large urban places but were not assimilated into the economic mainstream. Consequently, unlike the majority of their counterparts, they did not benefit from advantages associated with city size. Although this may not be a compelling argument for dispersal of industry, it does suggest that greater urban growth in existing centers is not the remedy to poverty.

Another argument for dispersal of economic activity is based on the alleged inability of existing urban centers to absorb continued increases in population. The population of the nation is forecast to expand by 100 million between 1970 and 2000. Many cities are already suffering from growth pains.

However, strong evidence supports the view that there is a minimum-size city as well as a maximum. The very small town is not as viable a settlement alternative as larger cities. It lacks scale economies for production and a limited range of consumption opportunities.

City size affects consumer welfare as well as, and partially because of, production economies. Small cities with poor access to large urban places have a limited range of consumer goods and services to offer residents compared with larger cities. An insufficient demand threshold exists to support many forms of entertainment, special medical services, or much variety in retail establishments.

Not only do wages tend to be lower in smaller towns, but also opportunities for economic improvement are less. Although living costs tend to be lower in small cities, they do not compensate for the wage difference. Per-capita income in metropolitan areas is about 27 percent greater than in the rest of the nation[2], while their cost of living is only 12 percent higher. However, many believe larger cities require the resident to absorb greater external costs such as travel time, pollution, congestion, and reduced personal safety. If this is true, the real income gap would be narrower. To consider such external costs, though, would also necessitate calculating external benefits associated with larger cities.

Concentration or Dispersal

Closely related to the optimum-city-size question is one of promoting increased concentration or greater dispersal. Numerous countries, notably England and France, have engaged in decentralization efforts. England's efforts to encourage industrial dispersal began in the 1930s and France implemented dispersal policies in the 1950s.

Economic concentration has demonstrated compelling advantages both for production and for consumer welfare. Yet the market forces responsible for these advantages also may be counterproductive, particularly when there are substantial diversions between private and public costs. These opposing observations are contained essentially in the city-size issue discussed above.

Dispersal of economic activity is considered for a variety of purposes—regional growth, national defense, rural-urban balance, and stabilization, among others. A prominent argument for dispersal is the alleviation of urban congestion and alleged diseconomies of scale.

2. Computed from *Survey of Current Business*, August, 1972, and *Monthly Labor Review*, June, 1972.

As indicated in Chapter 16, some breaks have occurred in the traditional pattern of greater concentration. Some industrial decentralization occurring in the past decade has added new vitality to small communities outside the major metropolitan areas. Those who argue for the feasibility of dispersal point to these recent examples as evidence that new communication and transportation technology allow the development of industries in small cities which once were tied to major urban centers.

Growth Centers

Within the context of settlement policy, several strategies to influence the spatial configuration of the economy have emerged. One attracting considerable attention is growth-center policy. Developed originally in France in the 1950s, growth-center concepts have had an impact on United States policy more recently.

Growth-center theory views economic activity as tending to agglomerate around certain key points in a region. The concentration of economic activity around these few points (or poles) dominates the economic functions of a much broader geographic area. A few "propulsive industries" form the core of the growth center and are distinguished from other industries by their ability to transmit direct and indirect effects to other industries in the center and surrounding region. Such effects are similar to the multiplier effects described in Chapter 3, coupled with the notion of spatial diffusion of economic progress which diminishes as the distance from the growth center increases. The growth center has or may easily attain the infrastructure and external economies conducive to growth. Surrounding areas benefit by spillovers of industries and by offering employment attainable by commuting or by short-distance migration.

One of the foremost proponents of growth-center policy has been Niles Hansen,[3] who has suggested that intermediate-size cities become the policy focus in efforts to stimulate growth in areas other than the large metropolitan areas. The growth center should be a rapidly growing intermediate-size city that can serve as an attractive labor market for potential migrants from lagging rural areas. An intermediate-size growing city has a sizeable infrastructure, labor force, and market. These are critical ingredients for self-sustaining growth.

3. Niles M. Hansen, *Rural Poverty and the Urban Crisis,* Bloomington: Indiana University Press, 1970. See also Niles M. Hansen (ed.), *Growth Centers in Regional Economic Development* (New York: The Free Press, 1972).

In this environment, subsidies and tax incentives may have positive stimulating effects. The expectation is that persons migrating from rural areas will be attracted to intermediate-size cities near them if jobs are available. This would also reduce the flow of persons, particularly the poverty-stricken, to the large metropolitan areas.

New or Renew?

Urban blight plaguing most large cities has brought renewal efforts to eliminate the decimated areas and replace them with new housing and business establishments. Many urban renewal efforts have been successful in their goal of rehabilitating a part of the city. Two striking examples of central-business-district renewal are Minneapolis and San Antonio. However, the majority of urban-renewal efforts have been severely criticized for accomplishing little more than displacing the problem.

The urban-renewal program became unaffectionately known as the "federal bulldozer." During the 1960s urban renewal demolished up to three times as many homes as it constructed. By 1969, when Congress required the construction of new housing units equal in number to those being eliminated, urban-renewal programs declined partly because of the unsavory image they had developed in the past. Nonetheless, renewal in some form will continue to be an important policy option for correcting urban blight and its associated problems.

As discussed in Chapter 17, new towns are another alternative for providing more living space and an environment for economic expansion. Part of the appeal of new towns is that they represent a fresh start with different if not fewer constraints. New physical forms more compatible with current economic and social conditions seem possible. The new-town concept appears to be most feasible adjacent to existing metropolitan centers, although new towns within urban centers are being tried.

Jobs to People or People to Jobs

A perennial controversy in regional policy is the movement of people to jobs or jobs to people. In absence of any policy in a situation where substantial unemployment exists in region A and a shortage of labor exists in region B, people will tend to move from region A to region B, and job opportunities will tend to move from region B to region A. But this adjustment process may be both slow and incomplete as the long-standing problems of many depressed areas would suggest. If policy is to alleviate the problems of depressed areas, should it encourage labor migration or capital flows or both? The opposing views have been labeled place prosperity versus people prosperity.

If people are reluctant to move and if there are other negative effects from migration as suggested elsewhere in the chapter, development strategies should be designed to attract industry which will provide employment opportunities within the region. Our discussion in Chapter 9 indicated that the population tended to be mobile but not over long distances. Moving costs and personal attachment to an area, because of friends and relatives, discourage migration. Among many there is a strong belief that people should not need to move in order to have employment or advancement. Thus it is argued that policies should encourage the movement of jobs to people.

But not all regions are capable of long-run development. As discussed in Chapter 7, the internal structure and access to inputs and markets of some regions places them at a comparative disadvantage. Such an economic environment counteracts development strategies designed to attract industries into the area. If favorable conditions for self-generating growth do not exist in a region, a better approach might be to pursue a policy which would encourage outmigration. Such a policy could include training programs to upgrade skills and subsidies to encourage mobility.

Moving jobs to people is the solution sought by local interests irregardless of the sometimes overwhelming effects of other factors. An analysis of local potential by community leaders often turns out to be a lament rather than a useful appraisal.

The desirability of policies designed to encourage migration depends on policy objectives, current economic conditions, and the institutional structure. The case for migration is made on the basis of economic efficiency; resources should move to areas of greatest return which will optimize resource use.

Migration has several potential impacts on both the sending and receiving region. The neoclassical view of the world would contend that the exodus of people from a region, assuming full employment and a homogenous labor supply, would raise the wage rate in the sending region and lower the wage rate in the receiving region. The phenomenon is illustrated in Figure 18-3.

The outmigration from region 1 reduces the supply of labor from SS_1 to SS_2, causing a rise in the wage rate from W_1 to W_2. The supply of labor in region 2, the receiving region, increases by the amount of the decline in region 1, thereby bringing a drop in the wage rate from W_1' to W_2'.

The region experiencing outmigration may, if the migration is extensive, incur difficulty in supporting public services and experience a decline in property values. The public sector, particularly the infrastructure, was designed to serve a particular population size. If the population decreases through outmigration, the demands on the public sector will also decline. Although public services may be responsive to the lower population base, public capital is fixed and requires maintenance which to a significant extent is independent of usage. Numerous areas of heavy outmigration complain of the burden of maintaining obsolete infrastructure. Furthermore, this burden restricts the public sector's ability to provide new infrastructure or services required to support new industry. This constraint on the responsiveness of the public sector to new activities discourages the development of new activity in the region even though wage rates may be relatively lower.

Property values tend to be depressed in the outmigrant region because of the decline in the demand for housing and because of the decline in demand for goods and services previously sold to the migrating population. Dramatic examples of depressed real-estate

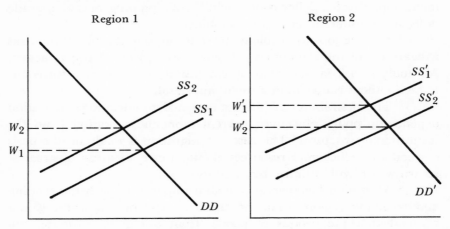

Figure 18-3 Impact on wage rates of migration

markets were the communities affected by military-base closings in the late 1960s, when in six months real-estate prices dropped 25 to 75 percent.[4] Long-term outmigration as experienced by thousands of small communities exerts the same type of depressing effects on property values in these communities.

Areas receiving the inmigrants also experience impacts on the public sector and property values. The new residents require more public services and infrastructure. Schools, streets, utilities, recreational facilities, and the like will need to be expanded if the population growth is significant. Public services will also experience greater demand. The inmigration may raise taxes of the original residents if the inmigrants do not pay taxes equivalent to the increased cost of the public sector for servicing them. The outcome depends on the characteristics of the migrants and the associated industry expansion. Nevertheless, the original residents may find the burden of supporting the public sector increased or decreased as a result of inmigration.

Although inmigration could lower average wage rates and raise per-capita costs of supporting the public sector for the original residents, property values will tend to rise. The benefits, of course, will accrue to property owners. Suggestions have been made that these windfall gains be taxed and the revenue distributed to the original residents as compensation for losses suffered as a result of the inmigration.

Although not always economically justified, policies to influence the location of new capital, new and expanded industries, are more acceptable than policies to encourage migration. The economic rationale is that the policies designed to reduce barriers to capital movements promote greater efficiency. Thus, if capital reluctantly moves into certain regions because of risk and uncertainty, policies to mitigate these unfavorable conditions would be desirable. Furthermore, a region with high unemployment and a population with a low tendency to migrate would be aided with a capital inflow which would provide jobs for persons who would otherwise be idle. The national economy would also benefit from such a policy. It is also argued that industrial location inducements can be justified if they replace or diversify the economic structure of the area to make it less subject to oscillations in demand or other external factors. This may be proper under a restricted set of circumstances, but often

4. J. E. Lynch, *Local Economic Development After Military Base Closures* (New York: Praeger, 1970).

the economic structure of the region is grossly underdeveloped and would require massive infusions of both public and private capital to reach a stage of self-sustaining growth.

As the city grows in size it is able to achieve economies of scale as a result of agglomeration and related factors. If the cost curves for cities of various sizes were as depicted in Figure 18-1, an effective case could be made for growth-promoting efforts until the population size reached point M, where average costs would be least.

The use of location subsidies was discussed in Chapter 12, where it was noted that industrial revenue bonds and similar devices are common in the United States. Location inducements have grown in variety and magnitude as states and areas compete for new industry.

An argument for intervention in the location-decision process is akin to the idea that cities and regions may be able to attain economies of scale if their growth is promoted.

PLANNING THE FUTURE

One way to obtain a desirable future for our cities, towns, and countryside might be to plan for it. As an activity to influence the design and function of cities, planning has been sporadically practiced since early colonial days with varying effectiveness. Because of its return to prominence in the past two decades, perhaps it will be a major force in the future of urban and regional economies. To understand the potential role of planning in guiding the growth of urban and regional economies, a brief history of planning in the United States is instructive.

The Evolution of Planning

Interest in planning has experienced numerous oscillations. Many colonial towns were developed from elaborate plans which subsequently influenced the pattern of development of other American cities. The interest in planning waned after the colonial period and remained minimal until nearly the start of the current century when the "city-beautiful" theme came into vogue. Not until the late 1950s did comprehensive planning gain acceptance as a guide to urban and regional development.

Colonial Town Planning. Early colonial settlements were strongly influenced by European, particularly English, town planning. The founders of Philadelphia arrived in 1681 with explicit instructions from William Penn for the selection of a site and layout of the town. The Philadelphia plan had three major features: a gridiron street system, a system of open spaces, and uniform spacing and setbacks for the buildings. The plan in general, and the gridiron street system in particular, had a strong impact on the spatial structure of other American cities. Because Philadelphia was an early transportation center, a large portion of persons entering the country for the first time or moving west became familiar with the Philadelphia system. The pattern was replicated as new towns were founded during the westward movement of the population.

Williamsburg, now restored to its colonial state, was the most detailed of the town plans of the colonial period. Francis Nicholson, governor of Virginia, planned Williamsburg for a new state capitol just four years after he had designed Annapolis. The Annapolis plan was in the baroque style with a square and two large circles from which diagonal streets radiated. The baroque style was also included in the Williamsburg plan, but the diagonal streets and circles were eliminated.

A final example was Pierre L'Enfant's plan for Washington, D.C. that was influenced by several European city plans, particularly that of Paris and its environs. The plan combined diagonal and radial streets with the gridiron system.

Early town plans such as Williamsburg reflected the technology and environment of the period. Manufacturing was nonexistent, and agriculture was the economic base of the community. Given this type of economy, the colonial town plan did a relatively successful job of planning the physical development of towns.

Postrevolution Antiplanning. Town planning came to an abrupt halt after the American revolution. New social and economic trends emerged which resulted in antiplanning, antigovernment, and antiurban political manifestations. Although cities grew, competition among cities for new commerce and industry superceded planning interests.

The development of the country during the century following the Revolution was outward-looking with regard to cities. Resources flowed into the development of canals, railroads, and similar efforts to expand commerce in developing regions. Interaction among cities and regions was intensified but little effort was devoted to improving the quality of life in the city.

The settlement of the West encouraged land speculation, which on occasion reached staggering dimensions. With the establishment of the rectangular survey system, land trading became common. Even cities like Washington, D.C., were victims of the land speculators.

Town planning was also discouraged by erosion of power of local governments in the postrevolution era. Colonial town governments had considerable power to promote policies associated with town planning. But city government authority was reduced to service functions in the period immediately following the revolution.

The "City-Beautiful" Movement. Modern American city planning usually dates from 1893 when a "White City" was opened to house the Columbian Exposition world's fair. The product of numerous architects, the "White City" received strong acclaim and rejuvenated a long dormant interest in planning.

The beautification of cities was the primary goal of this planning revival and has come to be called the "city-beautiful" movement. In addition to the Columbian Exposition, the Washington Plan of 1902 was a catalyst in this planning movement. Civic centers, thoroughfares, parks, boulevards, and parkways were the main elements of this effort. Hundreds of cities followed these leads with civic-improvement programs. But unlike Washington, which implemented much of the 1902 plan, most of the cities confined their efforts to a smaller scale, often a civic center. A notable exception was the 1909 Plan of Chicago developed by Daniel Burnham. This plan placed Chicago in its regional context and suggested the necessity of control of development beyond the city limits. Although primarily a physical planning effort, the city-beautiful movement initiated the trend toward more comprehensive planning.

The "City-Efficient" Movement. Between 1910 and 1920, automobile registrations increased from 458,000 to 8,132,000 and by 1930 had reached 22,973,000. The automobile changed the spatial structure of the city in a rapid and often disruptive manner. Suburbanization occurred at a rapid pace with the improved access provided by the automobile, and with it came the need for more and better roads.

The new problems moved planning into the era of the "city-efficient." Because of the fanning out of this city, emphasis also shifted toward regional planning. The Los Angeles County Regional

Planning Commission was set up in 1922, the Boston Metropolitan District Commission established a Division of Metropolitan Planning in 1923, and the New York Regional Plan Association was created in 1923. The first comprehensive state plan emerged in 1926 from a New York State temporary commission on housing and regional planning.

Zoning became a widespread technique to effectuate plans during the 1920s. Purported to be a means of stabilizing and protecting property values, zoning went through the cycle of enthusiasm and disenchantment of most new devices. Gradually it became part of the tools of planning.

The Depression. The take-off stage of comprehensive local planning was given both an additional thrust and a setback during the Depression of the 1930s. Faith in the "invisible hand" of *laissez faire* was shaken by the economic collapse and the long-dormant interest in government control was reawakened. The shift in political philosophy was also spurred by the Works Progress Administration which financed more than 100 planning studies. By the late 1930s WPA expenditures averaged $4.2 million annually, several times as much as local governments were spending.

But the economic crunch of the Depression choked off the privately sponsored metropolitan planning associations formed during the 1920s. The Regional Plan Association of New York and the Pittsburgh Regional Plan Association were two notable exceptions to this general demise of privately sponsored planning.

Comprehensive-Planning Movement. Federal funds from the Highway Act of 1962 and Section 701 of the Housing Act of 1954 as amended (the Planning Assistance Program) required plans as a prerequisite for funding. These not only provided an impetus for planning but also set the stage for a greater variety of planning requirements. The expansion in planning functions brought requirements for coordination among planning activities, as it became recognized that independent planning activities could have spillover effects on other plans.

The Planning Process

Planning endeavors to guide or control the activity of individuals and groups to minimize the adverse effects which may occur and to promote better performance in line with the objectives of a plan which reflects society's welfare.

As discussed in Chapter 12, the public sector has become increasingly involved in urban-regional economies because of market breakdowns, externalities, and collective consumption. But short-falls in the private-market economy do not necessarily mean that better solutions will be achieved through public-sector intervention. The success of the public sector in achieving "better" solutions rests on the effectiveness of its decisions. In order to improve this decision-making job, planning has emerged as a major force in almost every region of the nation. As indicated above, federal programs have provided considerable thrust for regional planning by requiring some form of planning for the receipt of federal funds.

As an evaluator of alternatives, a plan should be an integral part of policy formulation. The interrelationship of policy and plan is indicated in Figure 18-4. As an activity to foresee and guide change, the planning process generally consists of five components: goal formulation, an inventory, a forecasting model, a comprehensive plan, and implementation.

The process of effective plan-making generally should be a continuous system of analysis, considering linkages and feedback experience. Many plans have been one-shot rather than on-going efforts with resulting discontinuity that is often self-defeating. An essential characteristic of a plan is the ability to assess the consequences of alternatives.

Planning Goals. Planning is the systematic management of assets. As such, the goals of planning ought to include those areas of public and private facilities and services that society views as public-management areas. These would include transportation, land use, water and disposal systems, public-service systems, recreation, and the environment.

Transportation-planning goals should include all forms of transportation because of potential trade-offs between alternative modes. The private automobile has had a profound impact on the spatial structure of regions. Many of these impacts are considered to be undesirable, and uncontrolled growth may amplify these un-desirable conditions.

As explained elsewhere in the chapter, land use and trans-portation systems are interrelated. Land-use goals must consider this linkage and also include commercial and industrial development,

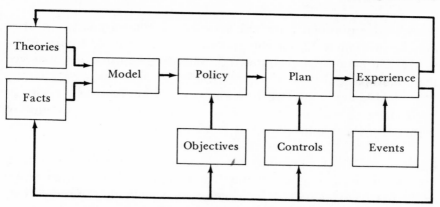

Figure 18-4 Planning in its environment

residential development (including racial and economic integration), and recreation and open-space requirements.

Goals for the design and implementation of water and disposal systems must be integrated with goals for the spatial structure of the region. Such a design would be long-term and match needs against financial resources.

Public-service-system goals include social services, education, health services, and public safety. Effective goal-setting is tied to the magnitude and characteristics of the population. Such factors as age structure, income levels and distribution, occupational characteristics, and racial mix influence the planning goals of public-service systems.

Recreation programs have lagged behind demand in most areas. An increase in leisure time, income, and freedom of movement are likely to continue to necessitate more effective planning for recreation.

The impact of all the development systems on the environment must be determined. If certain standards of clean air and water, noise, and aesthetics are to be attained, potential effects of alternate plans on environmental quality are a necessary part of the planning function.

The attainment of all initially specified goals is usually impossible because of resource constraints and an inconsistency of goals. The latter requires additional comment.

The interactions in an urban system create feedback effects which can mitigate or reverse a policy goal. As with so many choices, trade-offs are necessary in goal selection. A reduction in central-city traffic congestion and a revitalization of the central business district may be in conflict. Improving public services financed by property-tax revenue may work counter to attempts to improve and conserve the housing stock.

Although goals are important, and too often poorly formulated, they should not be established without prior knowledge of potential policies and their likely consequences.

Inventories. The background for effective planning is a thorough inventory of economic, social, physical, and geographic characteristics of the area. Since we are interested in the economics of the region, we will restrict our comments to an economic inventory.

All too many "economic-base studies" have attempted to satisfy the need for an economic description of the region on the basis of unrelated lists of income, employment, and production data. If the level of understanding of the economic processes at work in the regional economy is that low, it is difficult to perceive how an attempt to manage such economic forces can succeed.

Some type of analytical framework is necessary to give form and substance to the data-gathering effort. The framework should be influenced by the planning goals and the theories about regional structure and growth. A common, but not exclusive, framework is the input-output framework described in Chapter 2. In fact many of the applications of input-output described in Chapter 3 had a planning orientation. In the following section we will consider some of the frameworks employed to capture economic relationships necessary for planning.

Forecasting Models. A critical component of the planning process is the determination of the likely future dimensions of the regional economy and its population. A wide variety of instruments and techniques ranging in sophistication from a ruler to a complex econometric model have been used to make projections of a regional economy.

Planning can mitigate undesirable trends and accentuate desirable ones. But to do so requires an understanding of the variables which act to produce the likely future trends. Thus, a planning model functions best if it is something more than simply a predictive model. Planning models must be able to determine the impact of policy designed to bring about society's objectives. Planning attempts to change events in specified directions.

During the course of our earlier investigation of the structure and performance of regional economies, several models were introduced which can be and have been used in planning activities. These include input-output, export-base, income-expenditure, and shift-share models. The input-output model will be used to illustrate the basic structure of a planning model.

A strong appeal of input-output models for planning purposes is the interdependency captured by the model. As discussed in Chapters 2 and 3, input-output models facilitate impact evaluation and projections that consider industry interactions. Nearly as important is the consistency attainable from input-output analyses.

Basically, the input-output model is the core around which numerous additional segments are built or from which useful side calculations can be made. A possible model format is indicated in Figure 18-5. The model indicates that the economic structure and activity levels require public services and facilities and that in turn the provision of public services and facilities influence the structure and performance.

Suppose that we are interested in future housing needs for a region. We would like to know the future population, the type and location of employment, and income distribution, the age structure of the population, and the rate of aging of the housing stock. Figure 18-6 illustrates the role of the input-output model. The model is energized by the anticipated economic structure and level of activity. The results of this stage of the model indicate the anticipated output levels during the planning interval. The output values can be converted into employment in each industry by employment/output ratios corresponding to each sector. Population can be estimated from total employment by the labor force participation rate. The occupational mix of the employed population can be obtained from survey or published sources. Two basic characteristics of the population, age structure and income distribution, are then determined. These two elements are combined with an estimate of the replacement needs to form the demand for housing. Additional considerations would be included in a complete model, but this skeleton framework illustrates the approach.

Although considerable progress has been made in formulating theoretical relationships to explain urban economic growth and in constructing empirical models, the accuracy of forecasts is still far from acceptable. Economic projections are the product of a varied mix of factors, some of which are subject to substantial error. For most regional economies the activity levels of its industries are exogenously determined. This condition alone makes forecasting a

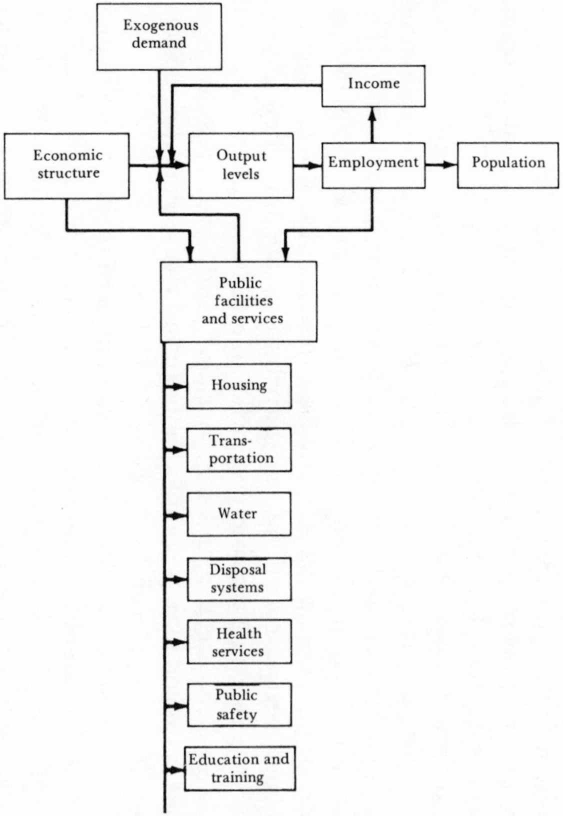

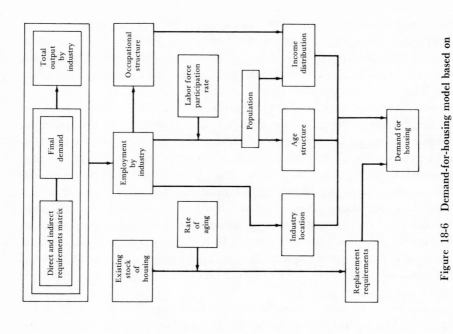

Figure 18-6 Demand-for-housing model based on input-output model

Figure 18-5 Single-demand model for public facilities and services

hazardous activity. The risk of error runs high in the best of forecasting frameworks.

The potential inaccuracy of forecasts necessitates considerable flexibility in plans for the future. This flexibility has been missing from much of the planning activity in regional and urban economies.

Simulation Models. A related approach to planning models is dynamic simulation, one form of which was discussed in Chapter 3. Based on methods of industrial dynamics, Forrester[5] has developed a provocative approach to simulating the dynamics of urban structure. Once developed, the simulation system can trace the effects of various policies on the system.

One of the most interesting conclusions of the policy simulations is that many of the common urban-management programs are counterproductive; they may worsen conditions that they were designed to improve.

Forrester simulates an urban area through 250 years of development, starting at the birth of a city and continuing through development, maturity, and finally stagnation. He finds a strong trend toward eventual stagnation based on the usual economic processes and policies. The aging process of housing and industry contribute to this situation.

A critical component of the model is the specification of feedback effects. Feedback loops, which form the basic structural components of the model, include stocks, flows, and a decision affecting or controlling the flow. The model focuses on housing, population, and industry. Changes in these three areas are involved with urban growth, stagnation, or decline.

A critical aspect of such a dynamic simulation model is the specification of individual economic processes and relationships which collectively comprise the simulation model. Of course this model is not unique to this effort, but there may be a greater tendency to forget that the reasonableness of the individual urban-sector descriptions and their interactions determines the validity of the simulations.

Some Criticisms

Despite rapid growth in the past two decades, regional planning has hardly been a resounding success. For instance, in

5. J. W. Forrester, *Urban Dynamics* (Cambridge: The M.I.T. Press, 1969).

evaluating several major metropolitan area plans, Boyce, Day, and McDonald[6] commented in the following manner about the Tri-State Transportation Commission of the New York Metropolitan Region: ". . . there does appear to have been a lamentable lack of purpose and integration to the Tri-State studies, both in the overall directions they have taken and in the detail and consistency of many of the contributory work items. One has the impression of two or three amorphous bodies of technical scholarship, somehow ending up by happy accident upon the same budget, and between them shaping it to buttress their various contributions, while what they were contributing to cannot have received much thought." Further on the authors observe that "good, clear discussions of veritable planning issues are few and far between."

A major problem has been an overextension of prescriptions to remedy situations, with insufficient knowledge of the consequences of the action. A basic justification for planning and planners should be superior knowledge of relevant relationships. Otherwise the planner's recommendations are not necessarily better than those of the nonprofessional. As planner Marshall Kaplan has stated: "Partly because of the marginal state of the planner's knowledge and partly because of the many isms governing his behavior, he has . . . concentrated much of his activity (or at least his rhetoric) in the long-range, comprehensive planning area. He has thus generally been able to substitute art for methodology and whim for technique. Unfortunately, his limitations have made his efforts almost irrelevant to current public decision-making processes concerning urban policy and programs. . . ."

FUTURE SCENARIOS

The ills of major urban centers have brought predictions of cataclysmic change or policy recommendations to drastically alter the spatial framework of the economy. Some see the city as a dying institution incapable of saving itself, others see the city as a powerful economic machine of great vitality. A few of these views of the future provide an interesting contrast.

6. David E. Boyce, Norman D. Day, and Chris McDonald, *Metropolitan Plan Making* (Philadelphia: Regional Science Research Institute, 1970), p. 403.

The Life-Cycle Hypothesis

Using techniques he developed to study the dynamics of industry growth, Forrester[7] has constructed an elaborate simulation model for cities. He models what he thinks to be the life cycle of the city—growth, maturity, and stagnation. Employing twelve sectors, the model simulates a 250-year life cycle of a city. Growth occurs because of feedback linkages in the system which accentuate growth until a land constraint is reached (the city is considered to be a fixed geographic size), which eventually produces stagnation. Some conventional programs to alleviate city maladies are incorporated into the model and found to be counterproductive.

Forrester's model suggests a growth curve for cities which can be avoided only with proper modification of ordinary economic forces and conventional policy. However, if Forrester's forecasts are correct, they are so without benefit of accepted economic relationships, which he shuns in formulating his model.

Projecting a Metropolis

An ambitious, thorough examination and projection of metropolitan growth was the New York Metropolitan Region Study. In one of the published volumes of that study, Raymond Vernon[8] sketches the likely future of the New York region. The outlook is neither utopian nor "gloom and doom," but rather a careful analysis of the basic economic mechanisms that have influenced and will influence the structure and performance of the New York region.

The projection framework initially ties the region to the national economy. National economic and demographic trends are viewed as partial energizers of the New York regional economy. From this starting point the internal growth of the region's economy is projected. The results indicated that the industry mix of the region would change toward nonmanufacturing activities and that the overall regional economy would grow more rapidly than the nation. Growth and change were viewed as a process of transition to changing economic conditions.

7. J. W. Forrester, op. cit.
8. Raymond Vernon, *Metropolis 1985* (Cambridge: Harvard University Press, 1960).

Ecumenopolis

The dynamics of urban growth are viewed by Doxiadis[9] as leading eventually to a worldwide city—an ecumenopolis. He sees population increasingly concentrated in the large urban regions with concomitant increases in externality problems, which will lead to disaster unless counteracted. He suggests that we not try to stop growth but to deflect it into settlement systems that reflect the quality of life that people want.

Dynamic Inertia

The future spatial patterns of growth in the United States will continue to be a mixture of inertia and flux. The existing spatial structure will strongly influence future trends. Large metropolitan areas will become larger because they have the public and private capital, the service base, the capacity to generate new technology, and related characteristics for self-generating growth. They also offer a larger range of choice in consumer goods and services as well as higher incomes.

Technological change, rising incomes, and consumer tastes have had a strong decentralizing effect on urban areas that seems unlikely to diminish. Areas peripheral to existing centers are likely to continue to experience the greatest growth from decentralization, although improvements in transportation and communication technology have increased the accessibility of nonmetropolitan regions.

As the suburbs gain people and economic activity, the functions of the central city change. The evidence indicates that the central city is becoming increasingly specialized in service activities and office centers, a continuation of existing trends.

Any straight-line extrapolation from past trends is likely to be misleading. The identification of basic trends from the maze of complex interactions is difficult, and even if they are properly identified, the time dimension adds to the uncertainty.

Relative prices and comparative advantage are continually changing and altering the optimum-location matrix. The search for new optimum locations changes the economic landscape in a gradual, but continual, manner.

9. C. A. Doxiadis, *Urban Renewal and the Future of the American City* (Chicago: Public Service Administration, 1966).

REFERENCES AND SUPPLEMENTAL READING

Advisory Committee on Intergovernmental Relations. *Urban and Rural America: Policies for Future Growth* (Washington, D.C.: U.S. Government Printing Office, April 1968).

David E. Boyce, Norman D. Day, and Chris McDonald, *Metropolitan Plan Making*, (Philadelphia: Regional Science Research Institute, 1970).

The report of the Commission on Population Growth and the American Future, *Population and the American Future* (Bergenfield, New Jersey: The New American Library, Inc., 1972).

J. W. Forrester, *Urban Dynamics*, (Cambridge: The M.I.T. Press, 1969).

William I. Goodman and Eric C. Freund (eds.), *Principles and Practice of Urban Planning*, Fourth Edition, (Washington, D.C.: International City Managers Association, 1968).

Niles M. Hansen, *Rural Poverty and the Urban Crisis*, (Bloomington: Indiana University Press, 1970).

Raymond Vernon, *Metropolis 1985*, (Cambridge: Harvard University Press, 1960).

Index

cost-pricing of, 262
Public utilities, relation to political
    fragmentation, 280–81

Rank-size rule, 98–101
Recreation, 311
Region:
    defined, 5
    homogeneous region, 5
    nodal economic region, 5
    significance of, 5–7
Regional concept, importance of, 6
Regional development structure, 142
Regional expenditure-income function,
    160
Regional income, definition, 26, 159
Regional spending, definition, 166
Regional tax matrix:
    definition, 224
    use in analyzing development, 224–25
Regional trade:
    definition, 27
    feedback effects, 162–63
    gravity models, 150–51
    price-differential models, 151–53
    reasons for, 149–53
    relation to growth models, 159–61
    relation to technology, 163–64
    relation to transport rates, 155–58
    terms-of-trade, 154–55
Rent-bid curve:
    households, 202–03
    industry, 199–202
    in land-use model, 199–206
Residential preference, 174
Retail trade, location of, 190–92
Revenue bonds:
    definition, 217
    effectiveness, 218
    as location incentive, 217
Richardson, Harry, 39, 64, 90, 148, 180
Romans, J. Thomas, 170, 180
Rose, A. J., 115
Rothenburg, Jerome, 206, 272
Rural, definition, 293
Rural Development Act, 293, 309–12
Rural development planning, 310
Rural housing, 310
Rural industrialization, 309–10
Rural poverty, 300

Sackery, Charles, 272
Sacks, S., 222
Scale economies:
    and agglomeration, 108–12
    external, 109–12
    internal, 108–09
    in urban government, 282–84
Schaap, Dick, 267
Scherer, F. M., 82, 90
Schmandt, Henry J., 196, 291
School integration, 241
Schreiber, Arthur F., 272
Sector theory:
    definition, 132
    in regional-growth theory, 132–33
    service activities, 60–61
    urban structure, 188

Shellhammer, K. L., 223
Shenkel, William M., 291
Shift-share analysis, 143–44
Siebert, Horst, 148
Simulation models:
    development, 37–38
    planning, 350
Smith, T. V., 186
Socially optimum market conditions:
    benefit externalities, 212
    cost externality, 212
Sonenblum, Sidney, 39
Spatial linkages, 141
Spatial price discrimination, 82
Spillover effects:
    definition, 210–11
    interjurisdictional, 214
    negative externality, 211–14
    positive externality, 211–14
    rationale for government intervention,
        210–14
    relation to socially optimum market
        conditions, 211–13
    urban government, 282–84
Stages-of-growth theory, 133–34
State and local government:
    dimensions of, 207–09
    expenditures, 209
    revenue, 208
    units, 209
Stein, C. S., 128, 317, 326
Stein, Jerome L., 180
Stewart, John Q., 150
St. Louis, urbanized area, 276
Strauss, Anselm L., 196
Striner, E., 39
Strout, A., 151
Struyk, R. J., 223, 226
Subsidies:
    efficiency of, 221
    influence on location decisions,
        218–20
    local government, 217–21
    for pollution control, 270
    of urban mass transportation, 262, 265
Suburban sprawl:
    effect of property tax on, 279–80
    shopping centers, 191
Supplying public services, 216

Taxes:
    impact on business, 224–25
    impact on growth, 222
    pollution, 269
    relation to housing, 247–48
    relation to services, 222–23
Technology:
    diffusion, 178–80
    diffusion and trade, 163–64
    effect on growth, 122–23
    and import substitution, 88–89
Terms of trade:
    definition, 154
    effect of changes on growth, 154–55
Thompson, J. H., 219
Thompson, Wilbur R., 134, 148, 253,
    272, 301, 302